AF478120

RELIGIOUS SCANDALS

RELIGIOUS SCANDALS

Judith M. Buddenbaum

GREENWOOD PRESS
An Imprint of ABC-CLIO, LLC

A B C · C L I O

Santa Barbara, California • Denver, Colorado • Oxford, England

Library of Congress Cataloging-in-Publication Data
Buddenbaum, Judith Mitchell, 1941–
  Religious scandals / Judith M. Buddenbaum.
    p. cm.
  Includes bibliographical references and index.
  ISBN 978-0-313-34688-0 (hard copy : alk. paper)—ISBN 978-0-313-34689-7 (ebook)
  1. United States—Church history. 2. United States—Religion. 3. Scandals—United States—History. I. Title.
  BR517.B83 2009
  277.3′08—dc22   2009016109

13 12 11 10 09   1 2 3 4 5

This book is also available on the World Wide Web as an eBook.
Visit www.abc-clio.com for details.

ABC-CLIO, LLC
130 Cremona Drive, P.O. Box 1911
Santa Barbara, California 93116–1911

This book is printed on acid-free paper ∞

Manufactured in the United States of America

CONTENTS

Series Foreword

Scandal is part of daily life in America. The evidence is everywhere, from the business world, with its Enrons, Ponzi schemes, and insider trading, to the political arena, where scandals are so pervasive that, for shorthand purposes, we simply add "gate" to each new one (Watergate, Contragate, Spitzergate, etc.). Cultural phenomena that are designed to entertain, inform, and distract us—television, film, popular music, sports, media—have also been touched by the fickle finger of scandal. Even religion, the one area of life that is intended to uplift and guide Americans, has not been immune to the taint of scandal.

Scandal, which can be defined as something that offends propriety or established moral codes and brings disgrace on anyone or any organization associated with it, is not a modern invention. It has been with us since the days of the Salem witch trials and Boss Tweed, and continues to resurface with the many breaking news events of today. To bring this subject into the open and to offer a wider historical view of such a major and often overlooked aspect of U.S. history—one that is of abiding interest to students—Greenwood developed this series of reference works. These volumes examine the causes and impacts of scandal within key areas of American life—politics, sports, media, business, popular music, television, film, religion, and more. Prepared by field experts and professionals, the volumes are written to inform and educate high school and undergraduate college students as well as to engage and entertain students and general readers alike. As reference tools, they place scandals within a wider social and cultural context, but as general histories, they are fun to read from cover to cover.

The volumes have been carefully written and edited to ensure that a diversity of viewpoints surrounding each scandal topic is included. Because many of the issues that caused scandals have never been resolved, the books in this series can be used to spark classroom debate as well as to examine the ethical issues that come into play. Each volume is enhanced with a timeline, illustrations, and a bibliography so that students can read further and in more detail about subjects that pique their interest, as well as to augment the reading and learning experience.

PREFACE

Surveys taken since the end of World War II show that the United States is the most religious of all Western nations. According to a 2008 survey by the Pew Forum on Religion and Public Life, 92 percent of Americans believe in God. At least half say they worship regularly.

Religious people are good people. Therefore, America's religious people couldn't possibly be involved in religious scandals. Or, could they be?

The fact that this book is part of a series is evidence that Americans are quite adept at doing scandalous things. While most Americans are Christian, no religion has a monopoly on scandal. Scoundrels sometimes masquerade as religious people; people of all faiths sometimes do bad things. They commit adultery. They cheat, steal, and lie. Sometimes they even murder. Scandals of this type are described in the chapters in Part I. Chapter 1 deals with sex scandals. Chapter 2 treats scandals stemming from the way people acquired or used money. Chapter 3 involves hoaxes and cases of stretched truth, while Chapter 4 tells of murders and other violent crimes.

On occasion these conventional religious scandals have received so much media attention that the coverage itself has seemed scandalous, especially to those whose religion was implicated in wrong-doing. And on occasion, those critics are right. The coverage can be sensational and overblown. It can adversely affect people's opinions about those involved in the scandals and sometimes also about the religions to which they belong. But even people who sometimes complain about the attention given to bad news about religion often find religious scandals fascinating the same way they find fascinating stories about the excesses and foibles of entertainers and athletes, the chicanery of business tycoons, and of politicians caught with their hand in the public till.

However much religious scandals may entertain and titillate, they also warn that appearances can be deceiving. People who seem to be religious may be hypocrites. Otherwise good people may turn out to have feet of clay. By labeling certain behaviors as scandalous, stories about all scandals, and especially about conventional religious ones, serve as a reminder that some things, no matter who does them, are unacceptable.

While conventional scandals that occur when people cause outrage by doing things that are contrary to the teachings of their faith and that also violate social norms or break the law are important, there is another kind of scandal that is even more important because it is rooted in the First Amendment's promise that "Congress shall make no law regarding an establishment of religion or prohibiting the free exercise thereof."

With freedom of conscience guaranteed by the First Amendment, religion and religiosity in America flourished. At the same time, religions proliferated. Nine out of ten Americans say they believe in god, but they do not all believe in the same god. Even though most Americans say they worship the same god and point to the same scriptures as authoritative, the Christian majority is divided among more than 200 churches, denominations, and sects. Today there are also well over 1,000 world, new, and alternative religions practiced somewhere within the United States. Differences among Christians can, in some cases, be as great as, or greater than, differences between other religions or those between some Christians and some members of other religions. Just how great is the potential for misunderstandings, controversy and conflict, and even scandals caused by differences in religious beliefs and behaviors can be seen by scanning some of the headlines posted online by the Council for America's First Freedom (http://www.firstfreedom.org) for just the week of September 14–21, 2008:

- Pro-Republican Telephone Push Poll Questions Offend Some Michigan Jews
- "Radical Islam" DVD Reemerges as Insert in Swing State Newspapers
- Pastor Leads Campaign Against Signing California's Gender-neutral Marriage License
- Turmoil at Nebraska Plant over Prayer Accommodations Reflects Nationwide Problem
- Florida Indian Tribe Files Suit Against County Permit Requirement for Powwow
- Texas County Settles Lawsuit with New Court Screening Policy for Religious Clothing

As the sociologist of religion Peter Berger points out in his seminal 1967 book, *The Sacred Canopy,* each religion's teachings create a plausibility structure. For those who live within a plausibility structure—under the sacred canopy of a religion—the beliefs that make up that structure make perfect sense in ways that they cannot and will not make sense to those outside the structure. What one person or one religious group may see as required or condoned by god will, on occasion, be taken as scandalous nonsense by others.

Scandals sparked by people speaking or acting in accord with the dictates of their conscience are treated in Part II of this book. Chapter 5, "Blasphemy and Its Progeny," deals with sentiments about god and religion that Americans have found scandalous. Chapter 6, "Religio-political Heresy," describes scandals resulting from expressions of religiously inspired opinions about America and its political, economic, and social structure. Chapter 7, "Rituals That Rankle," and Chapter 8, "Problematic Practices," examine instances of unconventional worship and lifestyle that a majority has labeled as both scandalous and dangerous.

Like the scandals discussed in Part I of this book, most of those in Part II have received heavy media attention. But unlike the scandals in Part I that stemmed from people violating social conventions and/or the law, those described in Part II gain their importance from the way they challenge social conventions and sometimes seemingly settled areas of law. These scandals of conscience focus attention on those first 16 words of the First Amendment in ways that raise important questions about how to recognize and define a religion, about the meaning and scope of religious freedom, and about how far citizens, religious and secular organizations, and the government must, should, or could go in tolerating, deferring to, or accommodating all religions or any particular one.

Because the number of religious scandals is huge and this book is a relatively short one, it deals only with two kinds of scandals—those that violated custom and law and those that posed a challenge to custom and law. As interesting and as illustrative of broader social trends as some might be, internal scandals derived from theological disputes over doctrine and practice are beyond the scope of this book. Missing, too, are most instances of hate speech and hate crimes targeting religious persons or groups because, as much as they scandalized people of faith, most of them were the work of those acting more out of xenophobia or for economic or political reasons than out of religious conviction.

But even with those exclusions, some difficult decisions had to be made in order to produce a book of reasonable length. Toward that end, every effort was made to include the most notorious religious scandals that a reasonably well-informed reader would expect to find in a book of this kind. However, some interesting scandals were necessarily left out in order to make room for other ones that would provide for greater diversity in kinds of scandals within a category of scandals, as well as in religious traditions represented by them. Within those parameters, decisions were also based on a desire to include scandals spanning the more than two centuries of American history that have elapsed since the adoption of the First Amendment.

Some of the scandals included in this book turned out to be so complex that deciding which section they belonged in, or even in which chapter within a section to put them, required making some judgment calls.

Because both religions and secular society have proscriptions against them, as a general rule scandals involving sex, money, hoaxes and lies, murder, and mayhem were placed in the chapter in Part I that corresponds to the kind of offense for which the perpetrator got into the most trouble. The Jim Bakker and Jimmy Swaggart scandals, for example, are often lumped together because both televangelists committed adultery. Swaggart was neither accused of nor admitted to any other kind of wrongdoing, so his story is in Chapter 1, while the Bakker scandal is in Chapter 2 because his adultery led to serious charges about the way he acquired and spent money.

However, if the person or group at the heart of the scandal claimed to be violating the law or societal norms as a matter of conscience and others within that faith agreed, the scandal went into Part II. Like Jim Bakker, whose scandal is in Chapter 2, the Rev. Sun Myung Moon was ordered to pay back taxes. His scandal, however, is in Chapter 8 because both members of his own faith and leaders from other religions, who generally believed Moon to be a dangerous cult leader, agreed that the religious defense he tried to raise on his own behalf deserved more serious consideration than either society or the courts were willing to give it.

In making those judgments about how to classify a scandal, every effort was made to avoid relying on my own beliefs about both the religions involved in a scandal and the words or deeds that people found scandalous. Instead, in describing scandals and in deciding how to categorize them, I have done my utmost to rely on external evidence such as a person's title, self-description, stated motivations, and contemporaneous commentary from those who shared the perpetrator's faith and those who did not.

While the scandals included in this book by no means exhaust the list of all possible American religious scandals, the ones included are intended to provide both students and members of the general public with a glimpse into the world of American religions and American religious history. By comparing early scandals with later ones of the same type, readers can seek out evidence for continuity and change in kinds of scandals and media coverage. They can also look for and find evidence of continuity and change in verdicts rendered in courts of law and in the court of public opinion. With that evidence in hand, they are invited to think critically about the meaning and social import of that continuity and change.

I thank the many colleagues and friends who told me of religious scandals, and the many authors and journalists whose work I drew on in writing this volume. Special thanks go to Dr. Debra L. Mason, director of the Center for Religion and the Professions at the University of Missouri and executive director of the Religion Newswriters Association, and to Sue Schuermann and Michael Hopkins, librarians at the University of Missouri, for the countless hours they spent tracking down obscure information about some of the scandals included in this book.

Timeline: Significant Religious Scandals in U.S. History

1811	New York Supreme Court upholds the conviction of Mr. Ruggles for blasphemy.
1833 December	Abner Kneeland publishes a letter explaining his differences with Unitarians, which leads to his arrest and conviction on charges of blasphemy.
1834 September	The Prophet Matthias is arrested and charged with fraud and embezzlement, assault and battery, and murder.
1840 March	Clergy and bankers launch a Moral War against newspaper publisher James Gordon Bennett and his *New York Herald*.
1847 October	John Humphrey Noyes is arrested in Putneyville, Vermont, and charged with adultery after word that he and his followers are engaging in what they call "complex marriage."
1852	After Church president Brigham Young tells Mormons of founder Joseph Smith's 1831 revelation, Mormons in Utah begin practicing plural marriage.
1872 November	Feminist and free love advocate Victoria Woodhull breaks news of the Rev. Henry Ward Beecher's adultery with parishioner Elizabeth Tilton.

1879
June Fearing imminent arrest on morals charges, Oneida Community founder John Humphrey Noyes flees to Canada.

1890
October The Ghost Dance sparks fear of an Indian uprising.

1901
May Followers of John Dowie go on trial for murder in Illinois and New York in cases stemming from the deaths of their children as a result of their parents' reliance on faith healing.

1902
November With church members on trial for the deaths of their children, Church of Christ, Scientist founder Mary Baker Eddy instructs members to comply with health regulations requiring the reporting of and quarantine for infectious diseases.

1913
September Father Hans Schmidt confesses to the murder of his "wife" and lover, Anna Aumuller.

1925
April *Scientific American* announces that spiritualist psychic Mina Crandon, who performed as "Margery the Medium," is a fraud.

1926
October Father Charles Coughlin begins a radio ministry that over time becomes increasingly anti-government and anti-Semitic.

1928
May Evangelist Aimee Semple McPherson disappears, only to reappear 35 days later under questionable circumstances.

1935
October Jehovah's Witness children, among them William and Lillian Gobitas, disobey rules requiring students in public schools to stand and recite the Pledge of Allegiance each morning.

1945
September Lewis Ford dies from a snake bite just over a year after *Life* magazine, at Ford's urging, brought the religious practice of handling snakes as a test of faith to national attention.

1947–1948
Winter During an interstate convention of snake handlers in Durham, North Carolina, Walter Bunn and others are arrested for ignoring the law forbidding the practice.

1951

December — Public showing of the movie, *The Miracle,* in New York is met with a wave of protest.

1964

March — Heavyweight world boxing champion Cassius Clay takes the name "Muhammad Ali" as he joins the Nation of Islam.

1965

February — Nation of Islam followers of Elijah Muhammad assassinate Malcolm X, a former Nation of Islam member turned Sunni Muslim.

1966

February — Muhammad Ali refuses to serve in the military.

October — Word that John Lennon told a reporter that the Beatles are more popular than Jesus leads to protests and boycotts.

1967

October — Father Philip Berrigan is among those who pour a mixture of their own blood and duck blood on Selective Service records as part of an anti-Vietnam War protest outside the Baltimore Customs House.

1968

May — Fathers Dan and Philip Berrigan and seven other Vietnam War protesters remove Selective Service records from the office of the draft board in Catonsville, Maryland, and burn them.

1972

March — Warren Buffett's *West Omaha Sun* newspaper publishes results from its investigation into Boys Town finances.

1975 — Liston Pack challenges an injunction forbidding the handling of snakes during worship services at his church.

1976

October — Presidential candidate Jimmy Carter finds himself enmeshed in a scandal when *Playboy* magazine publishes a story in which he says he has committed "lust in my heart."

1978

April–May — News of the so-called "Mormon Will" attributed to tycoon Howard R. Hughes raises more questions than answers.

November — Followers of Jim Jones, founder of Peoples Temple, kill Congressman Leo Ryan, three journalists, and one would-be defector before committing mass suicide in Jonestown, Guyana.

1981

July
A move to eastern Oregon by spiritual leader Bhagwan Shree Rajneesh and his followers develops into a political fight for control of Wasco County.

October
The Rev. Sun Myung Moon is charged with tax evasion.

1984

July
Fundamentalist Mormons Dan and Ron Lafferty kill their sister-in-law and her daughter because of her refusal to follow her husband's polygamist beliefs.

September
Ma Anand Sheela, a follower of Bhagwan Shree Rajneesh, engineers a bioterrorist attack in The Dalles, Oregon.

1985

October
Galen Black, a white man, is fired from his job at an Oregon alcohol and drug rehabilitation center for ingesting peyote during a ceremony of the Native American Church

Salt Lake City bombing murders lead to evidence that Mark Hofmann forged the Salamander Letter that raised questions about the origin of the Mormon religion.

1987

March
News of televangelist Jim Bakker's adultery touches off an investigation leading to charges of fraud, conspiracy, and tax evasion.

Al Smith, a member of the Klamath tribe, is fired from his position as a drug and alcohol counselor after taking unauthorized time off to attend services of the Native American Church during which he ingests peyote.

June
Ernesto Pichardo's application for a zoning permit for his Church of the Lukumi Babalu Aye sparks controversy; the City of Hialeah, Florida, passes ordinances banning animal sacrifice as part of Santerian worship.

1988

February
Televangelist Jimmy Swaggart confesses to visiting a prostitute.

1989

March
Pepsi Company cancels its contract with pop star Madonna when religious imagery in her "Like a Prayer" video sets off a wave of protests.

May
Contemporary artist Andres Serrano's "Piss Christ" sparks heated debate over public funding for the arts and humanities.

1991

November   An ABC *Primetime Live* story raises questions about televangelist Robert Tilton's calls for monetary "commitment vows."

1993

April   Believing the millennial Branch Davidians are an imminent threat, government agents attack their Mt. Carmel/Ranch Apocalypse community outside Waco, Texas.

1994

June   The Rev. Paul Jennings Hill kills Dr. John Britton in the second of a series of murders of abortion providers between 1993 and 1998.

November   Hit men hired by Rabbi Fred Neulander kill the rabbi's wife.

1995

May   A routine audit following Ellen Cooke's resignation as treasurer of the Episcopal Church turns up evidence of embezzlement.

1996

April   A fund-raiser for Democratic vice-presidential candidate Al Gore at a Buddhist temple in California raises questions about political activity by religious organizations.

July   Christian Identity sympathizer Eric Rudolph plants a bomb at Olympic Centennial Park in what turns out to be the first in a series of bombings.

1999

May   Wiccan ceremonies on the military base at Fort Hood, Texas, stir up controversy and a Congressional debate over religious freedom and military preparedness.

2002

August   A Massachusetts court orders Rebecca Corneau, a member of The Body, confined to a state-run birthing facility to ensure that the child she is carrying will be born with doctors present.

2001

June   Andrea Yates drowns her five children as an act of mercy, she says, to save them.

July   Continuing to defy court orders, Alabama Judge Roy Moore surreptitiously installs a monument inscribed with the Ten Commandments in the rotunda of the state judicial building.

2002

January   The *Boston Globe* launches a year-long investigation into sexual abuse by Catholic priests in the Boston Archdiocese.

June   Independent fundamentalist Mormon Brian David Mitchell, aka Immanuel, kidnaps Elizabeth Smart.

2004

December   People for the Ethical Treatment of Animals releases a videotape revealing conditions and slaughter practices at AgriProcessors, a kosher slaughterhouse owned by Aaron Rubashkin.

2005

February   Following his arrest, Lutheran congregation president Dennis Rader confesses to being the notorious BTK serial killer.

2006

October   Gay prostitute Mike Jones tells of sexual relations with the Rev. Ted Haggard, pastor of New Life Church in Colorado Springs and president of the National Association of Evangelicals.

2008

March   News reports treat sermons that Democratic presidential candidate Barack Obama's pastor, the Rev. Jeremiah Wright, delivered in 2001 as scandalous.

A call to a welfare agency from a woman claiming to be a young girl wanting help escaping from her abusive, polygamist husband leads to a government raid on the fundamentalist Mormon Yearning for Zion community in Texas.

May   Government agents round up undocumented immigrant workers at the AgriProcessors kosher slaughterhouse in Postville, Iowa.

Part I

Conventional Scandals: Violations of Sacred and Secular Custom and Law

Chapter 1

ADULTERY, PEDOPHILIA, AND HOMOSEXUALITY

In 1850, Nathaniel Hawthorne published *The Scarlet Letter*, his classic novel about an adulterous relationship between the Rev. Arthur Dimmesdale and Hester Prynne. Although the book is a work of fiction, the fact that it became an instant best seller is testimony to the fact that people found the story of a sex scandal involving a seventeenth-century New England clergyman quite believable. For that, the popular press of the era was at least partly responsible.

Until then, criticizing religious beliefs was both common and accepted. Speaking or writing critically about the behavior of religious people was not common or accepted—especially when those illicit behaviors involved sexual improprieties. But acceptance of that kind of attention to religious people did not come easily. Therefore, this chapter opens with the Moral War clergy and business leaders waged against Scottish, Catholic newspaper publisher James Gordon Bennett who instituted the scandalous practice of publishing satires, news, and commentaries linking religion to sexual, fiscal, and political improprieties.

Bennett and his *New York Herald* emerged unscathed from the Moral War. Religious scandals became so much a press staple that the Rev. Henry Ward Beecher, the subject of the second scandal in this chapter, found his liaison with congregation member Elizabeth Tilton in the public eye for more than a decade. A century later, televangelist Jimmy Swaggart found, as Beecher had a century earlier, that those who court public attention also invite very public scrutiny when they commit the kind of sins they preach against. "I Call It Sin," the third section in this chapter, tells his story.

Other well-known religious leaders have committed similar sexual transgressions, but in their cases the sex turned out to be a relatively minor element in a different kind of scandal, so their stories are in other chapters. However, most sexual transgressions like the ones Bennett covered and Beecher and Swaggart committed get little media attention of the kind that can turn a local scandal into a national one. Partly this is because they involve people who are not well known outside their local community. And, partly it is because adulterous affairs are quite common.

Although neither divorce, nor premarital, nor extramarital sex produce the outrage they once did, there are still sexual taboos that do cause outrage. Violations of these taboos are the subject of the last two entries in this chapter—the case of the pedophile priests and the case of Ted Haggard, "A Deceiver and a Liar," whose visits to a male prostitute revealed the same kind of hypocrisy about gay sex that Beecher and Swaggart displayed in committing adultery.

A MORAL WAR

The January 19, 1836, headline in James Gordon Bennett's *New York Herald* screamed, "Awful Disclosures." The story, extracted from a book attributed to Maria Monk, told of unspeakable doings in an unspecified religious order in Canada. Immediately after "taking the veil" that made Maria a full-fledged member of the order, her superior informed her that she was expected to "act like the most abandoned of beings, and that all my future associates were habitually guilty of the most heinous and detestable crimes." Like other members of the order, her duties as a nun would include performing "criminal intercourse" with priests.[1]

Bennett published just one more installment of "Awful Disclosures," but he kept the story alive for years with frequent references to Maria and her tale of illicit sex. That he freely admitted "Awful Disclosures" was a work of fiction didn't matter.[2] The Protestant establishment latched onto it as confirmation of their worst fears about Catholics and the Catholic Church.

But Bennett wasn't writing for the establishment. He wrote for the workers who came to New York from rural America and increasingly from Ireland to take advantage of the economic opportunities the city's burgeoning industrial base offered them. At a time when serious papers generally insisted that readers pay $6 or $8 in advance for an annual subscription, Bennett sold his paper for just a penny per copy.

Employing a style that can best be described as a cross between the *National Enquirer* and a personal blog, Bennett freely mixed fact and fiction, news and opinion, and satire and serious commentary, often in the same story, in ways that both informed and titillated on every subject imaginable: business, education, crime and the courts, entertainment, sports and religion—and he did it all from an outsider's perspective.

Bennett was Scottish and Catholic, albeit of a rather independent and idiosyncratic kind. It was the unique perspective that Bennett brought to his work that made his paper a "must read" even among those who found him and his paper offensive. But it was Bennett's approach to news—especially as it applied to news about religion—that also sparked controversy.

Instead of writing to defend or promote a particular faith or even religion in general, Bennett reported religious behaviors and their consequences for believers and unbelievers alike. In contrast to establishment opinion, he was a staunch supporter of religious freedom for all, including Catholics. He was an equally staunch opponent of hypocrisy wherever he found it. In that respect, he criticized his own church with as much glee as he did the big and powerful Protestant ones.

In the *Herald,* Bennett poked fun at his own lack of conventional religiosity. He gave neutral to favorable attention to church histories and charitable activities. In the *Herald* there was gavel-to-gavel coverage of the annual meetings of Bible and missionary societies that were a common feature of the era. But there were also satires, news stories, and commentary highly critical of religious people and organizations. Bennett lambasted politicians and Protestant clergy for attempts to make America into a religious, that is, a Protestant, nation at the expense of Catholics and other religious minorities; he also lambasted Catholic clergy for attempting to meddle in politics. He reported crimes against and by religious people. He mocked a coalition of clergy and publishers of other newspapers for using money from churches to speculate in land. He accused the most influential Episcopal Church in the city of accumulating its great wealth by unethically wresting property from its rightful owners and then failing to use its money and power for the benefit of the poor.

Then there were the stories of religion and sex. Bennett used the same sensational tone that he used in referring to Maria Monk's "Awful Disclosures" in stories reporting real sexual improprieties by both Catholic and Protestant clergy. There were at least 20 such stories during 1836 alone. Perhaps in reaction to them, Bennett also published three stories about the "Kissers," a religious sect he invented that incorporated kissing into its worship services.[3]

He also launched a campaign against prudery. Instead of using the polite term, "limbs," he mentioned women's "legs." In the pages of the *Herald,* "inexpressibles" became "petticoats."[4]

By 1840, it was all too much for the good people of New York to take. Clergy, business leaders, and other newspapers banded together in a Moral War against Bennett and his *Herald.* At the time, Bennett seemed like an easy target. He was an outsider, a Scot and a Catholic in an America that saw itself as a Protestant nation. His paper was more salacious than anything the public had ever seen. Clearly Bennett was up to no good. He and his paper posed a threat to true religion, decency, and good order. So a boycott was organized that was designed to put Bennett and his offending paper out of business.

For a while, the boycott seemed to work. But after a few months, the Moral War fizzled. With pennies a day from his lower-class readers, Bennett had a power base that made him and his paper virtually immune to a boycott led by bankers, the elite press, and middle- and upper-class clergy. Those pennies gave him the money that let him expand newsgathering by paying local reporters and correspondents from around the nation.

As Bennett devoted more time to management and less to writing, poetry and fiction became less common as fillers. There were also fewer satires. But beyond that, little changed. The reporters and correspondents knew what Bennett and his paper's readers expected, and they obliged with stories of religious scandals whenever the occasion presented itself.

In 1844, for example, a correspondent's account of a revival in Saratoga, New York, included reference to a "little backsliding" by one of the "brothers" that left a "dearly beloved sister ... burthened with a little responsibility."[5] In language more inflammatory than that used in connection with Maria Monk's "Awful Disclosures," the *Herald* published trial testimony and reporters' accounts of the seduction of Rhoda Davidson by the Rev. Joy H. Fairchild and of bigamy charges against the Rev. E. K. Avery.[6]

That kind of coverage remained a staple so long as Bennett was in charge. In journalism histories he remains linked to the Maria Monk story as an example of the kind of sensationalism that made him famous and infamous. Few people today would hold him up as a role model. Still, historians generally agree that his approach to religion reporting stands among his lasting contributions to journalism.

Where at one time covering religion from the standpoint of an outside, essentially neutral, observer seemed radical, today it is the norm. Bennett's church histories and detailed accounts of religious conventions and church events are now staples on the religion page. His hard news and investigative reporting showed that a newspaper can both survive and perform a public service by bringing religious scandals to public attention.

In 1924, Bennett's *New York Herald* merged with the New York *Tribune*. The combined *Herald Tribune* lasted until 1966.

A SAINT OR A SINNER?

The Rev. Henry Ward Beecher was the son of the Rev. Lyman Beecher, one of the most prominent mainstream Protestant evangelists of the era of religious revivalism that has become known as the Second Great Awakening. His sister, Harriet Beecher Stowe, wrote *Uncle Tom's Cabin*. As pastor of Plymouth Congregational Church in Brooklyn, the Rev. Henry Ward Beecher spoke to and for an era.

His message blended the idea of science-based reform with conventional religious piety in a way that called for both social change and personal, moral rectitude and self-improvement. People bought his books and eagerly read his magazine articles and columns. They flocked to his church to hear him preach.

Beecher embraced Darwin's theory of evolution and fervently supported the temperance movement. He was passionately anti-Catholic and contemptuous of the Irish-Catholic immigrants that at the time seemed to threaten the popular vision of a Protestant America. But he was also a consistent advocate for women's suffrage and a staunch foe of slavery.

Mock slave auctions at Beecher's church raised thousands of dollars to purchase the freedom of slaves. During the Civil War, Plymouth Church raised and equipped a volunteer infantry regiment. He pressed Lincoln to emancipate the slaves and went on a speaking tour in England to explain the North's aims and undermine support for the South. Near the end of the war, he was the main speaker at the ceremony when the Stars and Stripes was once again raised over Fort Sumter.

With the Civil War over and the North victorious, Beecher's popularity was at an all-time high as many credited him and his sister for their roles in popularizing and garnering support for the cause. Then, the unimaginable happened.

In July 1870, Plymouth Church member Elizabeth Tilton told her husband Theodore, also a church member and a business partner of the Rev. Henry Ward Beecher, that she had been having an affair with Beecher. In December of that year, Tilton confronted Beecher, who denied having any improper relations with Elizabeth. That would have been the end of it, except that at some point Tilton mentioned his wife's confession to his friend, Elizabeth Cady Stanton. Stanton told her friend and fellow women's rights advocate, Victoria Woodhull. Offended that Beecher was apparently engaged in the kind of "free love" relationship she advocated and that he railed against in sermons and writings, Woodhull published the story in the November 2, 1872, issue of her paper, *Woodhull and Claflin's Weekly*.[7]

Beecher issued a public statement denying that he had engaged in any kind of improper relation with Elizabeth Tilton. Mr. Tilton denounced Woodhull in statements to Brooklyn and New York City newspapers. Woodhull was arrested and imprisoned for sending obscene material through the mail. Elizabeth Tilton recanted her confession of adultery in writing.[8]

But the story refused to die. In 1874, the Church appointed a church council to investigate the matter. The council, made up largely of Beecher supporters, ruled the allegations groundless. Theodore Tilton filed criminal charges against Beecher and the matter went to court in January 1875.

The Beecher trial became the story of the century. The *New York Times* alone published more than 100 stories about it. Other newspapers in the area gave it equally heavy coverage and papers as far away as New Orleans and San Francisco regularly kept their readers informed about the latest developments in the case. Pamphlets both criticizing Beecher and supporting him flew off the presses.[9]

Throughout the trial Beecher consistently denied that he had engaged in adultery, while giving maddeningly vague answers to questions about the nature of his relationship with Mrs. Tilton. But in the end, most of the jurors couldn't bring themselves to believe that so prominent a preacher could be

Newspapers, magazines, broadsides, and pamphlets like this 1875 example kept the Beecher-Tilton affair in the public eye for over a decade. Library of Congress, James E. Cook drawing.

guilty of wrongdoing. In July 1875, Beecher was acquitted by a vote of 9 to 3. Still, the story would not go away.

In 1877, Elizabeth Tilton again confessed to an adulterous affair with Beecher. The church held another inquiry. Once again Beecher was exonerated. Through it all, Beecher's wife supported him. So did most of his family. And so did most members of his church. The Rev. Beecher kept his position as pastor of Plymouth Congregational Church until his death on March 8, 1887.

When Beecher died, national figures, including President Grover Cleveland, sent letters of condolence. The city of Brooklyn declared a day of mourning; the New York State legislature went into recess to honor him.

Beecher was, and still is, honored for his role in the abolition movement. But questions about the true nature of his relationship with Elizabeth Tilton remain unanswered, so the scandal also remains a part of Beecher's legacy.

Although the media no longer compare new instances of improprieties on the part of members of the clergy to events in the Beecher-Tilton saga as newspapers once did, their coverage of that saga helped make news of scandals involving clergy a standard part of religion news.

From that scandal the clergy learned they could no longer expect the press to look the other way when allegations of scandal surface. Newspapers learned anew that the public has an appetite for juicy clergy scandals; covering those scandals can be a money-maker and a public service (this chapter, "A Moral War").

As sensational as some of the coverage was, the story raised important questions about middle- and upper-class morality and family life. It also launched a national debate about the standards to which clergy should be held and to whom and by whom they should be held accountable that still has relevance (this chapter, "Pedophile Priests," "A Deceiver and a Liar").

I CALL IT SIN

In the late 1970s, when pressure from the National Association of Evangelicals led national television networks to open the airwaves to paid religious broadcasting, Jimmy Swaggart seized the opportunity, adding television to his ministry that already included radio broadcasts. By the mid 1980s, he had become the most popular of the new wave of televangelists that included Jim Bakker (Chapter 2, "Hush Money, Fraud, and a Lost Empire"), Jerry Falwell, and Pat Robertson.

Thousands flocked to services at Swaggart's Family Worship Center in Baton Rouge, Louisiana. An estimated 2 million people watched his television program. Swaggart's ministry alone contributed more than $10 million to the Assemblies of God mission budget; his popularity contributed immeasurably to the nearly 25 percent increase in membership that the denomination enjoyed between 1979 and 1985.

Swaggart spoke to and for the fundamentalist wing of Pentecostalism. In his church and on his broadcasts, he demanded that people turn to Jesus, avoid sins of the flesh, and shun worldly pleasures. He railed against adultery, adult entertainment, pornography, and rock-and-roll music. He both distanced himself from and spoke out publicly against anyone who didn't conform to his strict standards.

He broke with his cousin and boyhood chum after Jerry Lee Lewis created a scandal by marrying his 13-year-old cousin once removed. When Marvin Gorman, a popular Assemblies of God minister headquartered in Louisiana, was caught in adultery, Swaggart demanded he be given no special treatment just because he pastored a large congregation. He said much the same thing after the *Charlotte (NC) Observer* broke the story of fellow Assemblies of God minister and televangelist Jim Bakker's adultery and misuse of ministry money (Chapter 2, "Hush Money, Fraud, and a Lost Empire"). Saying Bakker was "a cancer that needs to be excised from the body of Christ," Swaggart called for him to be banned from preaching as an Assemblies of God minister for at least the one-year standard sentence.[10]

But if his words were often harsh, Swaggart, like his cousins Jerry Lee Lewis and Mickey Gilley, was also a born entertainer and gifted musician. Usually speaking extemporaneously and without notes, he whispered and shouted. As he preached, he danced and pranced, sang gospel songs, and played the piano. He didn't just lead a worship service. Week after week, Swaggart provided great theater.

But his most memorable performance had none of the shouting, dancing, singing, and piano playing that were his trademarks. On February 18, 1988, a subdued Swaggart spoke to his followers in a voice that sometimes fell almost to a whisper. He begged forgiveness from his wife, Frances, son, Donnie, the more than 8,000 congregation members who packed his Baton Rouge church, the countless thousands of others who watched on television, and finally from his Savior and Redeemer, Jesus Christ. "I do not call it a mistake, a mendacity. I call it sin," he said.[11]

At no time did Swaggart actually mention the sin by name, but he didn't have to. Everyone knew Swaggart's sin. Three days earlier, on February 15, 1988, Swaggart had been summoned to the Assemblies of God headquarters in Springfield, Missouri, to respond to evidence that he had been involved in improper sexual relations. The evidence came from the Rev. Gorman.

Gorman believed that Swaggart had brought his moral lapse to the attention of denomination headquarters at least partly to remove his chief rival in Louisiana from the scene. He sued Swaggart and the church for $25 million over his defrocking. Then, when his supporters began telling him that Swaggart might also be guilty of the sexual improprieties he railed against, Gorman hired a detective to see what he could find.

In October 1987, the detective found what he was looking for—Swaggart entering a house of prostitution. The detective took photos of Debra Murphree welcoming Swaggart into a room at the Travel Inn in New Orleans. He then called Gorman, who rushed to the motel where the detective took more pictures as Gorman confronted Swaggart.

Four months later, the photos showed up at denomination headquarters where they prompted the emergency meeting with Swaggart. During the meeting, Swaggart confessed to church leaders that he had struggled with an addiction to pornography since he was a teen. He also admitted to visiting prostitutes.

The Louisiana district of the Assemblies of God initially ordered Swaggart to step down from his position as pastor of the Baton Rouge church and refrain from preaching for three months, except for some preexisting commitments to preach in Europe. After that, he would be subject to a two-year "rehabilitation" process that would include clergy supervision. But the light sentence infuriated Assemblies clergy and lay members from around the nation; it also upset denomination headquarters because the district had acted alone. Bowing to pressure, the district imposed a one-year ban, which headquarters affirmed. Swaggart, however, announced plans to resume preaching on May 22, a move that effectively ended his career as an Assemblies of God minister.

Debra Murphree, the prostitute whom Swaggart had visited, got an advance of $75,000 from *Penthouse* for a story and photos in its July 1988 issue, and then disappeared from the scene.

Initially, research indicated a decline in the audience for religious television and respect for televangelists.[12] But 20 years later, Swaggart was still broadcasting radio and television programs from his Baton Rouge church. Figures published on its Web site and in annual editions of the *Yearbook of American and Canadian Churches* show that Assemblies of God was still growing, albeit not quite as fast as it was before the scandal.

Although lasting effects on the principals in the scandal turned out to be minimal, to some extent the televangelism scandals of 1987–1988 continue to taint the televangelism industry's image.

PEDOPHILE PRIESTS

There had been suspicions, hints, and allegations for years (this chapter, "A Moral War"). Occasionally, some of them had even been confirmed.

In 1985 in Louisiana, Father Gilbert Gauthe pleaded guilty to 11 counts of molesting young boys. In 1992, the Rev. James Porter of the Fall River, Massachusetts, diocese was accused of abusing children in five states; he later pleaded guilty to 41 counts of abuse. In 1993, legal proceedings began against the Dallas diocese over sexual abuse by the Rev. Rudolph Kos; in 1998, the diocese was ordered to pay $31 million to his victims.

But the scope of the problem of pedophile priests within the Roman Catholic Church didn't come to light until 2002 when the *Boston Globe* launched a year-long investigation as the Rev. John Geoghan, who had been a priest at St. Julia's parish in Weston, Massachusetts, went on trial for molestations that occurred in 1991.

Information revealed at trial and uncovered by the *Globe* through use of public records showed that similar complaints about Geoghan had repeatedly been brought to the church's attention during his 30 years as a priest. In each case Cardinal Bernard Law, like his predecessor Cardinal Humberto Madeiros, chose to deal with the problem internally instead of notifying secular authorities. On five occasions, Geoghan was reassigned to a new parish after allegations of pedophile behavior came to church attention. During that time, he had been treated off and on by private psychoanalysts and psychotherapists; he had also been treated for pedophilic inclinations at St. Luke's Institute in Maryland, the Institute of Living in Hartford, Connecticut, and the Southdown Institute in Ontario, Canada.[13]

But Geoghan was not an isolated case within the Boston archdiocese. In May 2002 the Rev. Paul Shanley, who had gained fame and glowing newspaper coverage from the *Boston Globe* for his street ministry to at-risk boys in Boston's poorer sections, was arrested in California and charged with three counts of child rape. Like Geoghan, he had been reassigned several times, apparently following allegations of sexual misconduct. A story on page A21 in the January 31, 2002 *Globe* telling the story of several men who claimed to be his victims led others to come forward with their own claims of sexual abuse by Shanley and other priests in Boston and throughout the country.[14]

While some of those allegations of sexual abuse are suspect, depending as they do on recovery of long-repressed memories, the *Globe* found court records documenting 18 cases against priests in addition to the one against Geoghan. An examination of clergy rosters turned up the names of 102 priests who in the 1990s had been placed on sick leave or removed from the clergy roster; there were settlements of sexual abuse claims involving 30 of those priests. Attorney Roderick MacLeish Jr. told the *Globe* of cases against 45 priests and 5 brothers from Catholic religious orders handled by his firm.[15]

Many cases were settled privately; in those that went to court, the names of the victim(s) were not part of the public record. In 10 cases in Middlesex, Suffolk, and Essex counties, the judge also removed the names of the priests from the public record. Therefore, it is almost impossible to tell how many priests abused how many victims, but according to a January 31 story in the *Globe*, credible sources estimated the number of victims in Massachusetts alone as in excess of 200. It also is difficult to determine how much the Boston archdiocese knew and when it knew about individual cases, but evidence in that story also revealed that in the mid-1990s the archdiocese paid a $400,000 settlement that kept allegations against Geoghan from becoming public.[16]

After 1992, Cardinal Law apparently more carefully avoided moving problem priests to assignments where they would have easy access to children. But in continuing to handle complaints internally, he, like bishops from around the country who admitted after a 1992 meeting in South Bend, Indiana, that some of them had hidden information about sexual abuse within their diocese, were acting in accord with Vatican policy. A directive ordering bishops and archbishops to deal with such matters internally originated with Cardinal Joseph Ratzinger, who was then the Vatican's prefect for the Congregation for the Doctrine of the Faith and is now Pope Benedict XVI.[17]

Only after the *Boston Globe* initiated its investigation did the Vatican begin to revise its policy concerning pedophilia cases. But even then it was at least as concerned with securing privacy for accused priests as it was with the harm they caused their victims.[18] But by then it was too little, too late.

News media around the country reported the findings from Massachusetts. Men and boys came forward telling stories of abuse that they had suffered at the hands of trusted priests. The media investigated the situation in their own areas. And the scope of the scandal mushroomed.

Hard numbers of pedophile priests and their victims are impossible to obtain, but a report commissioned by the Church and released in February 2004 put the number of priests accused of pedophilia in the United States in the last 50 years at more than 4,000 and the number of victims, mostly boys, at more than 10,000.[19]

On January 9, 2002, as Geoghan was standing trial on child abuse charges, Cardinal Law apologized to Geoghan's victims and promised to take a tougher line whenever new instances of pedophilia came to his attention. He apologized again on November 3 for having made decisions that caused so much suffering.[20] But on December 13, just 10 days after new allegations accusing eight priests of abusing women and girls and taking drugs and supplying drugs in return for sexual favors became public, he resigned as archbishop. The Vatican accepted his resignation, but Law kept his rank of cardinal, which is a separate position from that of archbishop. Pope John Paul quickly named him to a number of high positions within the Vatican bureaucracy. After Pope John Paul died in 2005, Law participated in the papal enclave that elected Joseph Ratzinger as pope.

On January 18, 2002, John Geoghan was convicted for indecent assault on a child and sentenced to 10 years in prison. On August 23, 2003, he was trapped in his cell at the Souza-Baranowski Correctional Center in Shirley, Massachusetts, strangled, and stomped to death by Joseph Druce, a fellow inmate and self-identified white supremacist.

On February 7, 2005, Paul Shanley was convicted on four counts that included rape and sexual assault on young boys and sentenced to 12 to 15 years in prison; he was acquitted on March 3, 2007, in a similar rape case.

On September 19, 2002, the Boston Archdiocese reached a $10 million settlement with Geoghan's victims; in 2003, it agreed to pay $84 million to settle 552 other cases.

Other dioceses and archdioceses faced similar financial problems as settlements in sex abuse cases mounted. Among the largest of those, the Diocese of Orange, California, paid $100 million to settle 90 claims and the Diocese of Covington, Kentucky, paid about $80 million to settle 552 claims. Five dioceses and archdioceses in California agreed to pay amounts ranging from $35 million to more than $600 million to settle still more claims. On July 7, 2004, the Archdiocese of Portland, Oregon, filed for bankruptcy rather than go to trial and face paying out the $155 million at stake in a lawsuit. The Diocese of Tucson, Arizona, followed suit, filing for bankruptcy in September 2004. A month later, the Diocese of Spokane, Washington, filed for bankruptcy. In February 2007, the Diocese of San Diego, California, also declared bankruptcy.

In 2003, the *Boston Globe* received the Pulitzer Prize for Public Service for its investigation and comprehensive coverage of the sexual abuse scandal. A year later, it published the full findings of its investigation in a book, *Betrayal,* written by the *Globe's* investigative staff.

Professional journalism organizations applauded the media's role in uncovering and writing about the pedophile priest scandal—so did The Vatican Survivors Network, along with other groups concerned with victims' rights. Although coverage was neither as heavy nor as sustained as it had been in the 1987 televangelism scandal involving Jim Bakker (see Chapter 2, "Hush Money, Fraud, and a Lost Empire"), many people inside and outside the Church criticized the media for excessive and sensational coverage. Catholic scholar Philip Jenkins called the coverage an example of anti-Catholic bias, which he described as "the last acceptable prejudice" in his book *The New Anti-Catholicism.*[21]

Certainly there were instances of misstatement, overstatement, and needless sensationalism in the coverage. But labeling the heavy, sustained coverage as evidence of pervasive anti-Catholicism ignores the reality that for over a century the media have covered scandals, relatively few of which have involved the Catholic Church. The thing that set the pedophilia scandal apart from those others was that it involved so many cases over such a long period of time that had been so systematically hidden from view by church officials who did not seem to take seriously the damage the illicit sex had done to victims.

But even if anti-Catholicism on the part of some journalists and some commentators may have been a contributing factor in some instances of poorly done or over-sensationalized coverage, the heavy, sustained coverage did not unleash a wave of anti-Catholicism anywhere near as virulent as the anti-Catholicism of 160 or even 75 years ago. In 1844, attacks on Catholic immigrants by Protestants, calling themselves "Native Americans," led to days of rioting in Philadelphia; by the end of the 1840s, the Native American party controlled local government in Pennsylvania and had made in-roads in other industrial states. In the 1920s and 1930s, the Ku Klux Klan targeted Catholics along with African Americans and Jews in its campaigns of terror and violence.

Instead of unleashing a wave of anti-Catholic sentiment, the scandal's only real effect on nonmembers may have been the force it lent to the burgeoning conservative Protestant opposition to any kind of civil rights or protections from hate crimes for homosexuals by making it easier for people falsely to assume that homosexuality is synonymous with pedophilia (this chapter, "A Deceiver and a Liar"). Beyond that, the scandal's main effect appears to have been internal to the Church.

Although few Catholics left the Church, the scandal had a big impact on Church resources. Even dioceses and archdioceses that weren't forced into bankruptcy by the massive settlements found themselves with cash flow problems as members redirected their financial giving to other Catholic institutions, and other charities, instead of making contributions that would flow into Church coffers. The scandal also exacerbated the persistent problem within the Church of finding enough priests to staff its parishes. Removing problem priests from the clergy roster decreased the number of available clergy by as much as 10 percent in archdioceses such as the one in Boston, while simultaneously making it even more difficult to attract young men to the vocation than it had been.[22]

A DECEIVER AND A LIAR

Ted Haggard studied at Oral Roberts University and served as associate pastor of Bethany World Prayer Center in Baton Rouge, Louisiana, before moving to Colorado Springs, Colorado. There, in a city sometimes described as "The Vatican of evangelical Christianity" because it is home to more than 100 evangelical church and para-church organizations including the Fellowship of Christian Athletes and James Dobson's Focus on the Family,[23] Haggard started New Life Church in January 1985 as an outreach ministry of Bethany Prayer Center. The Church thrived under his leadership, growing from a handful of worshippers meeting in the basement of his home to a mega-church with a 7,000-seat worship center and a claimed membership in 2006 of 14,000.

Haggard was a powerful pastor at the peak of his career. Though never as well known as Dobson or televangelists Jerry Falwell and Pat Robertson, he was president of the National Association of Evangelicals, the umbrella organization representing 30 million conservative Protestants. That position helped him put environmentalism on the conservative Protestant agenda, but he also used his position to garner support for other causes that have long been dear to the hearts of those who are part of the Christian Right.

Haggard strongly opposed abortion. And although he ministered to homosexuals through his New Life Church, he preached that homosexuality is a sinful lifestyle choice. He spoke weekly by phone with President George W. Bush, whom he regularly pressed for an amendment to the U.S. Constitution to ban gay marriage. He was a driving force behind Colorado's Amendment 43, which, if passed by popular vote in the November 7, 2006, election, would have banned gay marriage in Colorado.

But just a week before the election, Mike Jones, a male prostitute, revealed in an interview on KHOW radio that Haggard had regularly paid him for his services over a three-year period. Haggard had also bought and snorted crystal methamphetamine on a number of occasions.[24]

Haggard initially denied the allegations, saying he had never heard of Jones. Fellow evangelicals rallied to his support, but on November 2, 2006, New Life Church issued a statement saying Haggard was stepping down as senior pastor, at least temporarily, because he "could not effectively minister under the cloud created by the accusations."[25]

In a Focus on the Family news release issued that same November day, James Dobson called it "unconscionable" that "the legitimate news media" would report an allegation based on an accusation by just one man. "It appears," he said, "someone is trying to damage his [Haggard's] reputation as a way of influencing the outcome of Tuesday's election—especially the vote on Colorado's marriage amendment—which Ted strongly supports."[26]

On November 3, the *Denver Post* reported that results of a lie-detector test that Jones voluntarily took on the popular KHOW radio show hosted by Peter Boyle indicated deception in response to questions about whether he had engaged in sex acts with Haggard.[27] But there were also reports that voice analysis expert Richard Sanders had test results indicating that a sample of Haggard's voice taken from a television interview with him seemed to match samples from voicemails provided by Jones.[28]

The next day, the Overseer Board of New Life Church issued a statement saying that their investigation, along with Haggard's public statements, indicated he had "demonstrated immoral conduct." Therefore, "we have decided the most positive and productive direction for our church is his dismissal and removal."[29]

In a letter read in Sunday services at New Life Church, Haggard told congregation members, "I am a deceiver and a liar. There is a part of my life that is so repulsive and dark that I've been warring against it all of my adult life." Although he never described that "repulsive and dark" part, he admitted it was bad enough for him to have been "appropriately and lovingly removed from the ministry" and required "to submit to oversight by a team of church-appointed counselors.[30]

Gayle Haggard, Ted's wife and the mother of their five children, issued her own statement the same day. In it, she said she loved her husband and was committed to him and her marriage "until death 'do us part.'"[31]

Although Dobson feared and Jones hoped that the scandal would derail Colorado's gay marriage amendment, that didn't happen. In the November election, 52 percent of Colorado voters supported Colorado Amendment 43. That was just one percent less than the support Coloradoans gave in November 1992 to the more all-encompassing Amendment 2, which the U.S. Supreme Court subsequently deemed unconstitutional because it denied homosexuals the kind of equal legal protection required for all groups by the Fourteenth Amendment to the U.S. Constitution.

Nor did the scandal do anything to undermine the belief professed by Haggard and widely shared by conservative Protestants that homosexuality is a sinful lifestyle choice and not an inherent characteristic. In February 2007, Tim Ralph, a member of the team appointed by New Life to counsel Haggard, told the Associated Press that Haggard's relations with Jones were more an "acting out situation" than real homosexual behavior. If Haggard ever had homosexual inclinations, that was no longer true. Haggard is, Ralph said, "100 percent heterosexual"—something he fully realized only while visiting Jones, to which Jones responded that nothing in his three-year-long association with Haggard led him to believe that Haggard was anything but a gay man.[32]

Like Jones, others within the homosexual and transgendered community and many psychologists and medical professionals found Ralph's statement hard to believe.[33] Therefore, one effect of the scandal was to raise questions about the efficacy of the kind of reparation therapy some religious organizations offer.

In addition to sparking debate about the root causes of homosexuality and the claim of homosexuals to be entitled to the same kind of rights and protections available to other minorities, the scandal also again raised questions about the entrepreneurial spirit within American religion that allows televangelists, pastors of mega-churches, and other religious leaders to develop power bases from which they can operate independently of any meaningful oversight by a denomination or even an independent board of directors[34] (Chapter 2, "Hush Money, Fraud, and a Lost Empire"; Chapter 3, "Praying for Dollars").

Although Dobson criticized the media for so quickly reporting the story, Religion Newswriters Association, the professional organization for journalists who cover religion for the secular press, gave the Supple Award for excellence in religion writing to Eric Gorski, the religion writer at the *Denver Post* in 2006, for a body of work that included his coverage of the Haggard scandal.

Still, the scandal is so recent that it is too soon to know whether it will have any lasting effect on New Life Church. However, in March 2007, New Life Church announced that after 22 years of steady growth in attendance and financial contributions, it would have to lay off 44 staff members because of a decline in Sunday offerings since the scandal broke. And, further problems lay just ahead.

In late August 2007, Haggard sent messages to supporters and a letter to KRDO-TV in Colorado Springs asking that money be sent directly to him or channeled to him through Families with a Mission because his earning power had fallen so much since the scandal. Records in the Colorado secretary of state's office showed Family with a Mission sharing a Monument, Colorado, address with Paul Huberty. Although the organization was listed as a charitable organization in good standing in Hawaii as of February 2007, Huberty was listed in Hawaii as a registered sex offender who had moved out of state.[56]

The church was in the news again on December 9, 2007, when Matthew Murray, who had been dismissed from a suburban Denver minister-in-training program run by Youth with a Mission, shot and killed several people before traveling to Colorado Springs. There, he shot four people, killing two, at New Life Church before he was shot and killed by Jeanne Assam, a volunteer security guard at the church.

FOR FURTHER READING

Bjerga, Alan. 2001. The trials of faith: Discussion of religion and the Beecher adultery scandal, 1870–1880. *American Journalism* 18(1): 73–94.

Blumhofer, Edith L. 1987, May 6. Divided Pentecostals: Bakker v. Swaggart. *Christian Century*, pp. 430–431.

Buddenbaum, Judith M. 1987. "Judge … what their acts will justify": The religion journalism of James Gordon Bennett. *Journalism History* 14(2–3): 54–67.

Darman, Jonathan, and Andrew Murr. 2006, November 13. A pastor's fall from grace. *Newsweek*, pp. 34–37.

Entrepreneurs R us. 2006, December. *Christianity Today*, pp. 22–23.

Fox, Richard Wightman. 1999. *Trials of intimacy: Love and loss in the Beecher-Tilton scandal*. Chicago: University of Chicago Press.

Gillis, Chester. 2002, July 29–August 5. Cultures, codes and publics. *America*, pp. 8–11.

Gorski, Eric. 2006, November 5. Disgraced Haggard: I am a "deceiver and a liar." *Denver Post*. Retrieved January 22, 2008, from http://www.denverpost.com/search/ci_4607865.

Hougland, James G., Jr., Dwight Billings, and James R. Wood. 1990, September. The instability of support for television evangelists: Public reactions during a period of embarrassment. *Review of Religious Research* 32(1): 56–64.

Investigative staff of the *Boston Globe*. 2002. *Betrayal: The crisis in the Catholic Church*. Boston: Little, Brown.

Monk, Maria. 1836, January 19. Awful disclosures. In Judith M. Buddenbaum and Debra L. Mason, eds., *Readings on religion as news*. Ames: Iowa State University Press, 2000, pp. 91–93.

Ostling, Richard N. 1988, March 7. Now it's Jimmy's turn. *Time*, pp. 46–48.

Pfeiffer, Sacha. 2002, January 31. Famed "street priest" preyed upon boys. *Boston Globe*, p. A21.

Rossetti, Stephen J. 2002, April 22. The Catholic Church and child sexual abuse. *America*, pp. 9–15.

Sins of the fathers. 2002, March 4. *Newsweek*, pp. 48–53.

Stern, Madeline B., ed. 1974. *The Victoria Woodhull reader*. Weston, MA: M&S Press, sec. 2.

Chapter 2

MONEY, MARKETING, AND MANAGEMENT

Money, it has been said, is the root of all evil. Money can be a seductive temptress. Money brings with it access to all sorts of goodies. Having it translates into power or provides access to it. In a capitalist, consumer-oriented society like the United States, the desire for money can be strong both for people of faith and for those who profess not to believe in any god. Religious people, like everyone else, fall victim to greed, covetousness, and all sorts of financial chicanery.

In fact, some religious people may be especially susceptible to the lure of money because of their religious beliefs. Those who believe their god wants them to be prosperous or who believe that having the good things in life is a sign of god's favor can easily come to believe they deserve whatever they can get, no matter how they get it. Others may create, promote, or engage in all kinds of questionable money-making schemes in order to get the money that they believe is necessary to spread their religious message to those who are not yet committed to their god or to help what they believe will be a more god-pleasing society.

Although consumer advocates and financial advisers regularly remind people to check whether the nonprofit organizations, including religious ones, to which they donate money are trustworthy, few people take this advice when it comes to giving at the behest of a religious leader in whom they have confidence. They willingly and trustingly contribute to religions and religious causes promoted by a leader whom they have come to love and whose religious message they find genuine.

But even if donors were to check very carefully to make sure their gifts are going where the leader says they will go, there would simply be no way to tell for sure whether the leader and the causes she or he endorses are really from God. That, ultimately, is a matter of faith, and that is the message behind the first section in this chapter—the story of a self-styled religious prophet who, though probably mentally ill, managed to attract a following that included well-to-do, relatively sophisticated businessmen, who gave everything they had to support what they believed to be the Kingdom of God.

The second section, "The Richest City in America," is also a story of true believers who wanted only to raise money for what everyone agreed was a worthy cause. But they wanted so badly to do what was right that they found themselves embroiled in a scandal that turned on the questionable means they used to solicit funds. "Dollars for Democrats ... and Republicans," also is about religious people working for what they considered to be a good cause. But in that case, the seduction at the heart of the scandal lay in the access to power money can buy.

The remaining sections speak more directly to money as a temptress. The third scandal, "Hush Money, Fraud, and a Lost Empire," is the story of how an investigation into a popular televangelist's adultery mushroomed into a giant money scandal involving misappropriation, fraud, and tax evasion. Although the belief that God wants people to have good things and the attendant desire for goodies played a role in that scandal, greed played a bigger role in the remaining entries in this chapter.

"The Heiress Who Wasn't" is a classic case of financial wrongdoing—a case of outright theft committed by a trusted denominational financial officer with sticky fingers. The last section, "The Meat Mess," tells the story of an outwardly devout man who, like the televangelist described in "Hush Money, Fraud, and a Lost Empire," built an empire and lost it as a result of his business practices. But his story, like those in the second and fifth sections, is one of believing the ends justify the means.

THE KINGDOM, MONEY, SEX, AND MAYBE A MURDER

The pastor of the Scottish Calvinist church his family attended in Coila, New York, found Robert Matthews so appealing and so religiously precocious that he pronounced a special blessing on Matthews when he was only seven.[1] But if he was in tune with the divine, Matthews's life in the real world was anything but blessed.

In 1808, at age 20, he migrated from his home in Coila to New York City, where his incessant proselytizing led his fellow carpenters to call him "Jumping Jesus."[2] When they could no longer tolerate his religious harangues, they got Matthews fired from one job after another. Prone to foul moods and with a conviction for assault and battery against a woman on his record, he returned home. Back in Coila, he married, started a family, and enjoyed a few prosperous years as the proprietor of a general store before being forced into bankruptcy by bad business decisions. He also drifted away from the faith in which he was raised.

After briefly flirting with the Methodist and Quaker religions, Matthews became fascinated by Mordecai M. Noah, the editor of the *National Advocate* newspaper in New York City and self-proclaimed Judge of Israel and Messiah of the Jews. Deciding that he, like Noah, was descended from the Israelites, Matthews dreamed of using his carpentry skills to help Noah build his New Israel on Grand Island in the Niagara River.

When nothing came of Noah's scheme, Matthews moved his family to Albany, where he found steady work in the fast-growing state capital. There, resolving to be a better husband, he followed his wife into a church associated with the revival movement led by the Rev. Charles Finney.

All went well for a few months, but then Matthews's younger son contracted smallpox and died. Matthews's foul moods returned. He berated and beat his wife, claiming she was possessed of an evil spirit. She found emotional and physical support in a community of evangelical women. When he applied for membership in a Methodist church in Albany, he was rebuffed.

In mid-June 1830, Matthews quit his carpentry job, saying that the time for earthly work was over. He stopped shaving because, he said, God never intended for men to cut their hair. He went to City Hall and entered the mayor's office shouting to all present that God was about to dissolve all earthly institutions. He responded to his wife's pleas for money to pay the bills by saying only that there would be a way. When he tried to "baptize her in the Spirit," she rebuffed him. He turned on her and her evangelical community. They had no God, he said. The husband is the only Savior of his wife. He disrupted church services and disappeared with his sons to protect them from false gods.[3]

For his erratic behavior, Matthews was apprehended by the local authorities and confined for two weeks. He later described the event as the "Declaration of Judgment" that marked the beginning of his Kingdom.[4] Leaving his wife to fend for herself and their children as best she could, he set out to destroy the evangelicals who duped women and emasculated men by undermining the God-ordained patriarchal order in home, church, and society. Robert Matthews was now Matthias, Prophet of the God of the Jews.

In June 1831, he set out for Rochester, the heart of revivalism during the Second Great Awakening, to preach the Truth to the misguided. From there, he made his way back to Albany, west again, southeast to Washington, D.C., and then up the coast to New York City. In New York, he prowled the streets of lower Manhattan on horseback preaching to anyone who would listen. Few did.

Then on May 5, 1832, sporting a beard that made him look like conventional pictures of Jesus and a costume of green silk modeled after John of Leyden, who briefly presided over his New Jerusalem in the Reformation era Germany of the 1530s, the Prophet Matthias showed up at the Fourth Street home of Elijah Pierson.

Perhaps the Prophet remembered Pierson, who owned a mercantile business on Pearl Street, from the days when he ran a store in Coila. Or maybe he had learned about Pierson while making his sacred rounds in lower Manhattan. In any case, he must have known the visit was likely to prove very worthwhile.

Like the Prophet, Pierson was a religious seeker. Born into a strict Calvinist family in Morristown, New Jersey, he had made his way to New York City, where he started his mercantile business in 1820. Running his business by day and engaging in missionary work by night, Pierson prayed fervently and engaged in conversations with the Holy Ghost. In 1822, he married Sarah Stanford, the daughter of a Baptist minister. Together the Piersons explored the varieties of evangelicalism that were part of the New York religious scene. In Holy Club meetings at the home of Ann and Benjamin Folger, the Piersons came to see personal holiness and perfectionism as the way of the Lord. They gave up luxuries and worked tirelessly to help the outcasts of society learn to lead a God-pleasing life. They established schools, engaged in ministries to prostitutes and homeless alcoholics in New York's seedy Five Points area, and opened an asylum for prostitutes on Bowery Hill.

For eight years, Elijah and Sarah Pierson worked side by side in their mission to reclaim society's outcasts. When Sarah contracted consumption, her husband prayed, had visions, and suffered fits. From those intense religious experiences, he concluded he was really Elijah the Tishbite, commissioned to prepare the way of God on earth. At Sarah's funeral on July 1, 1831, Elijah announced he would raise Sarah from the dead.[5] When that didn't happen, many of his evangelical friends drifted away. Among those who stayed with him were the Folgers and his domestic servant, Isabella Van Wagenen, a freed slave who had attended services at his Bowery Hill mission.

After that first meeting between Pierson and Matthias the Prophet, both men had what they most wanted. Pierson had assurance that his visions were true. Matthias, the Incarnate Spirit of Truth, assured Pierson that he had known him to be a true believer even while Pierson had remained ensnared in that false religion, Christianity, that allowed women to preach and prophesy, thereby usurping the proper role for men. He, Matthias, had come to earth once again to establish a reign of Truth. The Spirit of Truth was that of male governance; the reign of Truth was that of the Father. The Father's Kingdom was at hand. It had begun the day Pierson had the vision proclaiming him to be Elijah the Tishbite. Together, Matthias and Pierson would build the Kingdom.[6]

Matthias had gained his first converts—Pierson and his servant, Isabella Van Wagenen. He also had a comfortable place to live and, of course, access to Pierson's money. For a month or so, Matthias preached to Pierson's associates from the chapel room in Pierson's Fourth Street house, but by the summer of 1832, he had moved into the home of another well-to-do convert, Sylvester Mills, deeming his larger home more suitable for a true prophet. There he taught them the Truth and revealed to them plans for a Kingdom with a mighty temple greater than anything Solomon had built. But first, there must be offerings.

Matthias demanded silverware and silver vessels custom engraved with the Lion of Judah. He demanded a wardrobe befitting his status: hats adorned with tassels representing the tribes of Israel; clothing of the finest silk, some costing as much as $14 a yard; leather boots; a fine two-edged sword; a fancy carriage for making his sacred journeys through the city; and, of course, fancy food.

Pierson and Mills provided whatever the Prophet wanted, but Mills's brother, Levi, got legal papers charging Matthias with practicing "a system of pretension & hypocrisy for the purpose of defrauding." When Levi Mills and his Christian friends—backed by police with a warrant claiming Robert Matthews and Sylvester Mills were "so far disordered in their senses as to endanger their persons, or the persons or property of others"—confronted the Prophet, a melee broke out. With the Prophet screaming that he was God Almighty, the police subdued him, cut off his beard, and transported him to a ward for the criminally insane.[7]

Pierson and George Matthews, the brother of the Prophet, got a bill of habeas corpus for the Prophet's release, but Matthias was quickly arrested again on grounds he had violated the blasphemy statutes by claiming to be God. However, the charges were dropped when officials decided it would be counterproductive to try to prove in court that Matthias was not whom he claimed to be.

The Kingdom temporarily languished, but within a few months it had attracted a handful of new recruits. Most notable among them were Catherine Galloway, the domestic servant of Sylvester Mills, and Ann and Benjamin Folger, who had been Pierson's friends and fellow missionaries ever since their Holy Club days a decade earlier. Like Pierson and Mills, Ben Folger was a prosperous businessman in New York City.

In the summer of 1832, the Folgers' country home near Sing Sing became Mount Zion, the first earthly home of the Kingdom. There the Prophet enjoyed the life of a prosperous country gentlemen.

As Father to his community, Matthias assigned indoor work to his female followers; men worked at "manly" outdoor tasks.[8] Pierson, now in generally ill health and suffering from recurring fits, puttered in the garden. Along with Ben Folger, he also handled the commune's finances. After communing with the Spirit of Truth, Pierson would propose stock purchases, real estate transactions, and business ventures; Folger would carry them out on trips to the city where he stayed at a house Pierson rented and made available to fellow believers.

Although neighbors were curious and perhaps a bit suspicious, the commune was safe from the outraged Christians and ever watchful police of New York City. Life at Mount Zion proceeded smoothly until Ann Folger seduced, or perhaps was seduced by, the Prophet Matthias.

From the beginning, the Prophet had taught that Christian marriages were invalid. Now he amended that teaching by saying that even those unions he had sealed were invalid; the only valid union was one between spirit matches. He and Ann Folger were a spirit match. Henceforth, she should be addressed as "Mother," even as he was "Father" to the Kingdom. Together they would produce a holy son who would further the work of their Kingdom.[9]

There was little Benjamin Folger could do other than sulk and spend as much time as possible in New York City on business. But he was a lonely man. When the Prophet sent Folger to Albany on an errand to find his children and bring them to Mount Zion, Ben Folger found solace with the Prophet's recently married adult daughter, Isabella Laisdell. When the Prophet found out that Ben and Isabella had spent a night alone together on the way back to Mount Zion, he berated the couple and beat his daughter on two successive days before switching course and proclaiming Ben and Isabella to be a spirit match.

That union upset Catherine Galloway who believed that Ann, the Mother of the Kingdom, had promised Ben to her as a spirit match. Then when Charles Laisdell showed up demanding to know why his wife had not returned home, it upset him even more to find her living with another man. Laisdell got a writ of habeas corpus demanding his wife's return. He also informed the people in the village of Sing Sing about the goings on at Mount Zion.

Following a judicial hearing in Sing Sing, the community—minus Isabella Laisdell—resumed its life at Mount Zion. Ben and Catherine were united as spirit matches. But Ben never quite gave up on his wife and she, although now pregnant with the promised holy child, apparently retained some feelings for him. On occasion when both were in New York City on Kingdom business, they resumed their previous relationship. But that was not enough for Ben.

Eventually Ben Folger confided in his old friends from the Christian community in New York City, telling them of the spirit unions and dalliances among the faithful and of his suspicions that the Prophet was a fraud and a con artist. He also told these things to people in Sing Sing, who attempted to take matters into their own hands, but Matthias got away unharmed.[10]

By early July, Elijah Pierson also had some doubts. Although in failing health and nearly blind, he now realized that he was also broke. Folger's business partner had gone to court and collected hundreds of dollars owed him as a result of Pierson's business schemes on behalf of the Kingdom. Perhaps even more galling to Pierson, he had not yet received his spirit match. While suffering from recurring fits, he made overtures to Mother, who calmed him as the others restrained him.

Then on July 29 Pierson became physically ill. Illness was, the Prophet taught, the result of disobediences, so no doctor was called. Pierson died six days later. A hasty inquest found no evidence of foul play, but when Pierson's body was sent to New Jersey for burial, coroners there took a second look.

Pierson was in failing health, but he had not died of natural causes. He had been poisoned.

In September 1834, when word reached the Prophet that the New Jersey coroners' report had been sent to authorities in New York, he fled to Albany where he was arrested and delivered to the prison ward at Bellevue Hospital to await trial on charges of murder, assault and battery, fraud, and embezzlement.

Police put the Prophet's wardrobe on public display. New York City newspapers reported and sensationalized the case. Other newspapers around the country picked up the story. Some writers pegged Matthias as insane. Others called him a fraud and a con artist. More charitably, a few said he was a victim of his own delusions. But all believed him guilty of something.[11]

Already convicted in the court of public opinion, the Prophet fared better in court. With respected New York attorneys Henry B. Western and N. Nye Hall defending him, the state's case against the Prophet quickly fell apart. The New Jersey coroners had presumed poisoning, but failed to perform tests that would have confirmed their suspicion, so there was no way to show definitively that Pierson, who was known to be in failing health, had been poisoned.

The Kingdom kept no financial records. Pierson's accounts were a mess. Folger had spent nearly $5,000 of his own money, but money given to the Kingdom was spent on the Kingdom. There was simply no way to provide empirical evidence that the defendant, Robert Matthews, was not the Prophet Matthias that he claimed to be, or that the money given to him and his Kingdom was anything other than a gift in support of the Kingdom.

In the end, only the charge of assault on Isabella Laisdell held up. The Prophet served three months in jail on the assault and battery charge, plus an additional 30 days on contempt charges stemming from his outbursts during the trial. The Prophet served out his sentence, but once free he quickly resumed his quest to establish his Kingdom.

In November 1835, he traveled to Kirtland in Ohio's Western Reserve territory. Using the name "Joshua. The Jewish Minister," Matthews obtained an audience with Joseph Smith, the founder of the new Mormon religion. Whether the Prophet hoped to convert the Mormons or find a place within that new religion is unclear, but nothing came of their encounter. Over the next few years, reports surfaced that the Prophet had been seen preaching in Little Rock, in St. Louis, and finally in the Iowa Territory, where he probably died in 1841.

The holy child Ann Folger was carrying turned out to be a girl. She and Ben Folger apparently reconciled. Like most of the others, they returned to the conventional life they had known before joining the Kingdom.

Isabella Van Wagenen went on to become a well-known speaker in the abolitionist movement. Although she never traveled with the Prophet after he set out for Kirtland, she remained a true believer to the end of her life.

Although bits and pieces derived from contemporary accounts of Matthias and his Kingdom turn up in literary works such as Nathaniel Hawthorne's

The House of Seven Gables and Herman Melville's *Moby Dick*, Matthias and his Kingdom rarely get even a footnote in most standard histories of the era. Even so, the story illustrates how easy it is for a charismatic religious leader to gain a following and how little effect verdicts in the courts of law and of public opinion may have on true believers (Chapter 1, "A Saint or a Sinner?" "I Call It Sin"; Chapter 2, "Hush Money, Fraud, and a Lost Empire"; Chapter 3, "The Missing Evangelist," "Praying for Dollars"; Chapter. 8, "The Revoked Revelation," "Of Miracles and Medicine," "Virgins and Guns").

THE RICHEST CITY IN AMERICA

For most Americans, their image of Boys Town most likely came from the 1938 movie of that name with its touching scene in which a small boy, carrying an even smaller boy on his back, tells Father Edward J. Flanagan (played by Spencer Tracy, who won an Oscar for the role), "He ain't heavy, Mister. He's my brother."

For others, their image of Boys Town probably came from the fund-raising letters they received each Christmas and Easter telling them that Boys Town, a residential facility for orphans and homeless boys, received no money from state or federal government or from churches. It needed their donations of "$1, $2, $5 or any amount you care to give" if it was to continue caring for its boys and giving them a bit of the good things more fortunate boys routinely get.[12]

That movie-based image was undoubtedly as close to the truth as a Hollywood movie is likely to provide. Under Father Flanagan's guidance, the Home for Homeless Boys he started in 1917 in a poor area of Omaha grew into Boys Town, a complex located on acreage 10 miles west of the city. There he provided a safe refuge where his boys could learn a trade and other skills that they would need in order to succeed in the adult world when they were old enough to go out on their own. That formula became the model for residential facilities throughout the nation and the world. In 1947, the year before his death, Father Flanagan traveled to Korea and Japan to share his expertise with his counterparts in those countries.

In the early days, Boys Town did struggle financially. Father Flanagan started his first home with little more than $90 and a prayer. He and several contributors mortgaged property in order to acquire the Boys Town site outside Omaha; other loans built the facilities. And until his death, Boys Town did depend on donations.

But in 1972, when the millionaire Warren Buffet, who at the time owned the weekly *West Omaha Sun* newspaper, gave his reporters the green light to look into Boys Town finances, they discovered that the image created by the fund-raising letters was one carefully crafted by Ted Miller, who became the organization's chief fund raiser in 1939. The message and the semiannual appeals remained in place under Father Flanagan's successor, Msg. Nicholas H. Wegner, even after Miller's death in 1962.

Records that became public after Congress passed the Tax Reform Act of 1969 requiring tax-exempt nonprofit organizations to file financial statements made it clear that Boys Town had grown wealthy beyond Father Flanagan's wildest dream. According to the account published in the *West Omaha Sun*, Boys Town may well have been America's richest city[13]—and it really was a city. Boys Town is located in Boys Town, Nebraska, a legally incorporated town.

While Boys Town may not have received any grants or gifts from state or federal governments, that did not mean it received no public funding. Boys Town received money from at least five government agencies. And like other municipalities in Nebraska, it received a share of sales and gasoline taxes.

The amount of public funding, however, was a mere pittance—just $200,000—when compared to its investment portfolio that was valued at over $150 million in 1970. With an annual income of $8.1 million in 1970 from that portfolio, Boys Town had more than enough money to cover its operating expenses without resorting to fund-raising appeals. But those semiannual letters netted at least $15 million after factoring in fund-raising expenses of approximately $3 million.

Boys Town's investment portfolio was four times as large as the University of Notre Dame's endowment fund. If Boys Town had been a business instead of a nonprofit organization, its wealth would have placed it at 372 on *Fortune* magazine's top-500 list.

Figures taken from the 1970 financial report and the 1970 census showed that Boys Town had an income of $16,500 for each boy in its care and a net worth of $190,000 per person—and those per capita numbers were likely to increase. Over the 20 years preceding the newspaper investigation, the number of boys being served had fallen by nearly 25 percent as the kind of long-term residential care Boys Town provided had lost its appeal.

Although the financial data uncovered by the *West Omaha Sun* were surprising, the story attracted relatively little attention. Without evidence of any real wrongdoing beyond sending out misleading letters asking for donations, it was at best a mini-scandal. Larger newspapers carried a story or two based on the *West Omaha Sun* report. Most major magazines ignored it. *Time* and *Newsweek* each gave it less than a page in their April 10, 1972, issue.[14]

In the absence of sustained media attention, there was no public outrage over Boys Town's fund-raising tactics or its great wealth. However, the story that the *West Omaha Sun* broke does neatly illustrate the importance of both open record laws and enterprising journalists for uncovering problems that sometimes crop up in even the most respected institutions, and for instigating beneficial reforms.

After the *West Omaha Sun* broke the story, Boys Town quickly hired a consultant to make recommendations that led to meaningful changes. While

Boys Town continued to solicit funds, it abandoned the misleading "wolf is at the door" approach it had been using. After some soul-searching, Boys Town changed its name to reflect a new, broader mission. Today, as Girls and Boys Town, the institution Father Flanagan started in 1917 to care for orphan boys serves at-risk youth of both sexes.

For their role in bringing about reforms at Boys Town, the 1973 Pulitzer Prize for local investigative reporting went to reporters Douglas R. Brown, Wesley B. Iversen, H. Michael Rood, Douglas D. Smith, and Paul N. Williams of the *West Omaha Sun.*

HUSH MONEY, FRAUD, AND A LOST EMPIRE

Jim and Tammy Faye Bakker got their start in the early 1960s when, fresh out of Northwest Bible College in Minneapolis, they began doing Christian-themed puppet shows for children in churches and at revivals. Together they built an empire.

Their first big break came in 1965 when Pat Robertson hired them to do a children's show for his fledgling Christian Broadcast Network (CBN) and then moved them into a gig hosting a talk-and-variety show that, along with their fund-raising success, helped put CBN on solid financial footing.

From there, the Bakkers moved to Orange County, California, where they joined with Paul and Jan Crouch to create Trinity Broadcasting. Although their union with the Crouches was short-lived, it gave the Bakkers their second big break. They got to keep the PTL name they had used in their program for Trinity.

"PTL" stands for either "Praise the Lord" or "People That Love." Under that name, they created their own television network with headquarters in Charlotte, North Carolina. With this network, they were finally in charge of their own ministry. On their own network, they were the stars.

Where Jim Bakker's fellow Assembly of God televangelist Jimmy Swaggart told his followers that Christians must walk a straight and narrow path (Chapter 1, "I Call It Sin"), Jim and Tammy provided a softer, more culture-friendly message. On the PTL flagship program, "The Jim and Tammy Show," their message was part Christian hope, part upward-striving, and part soap opera.

Although they never really preached a "prosperity Gospel" (Chapter 3, "Praying for Dollars"), Jim and Tammy gave people permission to enjoy the finer things in life in a way that certainly helped the Bakkers expand their empire and become rich. When, for example, Tammy Faye told viewers how she expected God to strike her dead when she first wore cosmetics, but now realized looking good was okay, people responded by making purchases from her line of cosmetics. When the Bakkers told of their vacations and vacation homes and then invited viewers to visit the Heritage USA theme park they had built in Fort Mill, South Carolina, viewers helped make it the third-most-visited theme park after Disneyland and Disney World. Their purchase of what amounted to time shares in the hotel the Bakkers built at the resort complex brought in millions of dollars.[15]

For the soap opera part, the Bakkers shared the ups and downs of their life together. Viewers rejoiced with them over triumphs. They cried with them and prayed over their problems[16]—and many of those problems were real. Although Tammy Faye was always an integral part of the Bakker empire, by the late 1970s she had come to feel neglected. Her husband, she said, spent too much time on work and not enough time with her.[17] While Tammy Faye sought solace alone at one of their homes, her husband sought solace elsewhere.

As early as 1984, Richard Dortch, second in command at PTL, received word that Bakker had committed adultery. By late 1986 or early 1987, news of a one-night stand had spread to other televangelists and to the headquarters of Bakker's parent denomination, the Assemblies of God. By March, the *Charlotte Observer* knew of the adultery, and from there, the story spread. In 1980, while Jim and Tammy Faye were separated, Jim had, indeed, had a fling with Jessica Hahn, a church secretary from New York. She said Bakker had raped her; he admitted to a one-night stand, but denied the allegation of rape. Although PTL officials believed his version, they authorized paying Hahn $265,000 in hush money.[18]

On March 19, Bakker stepped down as head of his PTL empire. By late March, Jerry Falwell of Moral Majority fame had ended up in control. In one of his first decisions as head of PTL, Falwell placed Dortch in charge. With that decision, what had started out as a rather routine adultery case quickly turned into a major money scandal.

Dortch had authorized paying the hush money to Jessica Hahn, so a closer look at PTL finances seemed warranted. Through interviews and an examination of PTL records from 1984 through 1987, the *Charlotte Observer* turned up evidence of fiscal mismanagement and malfeasance.

Even as PTL was paying hush money to Jessica Hahn, Bakker received a salary of $1.9 million in 1986 and $640,000 during the first three months of 1987. PTL had also picked up much of the tab for the Bakkers' cars, houses, and furnishings. At least some of that money came through the sale of "exclusive partnerships" in Heritage USA that for $1,000 would entitle the partner to a three-night stay in a luxury hotel at the complex. Although much of the money raised that way did go to operating Heritage USA as partners were told it would, there simply was no way most of them could enjoy the fringe benefit to which they were entitled. There were thousands more partners than the one 500-room hotel at Heritage USA could possibly accommodate, and there were no plans in place to build more hotels.

The revelations forced the Bakkers and PTL to sell cars, furniture, and assorted kitsch at auction. On June 13, 1987, PTL filed petitions in bankruptcy court for a Chapter 11 reorganization.

During a June 22, 1987, press conference in Tega Cay, South Carolina, Jim and
Tammy Faye Bakker look on as attorney Melvin Belli answers reporters' questions
about their lifestyle, finances, and the management practices of their PTL ministry and
its enterprises. AP photo, Sam Jones.

In December 1987, Jim Bakker was indicted on 24 counts of fraud and
conspiracy and income tax evasion. Richard Dortch was also charged. Tammy
Faye was not. Dortch admitted guilt and cooperated with federal prosecutors.
In 1990, his eight-year sentence was reduced to two and a half years. Following a trial that lasted five weeks, Bakker was convicted, sentenced to 45 years
in federal prison, and ordered to pay a fine of $500,000. On appeal, the fine
was voided and the sentence reduced to 18 years. Bakker served five years
before leaving prison in July 1994 for a halfway house operated by the Salvation Army.

In 1988, a *Charlotte Observer* reporting team led by Charles E. Shepard
received the Pulitzer Prize for meritorious public service for exposing the PTL
scandal, but the coverage angered Jim and Tammy Faye's fans, many of whom
cancelled their subscriptions in response to the paper's heavy coverage that
they took as evidence of media bias against religion in general and their kind
of Christianity in particular.

Although the paper never engaged in sensationalism, its coverage was heav-
ier and more sustained than the coverage the *Boston Globe* devoted to the
pedophile priest scandal (Chapter 1, "Pedophile Priests") 15 years later. In
1987 alone, the *Charlotte Observer* published more than 600 stories about the
scandal—and the coverage had an effect that went beyond the cancelled subscriptions the paper endured.

Congress held hearings to determine whether stronger regulations governing religious broadcasting were warranted, but ultimately declined to take action. The National Religious Broadcasters (NRB), however, stepped up its efforts to get religious broadcasters to subscribe to a code of ethics and submit audited financial statements to the Evangelical Council for Financial Accountability.

Research conducted independently by Steve Winzenburg and Quentin Schultze found that compliance with the standards was higher in the early 1990s than it had been just five years earlier, but they also found the reporting standards had, at best, a minimal effect.[19] Membership in NRB is voluntary. Therefore, it simply has no way to require compliance with its standards or to impose effective punishment for ethical lapses on nonmembers, or even on those who are members.

Research conducted in the wake of the scandal found that televangelists lost credibility and viewers in the wake of the scandals. But the effects were stronger among casual viewers and those who watched for surveillance purposes than they were among the conservative Protestant core audience who were generally more willing to forgive the Bakkers than they were to forgive the secular media.[20]

In 1992, Jim and Tammy Faye divorced at her request. On October 3, 1993, she married Roe Messner. Under her new name of Tammy Faye Messner, she did infomercials, made guest appearances on television entertainment shows, and told the world of her 11-year battle with cancer in magazine articles, on television talk shows, and in a best-selling book, *I Will Survive ... and You Will Too.* She died from the cancer on July 20, 2007.

In his 1996 book, *I Was Wrong*, Jim Bakker confessed that his version of the prosperity gospel that led him to believe he deserved the money and other goodies he derived from his PTL days was based on an erroneous understanding of scripture.[21] In 1998 he published a second book, *The Refuge: The Joy of Christian Community in a Torn-apart World.* By 2003, he was back on the air with second wife Lori (Graham), broadcasting the new *Jim Bakker Show* from a studio near Branson, Missouri. In 2008, the show moved into studios located in a 600-acre development known as Morningside. Although Bakker doesn't own the development, Morningside looks very much like Heritage USA. As late as 2005, Bakker still owed as much as $3 million in taxes on money he received when he headed PTL.

THE HEIRESS WHO WASN'T

In 1986 when Ellen Cooke applied for the position of national treasurer of the Episcopal Church, she listed as credentials for the job a degree in economics from Georgetown University and almost 20 years of experience in increasingly prestigious finance jobs within the Church. At a time when mainline

Protestant churches were reaching out to women and minorities in an effort to offset losses in both membership and money, she seemed like the perfect pick.

Within a few years, Cooke managed to narrow the salary gap between the clergymen who worked in the national office and laywomen on the staff, all while improving church finances. She insisted that departments stick to their budget and justify even minor expenses. She convinced the church it could save money by eliminating the position of executive officer for administration and finance and giving her those duties along with the ones she already performed. The church could save even more money and also receive a bit more interest income by transferring its accounts to a different bank.

True, Cooke could be a bit difficult to work with. Occasionally she seemed frazzled. Requests for funding authorization sometimes went astray, but people chalked it up to overwork; Ellen Cooke arrived at church headquarters early each day and often stayed late. And in an office that prided itself in being both collegial and informal, she seemed both too imperious and too formal. She ordered people around more often than was the office norm. While others at denomination headquarters went by their first name, she insisted on being called "Mrs. Cooke." "Mrs. Nicholas T. Cooke III" was the name she signed to checks and other church documents.[22] But people chalked those quirks up to her upbringing and her justifiable pride in her husband.

Everyone knew of her impeccable Episcopalian, upper-class bloodlines and the generous inheritance that was hers. They also knew all about her husband, Nicholas T. Cooke III. During his relatively short ministry, he had become rector first at St. Luke's Episcopal Church, an historic Episcopal church in Montclair, New Jersey, and then at St. John's, a 1,700-member parish in McLean, Virginia, an upscale suburb outside Washington, D.C. The Rev. Cooke was on a fast track to become a bishop in the Episcopal Church.

If people at St. Luke's had been a bit upset when the Cookes moved out of the rectory and into a nearby historic home for which they paid $465,000 and spent thousands more to refurbish, they didn't complain much. People just assumed their fancy house better suited Mrs. Cooke's style and that she could afford it. They didn't even mind much that the couple spent much of their time at a second home in Virginia. The Rev. Cooke was a good pastor. The churches he led received grants from denominational headquarters to pay for things his churches wanted or needed. The Rev. and Mrs. Cooke were also very generous with their own donations to the congregations he served.

For almost eight years Ellen Cooke seemed to be both competent and a good steward, frugal with church money and generous with her own. But by early 1994 her demanding, imperious ways had taken their toll. In December, after a year of increasingly acrimonious budget disputes, presiding bishop Edmond L. Browning fired Ellen Cooke.

In one of her last duties at church headquarters, Cooke prepared the introductory letter for a new manual for church workers. In that letter she wrote,

"The Church has entrusted us with funds…. This trust is deserving of our nurturing and careful attention to detail, and demanding of our accountability."[23]

But that was advice she had failed to follow. Ellen Cooke was not what she appeared to be. Ellen Cooke was a liar. She had held the financial positions within the church that she listed on her resume. But there was no economics degree from Georgetown. As a college freshman, she had flunked out of George Washington University. And her roots were not upper-class Episcopalian. She came from a working-class Catholic family. She had no inheritance.

Ellen Cooke was a thief. During her eight years in control of church finances, she had helped herself to $2.2 million in church funds by transferring money from the church accounts she had set up at the new bank into her own accounts at the same bank, by directly depositing church money into her accounts, and by making unauthorized charges on her church credit card. Most of that money went to pay for the Cookes' lifestyle: the house, furnishings, jewelry, clothing, gifts, travel and vacations, and private school for her sons by her first marriage. Some of it also financed her supposed generosity. She had funneled money from denominational headquarters into St. Luke's by making unauthorized grants to the church and by making unauthorized payments into a discretionary fund controlled by her husband.

Confronted with the evidence against her, Ellen Cooke claimed stress-induced depression led her to actions of which she had no memory. Some people believed her. Some also felt sorry for her and for her husband. Some wanted to forgive her. But her deception and her theft shocked almost everyone, and there were repercussions.

On January 24, 1995, Ellen Cooke admitted to charges of embezzlement and tax evasion. Judge Maryanne Trump Berry of the Federal District Court in Newark, New Jersey, sentenced Cooke to five years in prison and ordered her to pay $75,000 as restitution. Nicholas T. Cooke III claimed no knowledge of his wife's actions. Although he was never charged with any crime, he resigned from the ministry.

Within the Episcopal Church there were calls for the presiding bishop's resignation and a general housecleaning at church headquarters. The bishop kept his job, but the Church changed its accounting practices. The Episcopal Church recouped most of the money Ellen Cooke stole through insurance payments and the court-ordered restitution. But as a result of this scandal, the Episcopal Church and other religious institutions had a hard time regaining the trust of people who quite naturally wondered how such a venerable institution could so easily be duped by an employee.

Although the Episcopal Church and many others took a hard look at their financial practices and instituted reforms intended to reassure their members that their contributions would go for their intended purposes, scandals like the Ellen Cooke case continue to pop up. In March 2008, for example, Barry

R. Herr, the former treasurer of the Lower Susquehanna Synod of the Evangelical Lutheran Church in America, was arrested on charges of diverting more than $1 million in church funds to his own use.

DOLLARS FOR DEMOCRATS ... AND REPUBLICANS

It was a rather routine fundraiser, but it was one that raised more questions than money. In April 1996, Vice President Al Gore delivered a speech at the Hsi Lai Buddhist Temple in Hacienda Heights, California, that netted $140,000 for the Clinton-Gore reelection campaign.

Neither Clinton-Gore nor the Democratic Party had paid to use the temple, so free use of the facility amounted to the kind of soft money contribution that would have been legal if it had been given to a political party, but would have been illegal if, as in this case, the beneficiaries were political candidates. Nonprofit organizations risk losing their tax-exempt status if they raise funds or work on behalf of a candidate.

An investigation by the *Wall Street Journal* and the *Los Angeles Times* provided some evidence that the Temple might have engaged in money laundering.[24] Many Buddhist nuns and monks who had taken vows of poverty were listed as giving far more at the fund-raiser than they most likely could have afforded. In order to avoid losing its tax-exempt status by contributing money directly to the candidates, the Temple had most likely supplied the money its monks and nuns contributed in their own names.

If questions about illegal political activity were not enough, there were also questions about foreign entanglements and influence peddling. The Hsi Lai Temple, the biggest Buddhist temple in the United States, was part of the Fokuangshan Buddhist Order, legendary in Taiwan for its involvement in Taiwanese politics. John Huang, a naturalized Chinese American citizen, held various positions in the Clinton administration before resigning to return to the fund-raising on behalf of the Democratic Party that had first brought him to Clinton's attention. Huang had previously worked for and with James Riady, an American of Indonesian and Chinese extraction. Riady made his fortune in banking and used both his money and his connections to further his business interests in Asia. Riady helped both Bill and Hillary Clinton start their careers in Arkansas; he regularly made campaign contributions to Clinton and many other candidates. It was John Huang, friend and coworker with both Clinton and Riady, who had arranged for Gore to speak at the Hsi Lai Temple.

Republican presidential candidate Bob Dole seized on the Buddhist Temple fund-raiser to label the Clinton-Gore team as ethically challenged, but to little avail. Dole, other top Republicans, and the party itself had similar problems.[25]

Although Riady generally supported Democrats, his wife had donated $1,000 to Dole campaign coffers in 1988. Riady, himself, had hosted and partly underwritten a lavish dinner in 1993 at which Dole was an honored guest. Dole and other top Republicans had also received other "foreign" money. Cuban Americans contributed heavily to Dole and other Republican candidates. House Speaker Newt Gingrich, whose campaign strategy helped Republicans gain control of both the U.S. Senate and House of Representatives in the 1994 off-year election, had used Russia's and Saudi Arabia's embassies for his fundraisers. According to the *Atlanta Constitution,* the World Sikh Organization had also hosted a fundraiser for Dole in 1995 that was very much like the one the Buddhists had held for Al Gore.

Just as the amount of money raised at the Buddhist Temple was relatively small in comparison to other fund-raisers on behalf of Democrats, so was the money raised at Gingrich's Sikh fund-raiser. In any case, it paled in comparison to the political support funneled through and perhaps laundered by the Christian Coalition.

Televangelist Pat Robertson founded the Coalition as a political advocacy and voter mobilization organization after failing to become the Republican Party's presidential candidate in 1988. In every election since then, the Coalition has distributed voter guides that are generally crafted to favor conservative Republican candidates and that are distributed almost exclusively in conservative Protestant churches. In every election these voter guides have been the subject of complaints about impermissible political activity.

In 1992, the Internal Revenue Service announced plans to revoke the Christian Coalition's tax-exempt status, but took no action. As a religious non-profit organization, the Christian Coalition cannot legally support or promote a candidate; its voter guides, though slanted, are permissible educational material. But in 1996, the IRS again took a look at the organization's political activities after reports of money laundering came to light. According to an article in *Newsweek,* the Christian Coalition funneled money that it received from an Ohio tycoon who had already made the legal maximum campaign contribution to former President George H. W. Bush into "educational" programs designed to help Bush in his 1992 bid for reelection.[26]

In spite of all the charges and countercharges of foreign influence, money laundering, and illicit religious political activity, the scandals had little bearing on the outcome of the election. Neither did the scandals have any real effect on the religious organizations caught up in them. All kept their tax-exempt status. As of the 2008 election, the Christian Coalition was still distributing voter guides in some states. So was the Fundamentalist Church of Latter Day Saints.

The scandals did, however, fuel public demands for "campaign finance reform" of a kind that may be impossible to accomplish. The laws in effect at the time were both complex and vague. At least six times since it passed its first attempt at campaign reform in 1971 Congress has passed new laws aimed at preventing the kind of problems that popped up during the most recent election campaigns. Each effort has managed to curb some methods of buying influence, but each law has been as complex and as vague as the one it sought to fix. Each reform measure has also raised serious constitutional questions about freedom. While religious organizations have never been the target of any reform effort, any efforts to restrain their political activity also raise thorny constitutional questions about religious freedom.

Those questions about the relationship between the First Amendment and the law governing political action by tax-exempt religious organizations resurfaced during the 2008 presidential election campaign, first over an invitation for Democratic candidate Barack Obama to speak at the national meeting of the United Church of Christ and over some sermons his pastor, the Rev. Jeremiah Wright, had made from the pulpit (Chapter 6, "God Damn America."), and then when at least two dozen conservative Protestant pastors openly endorsed presidential candidate John McCain from the pulpit on September 28 as part of a nationwide challenge to tax law organized by the Alliance Defense Fund.

THE MEAT MESS

Aaron Rubashkin was a Russian immigrant, a Hasidic Jew, who parlayed a kosher butcher shop in Brooklyn into a business empire with headquarters in St. Paul, Minnesota. In 1987, he bought the long-abandoned HyGrade slaughterhouse in Postville, in the northeastern corner of rural Iowa. It would be a good deal for everyone, he said.[27] But it didn't quite work out that way.

Rubashkin got the lower operating costs he wanted when he bought the HyGrade plant and began operating it under the name AgriProcessors, Inc. Being nearer the herds of cattle and flocks of chickens processed at the plant meant lower transportation costs. Of course, in rural Iowa, unions weren't strong, so he didn't have to deal with them or pay union wages.

By 2008, AgriProcessors employed 900 people. It purchased and processed more than $100 million in livestock annually. Its "Aaron's Best," "Rubashkin's," "Shor Habor," and "Supreme Kosher" labels carried assurances from the New York-based Orthodox Union that AgriProcessors slaughtered and dressed cattle and poultry according to the strictest standards of Jewish law. With a 60 percent market share, AgriProcessors was America's leading provider of kosher beef and poultry. And as profitable as the kosher side of the business was, more money came from selling meat that did not meet kosher standards under the "Iowa's Best Beef" label.

But the town didn't get quite what it hoped for. AgriProcessors did bring jobs to the area. The town grew from about 1,400 in 1990 to almost 2,300 by the time of the 2000 census. But most of the jobs and the growth came as a result of immigrants from Russia who found their way to AgriProccesors after first showing up at Rubashkin's Brooklyn butcher shop looking for jobs, and from other immigrants brought in from Mexico, Guatemala, and the Philippines. And then there were the Jews: Aaron Rubashkin's sons, Sholom who came to Postville as the CEO of the company and Heshy who ran the facility; other members of the family; and an ever-increasing number of observant Hasidic Jews who came to conduct or supervise the ritual slaughter of animals for the kosher market. The Jews were easily recognized by their beards and the black Hasidic clothes they wore; they stuck together. In a town that for generations had been Catholic and Lutheran, there were now at least 300 Jews with their own synagogue, parochial school, and ritual bathhouse.

The presence of so many outsiders created a clash of cultures, as Stephen G. Bloom, a Jewish writer from the West Coast who taught journalism at the University of Iowa, first pointed out in his 2000 book, *Postville: A Clash of Cultures in Heartland America.*[28] The Jews of Postville referred to the townspeople by the derisive Yiddish term "goyim."[29] The Lutherans and Catholics sniffed that the Jews were dishonest and unscrupulous.[30]

The Yiddish term for the townspeople had its roots in a 1797 Chabad Hasidic religious text saying, "the souls of the nations of the world, the idol worshippers, derive from unclean husks and have no goodness in them whatsoever."[31] The Catholics' and Lutherans' opinions about the Jews in their midst smacked of the kind of unsavory anti-Semitic charges that Christians have leveled against Jews for centuries. But in this case, the townspeople of Postville turned out to be correct.

Although most of the people Bloom talked to for his book probably did not know it at the time, in August 1995 the National Labor Relations Board had found Aaron Rubashkin and his son Moshe guilty of collecting union dues from workers at their Cherry Hills Textile company in Brooklyn and failing to turn the money over to the United Production Workers Union as the law requires.

But the first real information about problems at the Postville plant did not come to light until 2004. First, Postville town officials announced that they were looking into allegations from local residents that the company was discharging untreated wastewater from its abattoir into local rivers in violation of state and federal environmental law. Then, in December, People for the Ethical Treatment of Animals (PETA) released a 30-minute video showing gruesome pictures of animals being slaughtered at the Postville plant, followed by another one showing similar conditions at the Rubashkin family's Local Pride slaughterhouse on the Oglala Sioux tribal reservation in Gordon, Nebraska.

In December 2004, the Department of Justice and the Environmental Protection Agency filed a civil lawsuit against the company for numerous violations of the Clean Water Act that ultimately resulted in AgriProcessors signing a consent decree and agreeing to pay $600,000 in fines. PETA's allegations of animal cruelty, however, were not as easily dealt with. Not only did the video spark outrage among animal rights activists and ordinary citizens who found working conditions at the plant appalling and the pictures of animals being killed gruesome beyond belief,[32] but it also upset observant Jews. They, too, found the working conditions at AgriProcessors' Postville plant upsetting, but they were even more distressed to find that the meat they had been buying might not have been produced according to kosher standards. PETA's video clearly showed that many animals died in agony when the single hand-delivered cut with a sharp, nick-free knife specified in Jewish law failed to sever the major nerves and arteries connecting an animal's head and body.[33]

The video sparked a debate in the Jewish community over the meaning of kosher slaughter and whether there should be a new definition, or perhaps a separate designation, that would indicate the producer of kosher products also conformed to high ethical standards.[34]

To deal with the uproar over conditions at its plant and over the way animals were being slaughtered, AgriProcessors brought in Temple Grandin, an animal science professor at Colorado State University who specializes in slaughterhouse design, to help them deal with the controversy by improving their plant. When in 2006 Grandin professed satisfaction with the improvements, the Orthodox Union trumpeted its role in bringing the Postville plant up to kosher standards.[35]

But the controversy wasn't over. PETA issued another video showing that AgriProcessors was still using the "second cut" instead of the single, clean cut specified in Jewish law.[36] Finding the news troubling, Grandin recommended installing video cameras to monitor procedures in the kill room.[37] Over the next four years, the story of the "not quite kosher" kosher killings in Postville remained a big story in the Jewish press, as did the debate over the meaning of the kosher label. It also popped up from time to time in major newspapers.[38] In 2008, however, that story was supplanted by an even bigger one.

On March 21, 2008, the *Des Moines Register* reported that the company had been cited for alleged health and safety problems.[39] On May 12, Immigration and Customs Enforcement (ICE) officials carried out two federal search warrants on the AgriProcessors plant and arrested 400 undocumented immigrant workers. It was the largest illegal worker roundup in ICE history. The raid touched off allegations of other labor violations at the plant. The company responded by hiring a New York public relations firm that quickly created new problems for AgriProcessors when information about its own ethics problems surfaced.[40]

August brought charges of violations of child labor law. On an August 26 visit to the area, Democratic presidential candidate Barack Obama cited the company for its employment practices and its unfair treatment of workers.[41]

A week later the Iowa attorney general filed 9,311 criminal misdemeanor charges for violations of child labor laws against AgriProcessors, its owner, Aaron Rubashkin, his son Sholom, and three human resources department employees. At the same time, the federal government entered charges for harboring illegal immigrants against two human resources managers at the plant.

Rabbi Menachem Genack, the head of the Orthodox Union, announced his organization would stop dealing with AgriProcessors unless it installed a new management team.[42] In response, the company announced that Bernard S. Feldman, a Long Island attorney who had defended family members in other cases, would replace Aaron Rubashkin.

On October 28, state labor authorities levied fines totaling $10 million against the company for illegally deducting "sales taxes" and costs for workers' uniforms from their paychecks and also for failing to give final paychecks to 42 workers rounded up in the May ICE raid. Aaron and Sholom Rubashkin were arrested on October 30, and AgriProcessors filed for bankruptcy on November 5.

Among Jews and in the Jewish press AgriProcessors was a major story, but one that was primarily about kosher food and the debate over the meaning of the kosher label. The *Washington Post* and *New York Times* each carried fewer than a dozen stories about AgriProcessors between 2004 and 2008—most of them framed to tap into the public's on-going debate over immigration policy and the government's treatment of undocumented workers. In Iowa, the scandal was big news. The *Des Moines Register* carried more than 150 stories between the May raid and the November bankruptcy filing. In them, the story was both business news about the effect of AgriProcessors' mounting problems on the community and a human interest story about the immigrants caught up in the scandal and a community trying to help them cope with their financial and legal problems in the wake of the ICE raid at the AgriProcessors plant.

But the story of AgriProcessors was and is also the story of a seemingly devout man who made a fortune and then lost everything by flouting the standards of his own faith and the law of his adopted country.

FOR FURTHER READING

Abelman, Robert. 1991, Spring/Summer. Influence of news coverage of the "Scandal" on PTL viewers. *Journalism Quarterly* 68(1/2): 101–110.

Bloom, Stephen G. 2000. *Postville: A clash of cultures in heartland America.* New York: Harcourt.

Boys Town bonanza. 1972, April 10. *Time*, pp. 17–18.

Brown, Douglas R., Wesley R. Iversen, H. Michael Rood, Douglas D. Smith, and Paul N. Williams. 1972, March 30. Boys Town: Lucrative income of a well-known child-care home. In Heinz Dietrich Fischer, ed. *Local reporting, 1947–1987: From a county vote fraude [sic] to a corrupt city council.* New York: K. G. Saur, 1989, pp. 170–180.

Downing, Larry. 1996, October 28. The Asian connection. *Newsweek*, pp. 25–32.

Episcopal coffers plundered. 1995, May 17. *Christian Century*, pp. 533–534.

Goodstein, Laurie. 1995, June 4. Thou shalt not lie. *Washington Post.* In Judith M. Buddenbaum and Debra L. Mason, eds. *Readings on religion as news.* Ames: Iowa State University Press, 2000, pp. 428–437.

Hanley, Robert. 1996, July 11. Judge gives church treasurer more than maximum sentence. *New York Times*, p. B6.

Johnson, Paul E., and Sean Wilentz. 1994. *The kingdom of Matthias.* New York: Oxford University Press.

Kiener, Ronald C. 2008, Fall. The Postville raid. *Religion in the News* 11(2): 2–5, 24.

Kopkind, Andrew. 1987, April 6. Jim Bakker's lost America. *Esquire*, pp. 174–183.

Moore, Jonathan. 1996, November 18. Buddhism gets down to business—and politics. *Business Week*, p. 65.

Stern, Marc. 2008, Spring. IRS: Bipartisan tool. *Religion in the News*, pp. 9–11, 26.

Walczak, Lee. 1996, August 12. Campaign-finance reform needs a miracle. *Business Week*, p. 31.

Wall, James M. 1987, April 8. The fall of the House of Bakker. *Christian Century*, pp. 323–324.

Ward, Christopher. 1934, December 8. Mr. Pierson and the new Messiah. *New Yorker*, pp. 43–48.

Watson, Jimmy. 1987, June 8. Heaven can wait. *Newsweek*, pp. 58–72.

Chapter 3

HOAXES AND HUMBUG

Like everyone else, religious people sometimes lie. They tell little white lies to protect other people's feelings. They dissemble or tell half-truths to further what they believe to be a good cause (Chapter 1, "Pedophile Priests"; Chapter 2, "The Richest City in America," "Dollars for Democrats … and Republicans"). Occasionally they tell whoppers in what is often a vain attempt to cover their involvement in major crimes (Chapter 4, "The Hudson River Mystery," "Murder for Hire"). Occasionally they craft complicated, seemingly true tales that turn out to be hoaxes. Some of those lies, half-truths, and hoaxes that turned into major scandals are the subject of this chapter.

"Margery the Medium" is about a woman, part of the Spiritualism movement that gained prominence in the late 1800s and early 1900s, who claimed the ability to communicate with the dead, but whose psychic gifts were really little more than parlor tricks. The second example involves a popular evangelist and founder of one of America's more than two hundred Christian denominations whose disappearance and mysterious reappearance was a scandal when it happened and is still a subject of debate.

The next two scandals, though not caused by the Church of Jesus Christ of Latter-day Saints, had the Church at its center. The first of those, the case of The Mormon Will, has never been solved, but actions by Mormons created the conditions that made the hoax possible. The second scandal is the story of the Salamander Letter foisted on the Church by two Mormons, one of whom apparently thought he was doing a good thing for the Church.

"Praying for Dollars," the final section in this chapter, is about one of the many religious leaders who have been accused of raising money under false pretenses, but it is one of the few cases where a court apparently agreed with his critics that his money-raising scheme was a hoax.

MARGERY THE MEDIUM

Her husband was a respected doctor in the Boston area who had taught surgery at Harvard. They married in 1918, less than a year after he performed surgery on her and just a few months after she divorced her first husband on uncontested grounds of cruelty. In her private life she was Mina Crandon— Mrs. Le Roi Goddard Crandon. The public knew her as Margery the Medium, a spiritualist who channeled messages from the spirit world to those attending the séances that made her famous.

The Spiritualism Crandon practiced had its roots in the early nineteenth-century religious fervor of the Second Great Awakening as a kind of amalgam of the teachings of Emmanuel Swedenborg and techniques taught by Franz Mesmer. According to Swedenborg, people who died did not go to one of two discrete places, heaven or hell, as conventional Christianity teaches. Instead, they progress through a series of spheres. Spirits in those spheres mediate between God and humans through mediums, as Swedenborg claimed to have been able to do while in a trancelike state. To that, Mesmer added "mesmerism," as hypnosis was then known, as a technique for inducing the kind of trances conducive to receiving messages from the spirit world.

But as a movement, Spiritualism dates to March 31, 1848, when sisters Kate and Margaret Fox of Hydesville, New York, reported communicating with the spirit world. Because the Fox home had a reputation for being haunted, family and neighbors were fascinated and more than a little scared when the sisters claimed the rapping noises they heard in their home came from the spirit of Charles B. Rosma, a peddler who had been murdered and was supposedly buried in the basement of their house. When the spirit seemed able to follow the girls to locations outside their home and to rap out accurate answers to questions asked of him, people were ready to believe.[1]

News of the phenomenon spread quickly. Luminaries including William Cullen Bryant, James Fenimore Cooper, Horace Greeley, Sojourner Truth, and William Lloyd Garrison attended séances, in the process giving it credibility. But there were, of course, skeptics.

In the April 1853 issue of *The United States Democratic Review,* an anonymous writer reported that the "Rochester Rappers," as the girls were sometimes called because they conducted their first séances in the Rochester, New York, area, produced the rapping noises by cracking their knuckles. That the sounds seemed to come from different areas of a room wasn't evidence they were communicating with the spirit world; ventriloquists produced the same kind of effect when they worked in similarly darkened rooms.[2] But scattered reports like this one did little to dampen public interest. Neither did it matter much when news surfaced that there never was a missing, and presumably murdered, peddler named Charles B. Rosma.

Spiritualism continued to spread, first in the United States and then to England and beyond. While Abraham Lincoln was president, he attended a séance with his wife, Mary Todd Lincoln, who hoped to be able to hear from their beloved son, Willie, who had died in 1862. Like Mrs. Lincoln, who hoped to communicate with her dead son, people who had lost loved ones in the Civil War flocked to séances hoping to receive messages from their loved ones who had died fighting in the war.

Then in 1884, when the movement was at its peak, the University of Pennsylvania established the Seybert Commission named for Henry Seybert, a true believer in Spiritualism, to fulfill terms in his will that required the university to investigate "all systems of Morals, Religion, or Philosophy, which assume to represent the Truth, and particularly of Modern Spiritualism." In 1887, the commission, made up of eminent scholars from the university, issued its report: While unwilling to say that all mediums were frauds, the commission reported that they had found fraud or suspected fraud in every case they had examined.[3]

Although other investigators of the era concluded that at least some phenomena produced by mediums could not be the result of legerdemain, the Seybert Commission's findings sent Spiritualism into decline until the 1920s. Just as had happened in the aftermath of the Civil War, after World War I people turned to mediums in hopes of communicating with loved ones who had died in the war. But in this era, Spiritualism also tapped into the spirit of the Jazz Age, in the process becoming much more a blend of religion and entertainment than it had been before. It is to this later era that Margery the Medium belongs.

In the early spring of 1923, Dr. Crandon told Mina about "table tipping," a simple form of mediumship similar to that of a Ouija board. Although Mina didn't seem very interested, Dr. Crandon had a table built to the specifications in the book on paranormal phenomena that he had been reading. When the table was finished, she agreed to invite four of their friends to join them in an experiment to determine whether the table would work the way the book said it would.[4]

The experiment with table tipping was a success. Soon after the Crandons and their friends placed their joined hands on the table in accord with the doctor's instructions, the table inexplicably began to move. Demanding to know who had the power to communicate with the spirit world, Dr. Crandon then instructed his guests, each in turn, to remove their hands from the table. The table continued to rock and tilt until only Mina's hands remained. Mina was the medium.

Over the next few months, Dr. Crandon regularly told his wife about paranormal phenomena as he learned about them from his readings. At the séances the couple began to hold in their home for their large circle of friends, Mina began to display the powers her husband told her about: a bell placed in a box on the floor would suddenly begin to ring; a wand floated in mid-air pointing to the person with whom a spirit wished to communicate. To those who attended the séances, each new skill Mina exhibited seemed to underscore her legitimacy.

When, under hypnosis, she began to channel a male voice that she identified as that of her brother Walter, who had died in a railroad accident some years earlier, they were certain she was a powerful medium. The voice was deep. It didn't seem to come from where Mina was sitting. Moreover, the language was so coarse and the words so irreverent that the voice couldn't possibly have come from the doctor's wife.

That summer Dr. Crandon took Mina to Europe where she showed off her skills to a number of experts, including Sir Arthur Conan Doyle, the author of the Sherlock Holmes books. A true believer in Spiritualism, Doyle pronounced Mina "a very powerful medium."[5] He also commended her to the magazine *Scientific American*. Associate Editor J. Malcolm Bird, who shared Doyle's belief that Mina was legitimate, wrote articles for the magazine lauding her psychic gifts. In them, he called her "Margery the Medium," ostensibly to protect the couple's privacy.[6]

After that, Mina began performing publicly as Margery the Medium. She also applied for the cash prize *Scientific American* had begun offering in 1922 to anyone who, under test conditions, could demonstrate psychic powers.[7]

On July 24, 1924, working as Margery the Medium and wearing a diaphanous gown meant to show she had nothing to hide, she welcomed five guests to her home for her most important séance to date. Among the guests was Harry Houdini, the famous magician and escape artist.

Houdini had already attended hundreds of séances in hopes of being able to communicate with his mother who had died in 1913. Although his experiences with other mediums had convinced him that all of them were frauds, he came to the July séance with Mina/Margery willing to be shown that she had genuine psychic powers. At least partly for that reason, he had been named to the *Scientific American* committee that had been established to see if she qualified for the prize. But when the committee didn't notify him of its early meetings, Houdini conducted his own investigation.

After private séances, Houdini showed the Crandons evidence he said indicated that Margery was a fake. Dr. Crandon accused Houdini of sabotage and barred him from attending any further séances.[8] Sir Arthur Conan Doyle denounced Houdini, once again proclaiming his belief that Mina/Margery was a legitimate medium.[9] Houdini published a pamphlet in which he explained how Margery produced many of the phenomena her supporters attributed to her psychic gifts.[10]

In April 1925, *Scientific American* announced that Mina/Margery would not be receiving its prize. The magazine's investigation showed she was not a legitimate medium.[11] But Margery the Medium maintained a large and loyal following. She even demonstrated new skills.

Ectoplasm, a substance Margery said was the physical manifestation of visitors from the spirit world, began to appear during séances. Skeptics who touched the ectoplasm in spite of dire warnings that doing so would lead to their death within a year said it felt suspiciously like the kind of animal tissue Dr. Crandon could have obtained from his medical lab. Others speculated that he had surgically altered Margery during the operation he had performed on her before their marriage so that she could more easily retrieve the substance, whatever it was, from inside her vagina.[12]

But no one was able to provide a convincing explanation for the ectoplasm. Harry Houdini died in 1926, a little more than a year after he had touched the ectoplasm. Margery supporters remained convinced she was a genuine medium—until 1928. That year, at Margery's request, her dentist, Dr. Frederick Caldwell, showed her how the hot wax he had used to take dental impressions could be used to make an imprint of Walter's thumbprint. He also gave her the sample print and the equipment to make new ones.

At her very next séance, Walter left his print in wax. A fingerprint expert called in by the Crandons announced that it was similar to one left on a razor that had belonged to Walter. But another expert, the psychic researcher E. E. Dudley, took another look. The thumbprint was that of Margery's dentist.

The scientific community accepted Dudley's finding. Malcolm Bird admitted that the articles he had written about her for *Scientific American* were full of embellishments and half-truths.[13] Among her influential supporters, only Sir Arthur Conan Doyle, who in 1926 had published a two-volume history of Spiritualism, remained. Margery continued to conduct séances sporadically until her death at age 54 in 1941, but the public was no longer terribly interested in her or in the kind of spiritualism she represented.

Still, questions about the afterlife continue to trouble those who find the answers provided by established world religions unsatisfying. Spiritualists still accept Swedenborg's teachings about the nature of the afterlife. They still meet regularly to conduct séances to communicate with the spirit world. By the end of the twentieth century, Swedenborg's teachings about the structure of the spirit world and notions about reincarnation borrowed from Eastern religions had also merged to become a part of some strains of New Age religion. Most towns still have at least one psychic of the Mina/Margery type who purports to be able to channel messages from the spirit world.

Occasionally, efforts to communicate with those who have died receive widespread media attention, in the process generating new scandals. In 1966, James Pike, who had been Bishop of California, parted company with the Episcopal Church over differences in style, church direction, and theology, stemming in part from his well-publicized efforts to communicate with his son who had committed suicide. The most famous of those efforts was a September 1967 televised séance conducted by Arthur Ford, who at the time was a Disciples of Christ minister. Although people watched the show, it did little to change people's opinions or to revitalize Pike's ministry. He died in 1969 in the Israeli wilderness near Bethlehem when he became lost while conducting research for a book on the origins of Christianity.

THE MISSING EVANGELIST

Aimee Semple McPherson captured the public imagination in a way few people have ever done. As a woman and as a minister she was well ahead of her time. She was born in 1890 in Ontario, Canada, to James Kennedy, a devout Methodist and a widower, and his much younger second wife, Mildred (Pierce), whose religious inclinations were Salvation Army. Aimee began her public speaking career at age 13 as a self-proclaimed agnostic proponent of Darwinism. In 1907, she met her first husband, Robert Semple, a Pentecostal missionary, and had a conversion experience. In 1910, the couple embarked on a missionary trip to China, where Mr. Semple died in Hong Kong of dysentery, leaving his wife as the single mother of an infant daughter, Roberta. Back in the United States, Aimee joined her mother in Salvation Army work, met and married second husband Harold McPherson in 1912, and gave birth to a son, Rolf.

But the conventional role of housewife and mother held little appeal. After a bout with postpartum depression and other illnesses, the new Mrs. McPherson felt called to the ministry.

By 1916, with her mother as the driver, McPherson was touring the country in a 1912 Packard convertible with religious messages painted on its side. Between 1916 and 1923 they crisscrossed the country six times. On those trips Aimee Semple McPherson, or "Sister Aimee" as she billed herself, spoke to ever-growing crowds through a megaphone from the backseat of her "Gospel Car," and at tent revivals, boxing arenas, and entertainment halls.[14]

By 1918, however, McPherson decided she needed a permanent base for her thriving ministry. She and her mother settled on Los Angeles as the base for their evangelistic work. That same year, her husband, having grown increasingly frustrated by his wife's travels, filed for a separation on the grounds that she had abandoned him. They were divorced in 1921. At that time the idea of a woman leaving her home to travel the country was almost unheard of. Divorce on the grounds she had abandoned her husband could have made her a pariah in polite society. But, if anything, her travels and her new status as an independent, single woman made her even more fascinating.

Aimee Semple McPherson courted media attention and the media responded, publishing hundreds of stories about her and the crowds who came to see her. The publicity created bigger crowds and more generous donations.[15]

When Sister Aimee opened her Angelus Temple on New Year's Day 1923 at the intersection of Sunset and Glendale Boulevards in the Echo Park area of Los Angeles, it was already fully paid for through donations she had received on her cross-country travels. The Temple quickly became a local attraction, rivaling Hollywood itself.

With segregation the norm and suspicion of foreigners high, particularly Mexicans, Sister Aimee welcomed people regardless of social status, race, or ethnicity. She filled Angelus Temple's 5,300-seat auditorium for services three times a day, seven days a week. In the early years, she often preached at all of the services, almost always dressed in her trademark white gown and red military-style cape adorned with a corsage of fresh flowers.

People came, of course, to hear Sister Aimee preach. But she was only part of the appeal. Worship services at Angelus Temple were also a good show. There were guest preachers, both black and white, public recitations of religious poetry and stories, and lots of music. There were faith healings and demonstrations of speaking in tongues. There were also pageants and morality plays— "illustrations," Sister Aimee called them—complete with special effects, scenery, and costuming that rivaled anything available in theaters or the movies.[16]

Sister Aimee embraced the new medium of radio, adding it to a media ministry that already included a religious newspaper and two magazines. She was the first woman ever to preach a sermon on radio. On February 6, 1924, she became the first woman to receive a license to operate a radio station, station KFSG. By then, Angelus Temple had become home to a new denomination, the International Church of the Foursquare Gospel. The radio station's call letters stood for "Kall Four Square Gospel."

By 1926, the Church of the Foursquare Gospel had expanded to include a growing network of satellite congregations. However, on May 28 of that year, Aimee Semple McPherson disappeared while on an excursion to Ocean Park Beach on the California coast.

A secretary, who had gone to the beach with her, said Sister Aimee had been swimming close to shore when she left to make a phone call. When she returned about 15 minutes later, Sister Aimee was gone. A search was quickly launched, but turned up nothing.

That night, Sister Aimee's mother took her place in the pulpit. Presuming her daughter had drowned, she told the congregation, "Sister is with Jesus." Worshippers cried. Some fainted. The next day, people began showing up at the beach to watch and pray over search-and-recovery efforts. At least two people lost their lives as they searched in vain for their beloved Sister Aimee. For more than a month, the nation's media, led by William Randolph Hearst's *Los Angeles Times*, both reported and hyped the story.[17]

But Sister Aimee wasn't dead. On June 23, she showed up in Agua Prieta, just across the Mexican border from Douglas, Arizona, with a story even more incredible than that of her presumed drowning. She said she had been approached at the beach by three people she identified as Steve, Jake, and Mexicali Rose. At their request she had agreed to go with them to pray over a sick child. But instead of taking her to see the child, they had driven her to a shack in Mexico where they held her captive. She finally managed to escape, she said, by sawing through her bonds with the jagged edge of a syrup can and then making her way on foot to the border town.[18]

But the story was suspect. Sister Aimee had last been seen wearing a bathing suit. She reappeared wearing a dress and a wristwatch she hadn't taken to the beach. Her shoes were grass-stained, not covered in dust, and she was neither dehydrated nor sunburned as would have been the case had she trekked through the desert for 13 hours as she claimed to have done.

Sister Aimee's mother told authorities she had received a ransom note while her daughter was missing, but she had thrown it away because she was certain her daughter was dead and the note was a fake. The shack couldn't be located. Sister Aimee stuck to her story.[19] A grand jury that convened on July 8 to investigate the matter found too little evidence to press any charges against Sister Aimee or her mother. However, the investigation continued, and the grand jury reconvened when new evidence turned up.

Sister Aimee had been seen on several occasions with Kenneth Ormiston, the married radio engineer for station KFSG, who had disappeared at about the same time. Her handwriting was on hotel receipts from the period during which she was missing. Still, Sister Aimee stuck to her story. But when her answers about her relationship with Ormiston didn't satisfy investigators, she and her mother were arrested and charged with corruption of public morals, obstruction of justice, and conspiracy to manufacture evidence.

The trial in Judge Samuel Blake's courtroom became a media circus. Grandstands were built to hold the crowds. But in the end, all charges were dismissed. Sister Aimee returned to her ministry only to become embroiled in new scandals. In 1927, she created mini-flaps when she bobbed her hair in flapper fashion, shopped for fancy clothes in Paris and was caught, but not arrested, for trying to smuggle some of them past U.S. Customs.

Worse yet, Sister Aimee ignored her own teaching that a person should not remarry while a previous spouse was alive. On September 13, 1931, with Harold McPherson still very much alive, she married David Hutton, an actor and musician whom she had hired to play the role of the Pharaoh in a religious opera she had written. Two days after the wedding, Hazel St. Pierre sued Hutton for alienation of affection. Hutton claimed never to have met St. Pierre, but settled the case by paying her $5,000. Sister Aimee and Hutton separated in 1933; they divorced on March 1, 1934.

Through it all, Sister Aimee remained pastor of the Angelus Temple and head of the International Church of the Foursquare Gospel. During the Great Depression, she created soup kitchens and free clinics. During World War II, she lent her talents to war bond rallies.

On September 27, 1944, Sister Aimee was found dead in her hotel room in Oakland, California. Although there were rumors of suicide and even some allegations that once again Sister Aimee had staged a media event, the coroner ruled that she had died of an accidental overdose of prescription barbiturates.

Anthony Quinn, who had served as her translator and went on to become a movie star, credited her charitable work with keeping the Mexican

Aimee Semple McPherson, wearing her trademark white robe and red cape, ordains 200 ministers during a June 28, 1936, service at her Angelus Temple. AP photo.

community alive during the Great Depression.[20] Vehement critics during her lifetime such as the Rev. Robert Schuller, whose own Crystal Cathedral is a mega-attraction in southern California, spoke admiringly of her ability to recruit and mobilize an army of evangelists to spread the Gospel.[21]

At the time of Sister Aimee's death, the International Church of the Foursquare Gospel had 410 churches, 210 mission stations, and approximately 29,000 members. Today it has more than 25,000 churches and almost 2 million members worldwide.

THE MORMON WILL

Howard Robert Hughes set transcontinental flight records during the 1930s in the Hughes H-1 Racer that he designed and built at his Hughes Aircraft Company. For a time, he was the majority stockholder of Trans World Airlines and of the RKO motion picture company where he produced blockbusters such as *Hell's Angels, Scarface,* and *The Outlaw.* He set up the Howard R. Hughes Medical Institute in Maryland, bought up Las Vegas casino hotels, and created the Summa Corporation as an umbrella enterprise to manage his far-flung corporate enterprises.

But by the 1950s, Hughes had become a virtual recluse, living on the top floor of one or another of his hotels. Ensconced in his quarters, he surrounded himself with hand-picked aides, many of them Mormons, who catered to his every whim while screening his contacts with the outside world. He was so intent on guarding his privacy that he bought up the copyright to almost everything that had been written about him in a vain effort to keep writers from producing new works about him to satisfy public curiosity. The latest photo of him dates from 1952; after 1958, he never appeared publicly.

Howard Hughes died on April 5, 1976, in an airplane somewhere between Acapulco, Mexico, where aides had apparently taken him for medical care, and Houston, Texas, a hometown he had not visited in more than 20 years. At his death, Hughes left behind an estate estimated at $2 billion. There were two ex-wives, but no children, and so there was an immediate scramble to claim the fortune.

Noah Dietrich, who once was Hughes's chief lieutenant, said he had seen a will sometime in the 1950s. Hughes's current aides said Hughes had planned to sign an important document, which might have been a will, a few days before he died, but he had been too ill to do so. Executives from his Summa Corporation said they thought there should be a will that would name one of them as executor. For tax purposes, the will would probably leave all or most of Hughes's estate to his nonprofit medical center that Hughes had made the owner of his businesses.[22]

A diligent search of Hughes's living quarters, corporate offices, and of the banks where Hughes had or once had accounts turned up nothing. But three weeks after his death, a tattered yellow envelope addressed to Spencer W. Kimball, president of the Church of Jesus Christ of Latter-day Saints, showed up on a desk at Church headquarters in Salt Lake City. Inside the envelope was another envelope containing a will bearing the signature of Howard R. Hughes. The will, dated March 19, 1968, left one-sixteenth of the estate— $156 million—to the Church.

When Mrs. Leslie King, a handwriting expert whom the Church asked to look at the document because she had examined Hughes's handwriting in previous court cases, pronounced the signature genuine, Church officials filed the document with the probate court in Clark County (Las Vegas), Nevada, as a message accompanying the will instructed them to do. Even so, the Church remained skeptical as to whether the will was genuine.[23]

"The Mormon Will," as the press quickly dubbed it, was handwritten on lined legal paper of the kind Hughes was known to use when he wrote memos to his staff, but Hughes rarely made spelling or grammatical errors, and he had always been a stickler for detail. The will contained 11 misspellings. One provision was maddeningly vague. It left "the remainder" to be divided among unspecified "key men in my company's [sic]." There were no witnesses to the will. Dietrich and Hughes had been estranged since 1956, yet Dietrich was named executor of the will. Then there was the provision leaving one-sixteenth of the estate—another $156 million—to Melvin Dummar, who operated a service station in Willard, Utah.[24]

The story Dummar told reporters just added to the mystery surrounding the "Mormon Will." Dummar said that one night in December 1967, while he was driving across the Nevada desert, he had seen a skinny, dirty old man lying beside the road. He gave the man a ride to Las Vegas. Just before he let the man out at the back door of the Sands Hotel, the man asked him for some money. Thinking the man was a bum, Dummar gave him a quarter. Now, however, he said he thought the man must have been Howard Hughes. The provision in the will must have been Hughes's way of repaying him for the good deed he had done nine years earlier.[25] For a time, Melvin Dummar became something of a media darling even as journalists raised more questions about the discovery of the Mormon Will.

Just before the will turned up at Church headquarters, both John Connally, former governor of Texas, and Frank W. Gay, chief executive officer of the Summa Corporation and a devout Mormon, visited Church headquarters, but Church executives told reporters the men were there on unrelated, unspecified business.[26]

Dummar initially said he had never seen the will, but he changed his story when his fingerprint showed up on the document. Now he said that a well-dressed man, whom he did not know, had shown up at his service station and given him the envelope with instructions to take it to Church headquarters. He had looked at the documents, been surprised by the contents, and, not knowing what else to do, had taken the envelope to Salt Lake City where he had left it on a desk inside Church headquarters.[27]

In court, Hughes's cousins and Summa Corporation officials joined the Church and Melvin Dummar in pressing claims to the Hughes estate. Nevada, which had no inheritance tax, along with Texas and California, both of which had inheritance taxes, claimed to be Hughes's legal residence. Even the federal government, which had an interest in seeing the case settled quickly so it could claim its millions in estate taxes, got involved.

In June 1978, after a jury trial lasting seven months, the court in Las Vegas ruled that the Mormon Will was a forgery. Hughes had died intestate. In 1983, the Hughes fortune, less the amount that went to attorneys and tax collectors, was divided among his cousins, including William Lummis, who serves as a trustee of the Howard Hughes Medical Institute.

Both Dummar and The Church of Jesus Christ of Latter-day Saints lost their claim to millions of dollars. While the Church emerged otherwise unscathed from the episode, Melvin Dummar was not so lucky. Although he was never convicted, Dummar had once been arrested for cashing a forged check, so the one-time media darling found himself labeled a forger and would-be thief.[28]

But courts can answer only the questions before them based on the evidence they have available to them. No one has ever provided convincing evidence that Dummar forged the will. As improbable as it seemed that Dummar found Hughes in the desert in December of 1967, his story may be true.

On February 23, 2005, the Church-owned *Deseret News* reported that Gary Magnesen, a retired FBI agent, had learned that Hughes had purchased interests in mines close to where Dummar said he had found him. Furthermore, Magnesen claimed that some of Hughes's closest employees had told him that they remembered Hughes entering the Sands in December 1967 and telling them that Dummar had given him a ride to the hotel.[29]

On June 12, 2006, Dummar filed suit in the United States district court in Utah claiming that Lummis and Frank Gay, the former chief executive of Hughes's business enterprises, had presented perjured testimony and concealed evidence during the 1978 trial. On January 9, 2007, Judge Bruce Jenkins dismissed the lawsuit, saying it had been "fully and fairly litigated" in Las Vegas in 1978.[30] However, the decision left open the possibility that the case of the Mormon Will might be reopened if a lawsuit were filed in Nevada.

THE SALAMANDER LETTER

Between 1980 and 1985, the Church of Jesus Christ of Latter-day Saints acquired dozens of documents pertaining to its early history. Most of them received little attention outside Church circles. But when the Church published the text of a letter dated September 1830 sent by Martin Harris to William W. Phelps in its official *Church News* in April 1985, media outlets around the country picked up the story.[31]

According to official Church teachings, the angel Moroni led Joseph Smith to a site outside Palmyra, New York, where he found gold plates bearing writing in a language identified as Reformed Egyptian. With the angel's help, Smith translated the message telling of Jesus's ministry to the people of the New World.

The letter written by Martin Harris to William W. Phelps told a different story about Smith's discovery of the *Book of Mormon*. According to the letter, spirits appear to Smith in dreams. It is a white salamander, capable of transforming itself into a "spirit," and not the angel Moroni, who leads Smith to the gold plates.

The repeated mention of spirits, along with references to a stone of the kind Smith was known to use to hunt for buried treasure, seemed to outsiders to place the discovery of the *Book of Mormon*, which the Church considers holy scripture along with the Bible, into the same occult tradition that gave rise to the Rochester Rappers (this chapter, "Margery the Medium") in nearby Rochester, New York. Jerald and Sandra Tanner, former Mormons who made a career of trying to discredit the Church, had warned the Church that some documents it had acquired might be fakes.[32]

Still, the Church had little reason to believe that the "Salamander Letter," as the Harris letter became known, was anything but genuine. Harris was Joseph Smith's first convert outside members of the Smith family. He was one of three men to whom Smith showed the gold plates on which the *Book of Mormon* was written. He was also one of the men who wrote down the words in the sacred text as Joseph Smith read and translated them. Phelps, the editor of a newspaper in Canandaigua, New York, was also an early convert to the new religion, so it was quite likely the two would have corresponded. Experts who compared the letter to other samples of Harris's writing declared he was probably the author.[33]

On June 23, amidst growing speculation about the origin and consequence of the Salamander Letter for the Church, Church president Gordon Hinckley reminded the faithful that attempts by outsiders to discredit Joseph Smith and the Church were nothing new. Nothing in the Salamander Letter provided reason for anyone to doubt the divine origins of the *Book of Mormon*. Although the possibility existed that the letter was not genuine, there was certainly no reason to take the word of two disgruntled ex-Mormons over that of handwriting experts and Church leaders who had actually seen and handled the letter.[34]

Over the summer, media attention to the story dwindled, but it picked up again after October 15. That morning, Steven Christensen, a prominent businessman, picked up a package outside his office door in Salt Lake City. Inside the package was a pipe bomb, which exploded, killing him instantly. Three hours later, Kathleen Sheets died outside her home in Holladay, a Salt Lake City suburb, when she picked up a similarly booby-trapped package addressed to her husband, J. Gary Sheets.

Police initially thought the murders were the work of a disgruntled investor because Steven Christensen and Gary Sheets were partners in a failing real-estate investment firm. But when a third pipe bomb blast critically injured Mark Hofmann three days later as he was climbing into his car parked near Temple Square in Salt Lake City, they discovered a Mormon connection.

After serving as a Mormon missionary in England where he frequented antique bookstores, Hofmann made a name for himself as a dealer in antiquities. He had a seemingly uncanny ability to find valuable documents that he sold to private collectors, museums, university libraries, and the Church of Jesus Christ of Latter-day Saints. Christensen had paid Hofmann $40,000 for the Salamander Letter, which he then gave to the Church as a gift after he and Sheets had paid to have the letter authenticated. Both Christensen and Sheets were bishops in the Church of Jesus Christ of Latter-day Saints. They had been negotiating with Hofmann to buy a set of papers by William E. McLellin (sometimes written as M'Lellin), one of the original members of the Council of Twelve that governs the Church.

But Hofmann was apparently having difficulty producing the McLellin papers in a timely manner. The bombings may have been his way of dealing with customers who were becoming increasingly impatient and skeptical. After an ambulance took Hofmann to the hospital, police discovered equipment for manufacturing pipe bombs in his car. In the trunk were pages of Mormon documents. A subsequent search of Hofmann's home turned up equipment for forging documents.

In February 1986, Hofmann was arrested for the murders and forgery. He avoided the death penalty by pleading guilty to the lesser charges of second-degree murder and theft by deception, and was sentenced to life in prison. In prison he shares a cell with Dan Lafferty, a fundamentalist Mormon who murdered his sister-in-law because she refused to accept polygamy (Chapter 8, "The Revoked Revelation").

On July 31, 1987, the Church of Jesus Christ of Latter-day Saints issued a statement that was subsequently published in the October issue of *Ensign* magazine, reminding the faithful that the Church "has a divine mandate to record, acquire, and preserve documents and artifacts considered to be of importance to its history and the times and environment in which it developed." The Church had "followed time-honored professional practices and relied on competent authorities" in acquiring the 10 documents the Church now believed to be Hofmann forgeries.[35]

While the Church may have acquired more Hofmann forgeries than any other single institution, others had bought his forgeries of works by Abraham Lincoln, Mark Twain, and Emily Dickinson. Those purchases, based as they were on expert opinions about the genuineness of the documents, continue to trouble museums as they simultaneously work to reassure the public that the documents they hold and display are genuine and to increase their holdings of significant documents.

As a relatively new religion, the Church of Jesus Christ of Latter-day Saints may be more vulnerable than older religions to scams involving forged documents of the type Hofmann created. But all religions are vulnerable when con artists attempt to pass off as genuine religious artifacts of recent origin. News that the James Ossuary, a stone burial box with the inscription "James son of Joseph, Brother of Jesus," was to go on display at the Royal Ontario Museum on October 31, 2002, received intense media coverage. As with the Salamander Letter, the Ossuary became an even bigger story as scholars attending the annual meeting of the American Academy of Religion debated its authenticity as information about its condition when it arrived in Canada surfaced. Although the Royal Museum has adopted a "wait-and-see" attitude,[36] many scholars accept the Israeli Antiquities Authority finding that the inscription is a modern forgery applied to an ancient ossuary, while others maintain that both the ossuary and the inscription are genuine.

PRAYING FOR DOLLARS

After two years on the road as a traveling evangelist in Oklahoma and Texas, Robert Tilton settled in Dallas where, in 1976, he started Word of Faith Family Church in Farmers Branch, Texas. The Church grew steadily over the next few years, but neither it nor Tilton's efforts to expand his televised ministry beyond the Dallas area were growing as fast as he hoped—at least until after he had an epiphany while vacationing in Hawaii. He could expand his ministry by creating infomercials modeled after the ones he had seen on television in Hawaii, especially those that real estate tycoon Dave Del Dotto used in his business. So, in 1981, *Success-N-Life*, was born.

On television and in his church, Tilton began preaching the prosperity gospel. All problems, but especially poverty, are the result of sin, Tilton maintained. God wants people to have all the good things in life; He will abundantly reward those who commit themselves to Him and show their commitment. The way to do that, Tilton said, was for people to send him a letter explaining their problems and their needs. Tilton would pray over their request. If people also sent along a "commitment vow" in the form of a financial contribution, preferably of at least $1,000, God would hear the prayer and recognize their commitment by rewarding the donor with material riches and other blessings.[37]

With backing in the form of a $1.3 million loan from Dallas banker Herman Beebe, Tilton quickly became the biggest purchaser of air time for a religious program, buying 5,000 hours of time each month. At its zenith in 1991, *Success-N-Life* could be seen in all 235 television market areas. But by then, Ole Anthony, founder and spiritual leader of the Trinity Foundation, had become suspicious. In one of the poorer suburbs of Dallas, Trinity Foundation's core members lived together according to what they believed to be the practices of first-century Christians. There, they operated a halfway house for recovering addicts and ex-convicts, and a soup kitchen for those down on their luck.

By the mid-1980s, some of those who showed up at Trinity Foundation asking for help told similar stories of having failed to receive the promised riches after having sent commitment vows to Tilton. Among them was Harry Guetzlaff, a long-time donor who had been rebuffed when he went to Tilton's ministry for help with financial problems stemming from his recent divorce just a few weeks after he had sent another commitment vow—this time for $5,000.

Guetzlaff, a former marketing director of Coca-Cola, and Anthony, a licensed private investigator and former Air Force intelligence officer, set out to see what they could find out about Tilton's ministry. At about the same time, ABC news began investigating Tilton and two other Dallas televangelists, W. V. Grant and Larry Lea.

ABC News and the Trinity Foundation pooled their investigative efforts. On November 21, 1991, Diane Sawyer reported their findings in "The Apple of God's Eye," a *Primetime Live* segment produced by Robbie Gordon.[39] According to Sawyer, mass mailings of replies to prayer requests and unsolicited calls for donations were handled by Response Media. In a secretly recorded interview, its director, Jim Moore, told Anthony that Tilton never really intended to pray over the letters viewers sent him. His calls for "commitment vows" were a money-making scheme that brought in as much as $80 million a year. Unopened letters went to banks where Tilton's ministries had accounts. In Dumpsters outside the banks and at the office of Tilton's attorney, the ABC-Trinity investigative team found bank statements, thousands of prayer requests, and computerized lists of names carefully coded to indicate the nature of the requests so an appropriate mention of it could be included in follow-up letters sent out by Response Media.[40]

The day after the *Primetime Live* story broke, Tilton responded to the allegations on his *Success-N-Life* program. In a segment he called "Primetime Lies," and again the next week in a follow-up segment of ABC's *Primetime Live,* broadcast on November 28, he told viewers he had "laid on top of those letters so much that the chemicals actually got into my bloodstream.... I had two small strokes in my brain [from all the ink]." He also charged that the letters had been stolen and placed in the Dumpsters, perhaps by Anthony, whom he and other Dallas area preachers had come to view as a dangerous foe.[41]

Sawyer, however, asserted that the investigative team found unopened letters in Dumpsters 14 different times in a 30-day period. And, over the next seven months, *Primetime Live* updates aired new allegations about unopened prayer requests and unsavory fund-raising tactics from people who knew or worked for Tilton.

In 1992, Tilton sued ABC for libel. ABC religion reporter Peggy Wehmeyer, who knew Anthony from her previous work as religion reporter at television station WFAA-TV in Dallas, had warned ABC that Anthony was so obsessed with his crusade against televangelists that information from him might prove unverifiable.[43] In court, Anthony admitted that some of the prayer requests noted in Trinity Foundation logs were suspect. Nevertheless, trial court Judge Thomas Brett dismissed Tilton's case in July 1993. In 1995, appellate Judge Michael Burrage upheld that verdict even as he criticized ABC for its editing of the story. The U.S. Supreme Court refused to hear Tilton's appeal.

Several members of Tilton's Word of Faith Family Church and donors to his *Success-N-Life* television program sued Tilton in 1992 and 1993 for making fraudulent claims. Some of them may have received financial settlements that would not be public court records, but those who went to court did not prevail. The First Amendment's guarantee of religious freedom provides a strong shield against claims arising from religious teachings, no matter how outrageous or damaging they may seem (Chapter 2, "The Kingdom, Money, Sex, and Maybe a Murder").

In cases like this, oversight, such as it is, comes from the denomination to which a pastor or church belongs, or through membership in organizations like the National Religious Broadcasters (NRB) or the Evangelical Council for Financial Accountability (ECFA). However, many ministries have no ties to a denomination. Membership in NRB and ECFA is strictly voluntary. There is no way to compel membership or even to impose meaningful sanctions on members who fail to comply with ethical standards.

According to figures published in the September 13, 1993, issue of *Christianity Today*, Tilton lost 85 percent of his television audience after the *Primetime Live* exposé. Annual donations fell from $80 million to $25 million; 6,000 of the 8,000 members left his Word of Faith Family Church. By the end of 1994, *Success-N-Life* was off the air. In 1996, Tilton quit preaching at his Dallas church, but by then he had moved to Florida and started a new church.

Tilton returned to the airwaves in 1997. Through his new version of *Success-N-Life*, which airs regularly to a primarily African-American audience as part of a block of inspirational programs on the BET network, Tilton is still preaching his prosperity gospel, calling for "commitment vows," and accumulating computerized mailing lists of potential donors.[44]

Although other religious leaders have been found guilty of fraud in connection with their money-making schemes (Chapter 2, "Hush Money, Fraud, and a Lost Empire"), Tilton has never been convicted of fraud in connection with his activities. Nevertheless, the fact that the trial court threw out Tilton's libel case against ABC and no higher court accepted his appeal is clear indication that either the court believed the harmful information ABC and the Trinity Foundation presented against Tilton was substantially true or that the charges were made without actual malice, which would require showing either that the publishers of the information knew it was false or acted with reckless disregard as to whether it might be false.

FOR FURTHER READING

Bilger, Burkhard. 2004, December 6. God doesn't need Ole Anthony. *New Yorker*, pp. 70–81.

Bird, J. Malcolm. 1924, July. Our next psychic: A preliminary account of the case that now comes before us, as it appears to the naked eye. *Scientific American*, pp. 28–29.

Comstock, Sarah. 1927, December. Aimee Semple McPherson: Prima donna of revivalism. *Harper's Monthly Magazine*, pp. 11–19.

Faithful cling to waning hope. 1926, May 20. *Los Angeles Times*. Retrieved April 10, 2007, from http://xroads.virginia.edu/~UG00/robertson/asm/latimes.html.

Foy, Paul. 2007, January 9. Judge tosses lawsuit over Hughes will. Associated Press. Retrieved May 2, 2007, from http://www.signonsandiego.com/news/nation/20070109-1151-wst-dummar-hughes.html.

Hinckley, Gordon B. 1985, June 23. First Presidency message: Keep the faith. Published September 1985 in *Ensign*, pp. 3–6. Retrieved March 5, 2008, from http://www.lds.org.

Kennedy, John W. 1993, September 13. End of the line for Tilton? *Christianity Today*, pp. 81–82.

Lawton, Kim A. 1992, January 13. Broadcasters face ethics questions—again. *Christianity Today*, pp. 42–43.

Oaks, Dallin H. 1987, October. Recent events involving Church history and forged documents. *Ensign*, pp. 63–69. Retrieved March 5, 2008, from http://www.lds.org.

Ostling, Richard N. 1985, May 20. Challenging Mormonism's roots. *Time*, p. 44.

Rowe, Sean. 2006, June 11. Second coming: A jet-settin', Scotch-sippin' Robert Tilton washes up in South Florida and he still wants your money. *Dallas Observer.* Retrieved March 3, 2008, from http://www.dallasobserver.com/2006-11-06/news/second-coming.

Ryder, David Warren. 1926, July 28. Aimee Semple McPherson. *The Nation*, pp. 81–82.

Shipps, Jan. 1985, November 13. The salamander and the saints. *Christian Century*, pp. 1020–1021.

Sidey, Ken. 1992, February 10. Addicted to broadcasting. *Christianity Today*, p. 12.

Stashower, Daniel. 1999, August. The medium and the magician. *American History*, pp. 38–46.

The Hughes will: Is it for real? 1976, May 10. *Time*, p. 30.

The psychic investigation: Claims of Margery to produce supernatural phenomena are rejected by the Committee. 1925, April. *Scientific American*, p. 229.

The search for the phantom will. 1976, April 26. *Time*, pp. 20–21.

Updike, John. 2007, April 30. Famous Aimee. *New Yorker*, pp. 76–79.

Williams, Dennis A., Phyllis Malamud, and Anthony Mabro. 1976, May 17. Howard Hughes: Heirs apparent. *Newsweek*, pp. 39–40.

Chapter 4

MURDER AND MAYHEM

The United States may be the most religious of all Western nations, but it is also a very violent one. According to data compiled by the Federal Bureau of Investigation, there were just over 100,000 homicides in the United States in 2007. On average over the last decade, there have been between 6 and 7 killings per 100,000 in population—three times the rate for Canada. Although few of those violent crimes have ever been committed by people who would readily be identified as religious, religious people do sometimes murder. When they do, the murders almost always make the headlines.

Like others who kill, religious people sometimes do it just because they can, or in retaliation for some supposed offense, or in an effort to cover up some other wrongdoing. But religious people also sometimes kill for religious reasons—because they believe their god commands or condones their action. The examples in this chapter illustrate both variations in kinds of killings committed by religious people and in their motivations.

"The Hudson River Mystery" is the story of a problem priest who claimed he killed in response to a divine command, but whose crime was also a cover-up for adultery. "A Monster and/or a Martyr" tells of a charismatic and powerful religious leader whose involvement with and subsequent apostasy from the Nation of Islam lay behind his assassination, while "The Flavor-Aid Massacre" is about another charismatic leader who convinced his followers to try to murder the congressman looking into the cult and then to commit mass suicide. "Domestic Terrorists" tells the story of men who believed their god condoned the murder of abortion doctors, while "Another Domestic Terrorist" is about a man who, though not personally religious, also found justification for bombings in religious teachings. In between them is the story of an adulterous rabbi who arranged for the murder of his wife. The chapter ends with accounts of "The Good Mother" who murdered her children as an act of mercy, she said, to save their souls, and one of a congregation president and family man who led a double life as the serial killer "BTK."

THE HUDSON RIVER MYSTERY

At dawn on Tuesday, September 2, 1913, Lucy Grace Cure of Brooklyn, New York, was fishing from her boat off Constable Point when she heard and felt something bumping against her boat. The "something" was the neatly severed head of a young woman. Three days later, 11-year-old Mary Bann and her 9-year-old brother Albert found an oddly shaped package on the bank of the Hudson River near their Cliffside Park home. With the help of her friend, Alice McKnight, she pulled the package up out of the water and unwrapped it. Inside, the children found the upper part of a headless human torso.

Over the next week, more body parts washed ashore—arms, legs, and the lower part of the torso. As each body part surfaced, local newspapers provided updates on the story they dubbed "The Hudson River Mystery."[1] But it wasn't a mystery for long. Joseph Faurot, an inspector with the New York Police Department who had already made a name for himself by using fingerprints to solve an earlier murder, was on the case. This time, however, he didn't use fingerprints to solve the crime. Instead, it was a pillowcase that led to the identity of the victim and her killer.

All of the body parts that washed ashore had been wrapped in sheets or pillowcases. One of the cases had a price tag that led to the store where it had been purchased. That led to the name and address of the purchaser, A. Van Dyke of 68 Bradhurst Avenue. Carlton Booker, who lived in the first-floor apartment at that address, said he had rented an apartment to a Mr. Van Dyke who had paid for it in cash and had also asked him to accept deliveries for him—a mattress and several smaller packages from the store where the pillowcases had been purchased.[2]

Inside the apartment, the police quickly deduced that they had found the scene of the murder. The floor and walls appeared to have been freshly scrubbed, but there were traces of blood in corners and in the bathroom. The mattress was missing, so the victim had probably been murdered in bed and then carried to the bathroom where her killer dismembered the body. The only clothing in the apartment was a man's suit jacket with a label indicating it belonged to A. Van Dyke. However, there were a few pictures and letters with other names. The police now knew the victim was most likely Anna Aumuller. Her killer's name probably wasn't A. Van Dyke. A. Van Dyke was almost certainly Father Hans Schmidt. Addresses on the letters led the police first to the Church of St. Boniface and then to St. Joseph's.

At St. Boniface, Father John Braun recognized the picture the police had found at the Bradhurst Street apartment as that of Anna Aumuller who had worked as a housekeeper at the church until about May 1912 when Father Schmidt had transferred from St. Boniface to St. Joseph's parish on 125th Street. Father Braun described Father Schmidt as having a "Dr. Jekyll and Mr. Hyde" personality that made him uncomfortable. He was not sorry to see

Father Schmidt move to another church. He was, however, sorry to see Anna leave, but she wanted to continue working for Father Schmidt, so she left St. Boniface when he left.[3]

When the police found Father Schmidt at St. Joseph's and confronted him with the evidence that they had accumulated thus far, he readily admitted killing Anna. He had killed her because he loved her, he said, adding, "You wouldn't understand, but God understands."[4]

While Anna Aumuller may have been the love of Father Schmidt's life, she was not his only lover. And, her murder was not his only crime. After Father Schmidt's arrest, a search of his living quarters at St. Joseph's turned up evidence that Father Schmidt and Ernest Muret, a dentist, were producing counterfeit $10 bills at an apartment on West 134th Street. Dr. Muret and Father Schmidt were also lovers. As newspapers recounted each new detail of the Hudson River Mystery, allegations surfaced of improper relations with young people of both sexes in congregations Father Schmidt had served in Germany.[5]

Then there was also Alma Kellner. In what Louisville, Kentucky, papers called the "case of the century," the 8-year-old girl had disappeared after leaving for school on the morning of December 8, 1909.[6] After an intense search and weeks of even more intense media coverage, Kellner's mutilated body was found on May 26, 1910, in the cellar of St. John's Church. The church janitor, Joseph Wendling, was convicted of the crime. At the time, Father Schmidt, who was a priest at St. Joseph's, professed not to know the girl, but he was one of very few people at the church who had a key to the cellar. In retrospect, the murder of Alma Kellner seemed eerily similar to that of Anna Aumuller.

In the face of constant newspaper reports of evidence and allegations, Father Schmidt's attorney in the Aumuller case, Alphonse Koelble, concluded that the only possible way to avoid the death penalty for his client was to prove him insane.[7] That strategy seemed likely to work. A court in Germany had proclaimed Father Schmidt insane following his arrest and trial there for forging documents proclaiming him a priest while he was still a seminarian.

In the New York court, Koelble produced sworn testimony from Father Schmidt's father, brother, and cousin in Germany stating that there were suicides and insanity in both his mother's and his father's families. They also testified that, as Father Braun had discerned, Father Schmidt had always been a Jekyll-and-Hyde character.

As a child he had been pious and prone to religious visions even as he found bloody slaughters fascinating and sexually arousing. While his siblings avoided attending mass more often than absolutely necessary, he went to mass with his mother every day. At home he prayed incessantly. Wearing clerical garb that his mother made for him, he delighted her by reciting the mass in Latin. He announced that he had a vision saying he was to become a priest. He claimed he had conversations with Christ and with St. Elizabeth and that he had seen sacred images in blood on an altar cloth that others identified only as a wine stain.

But in Germany he also killed and dismembered geese and other small animals and stuffed their parts in his trousers. He spent hours at a slaughterhouse near his home and persuaded a boy from the neighborhood to visit it with him; there, the two boys engaged in homosexual acts while watching pigs being slaughtered.

As a seminary student, Schmidt wandered the streets at night, exposing himself and handing people bread he had stolen from the seminary kitchen. So troubling was his behavior that his classmates demanded he be expelled, but instead he was ordained in a private late-night ceremony on Christmas Eve 1906. Other priests at the first church he served in Germany also found his behavior troubling, so he was moved to another church and then another before leaving Germany in July 1909 for the United States. But instead of the fresh start he apparently hoped for, priests and congregants in each congregation he served found him both difficult to work with and very strange.

Expert witnesses for the prosecution tended to think Father Schmidt's confession might have been cunningly crafted so that he would appear to be insane. Experts for the defense had no trouble finding him insane. The most powerful testimony to that effect came from Dr. Smith Ely Jeliffe, an "alienist" as psychiatrists at that time were known. In court he told of conversations with Father Schmidt that both corroborated the basic outline of the priest's confession to police at the time of his arrest and also added telling details about his relationships and reasoning.

According to Dr. Jeliffe, Father Schmidt said he loved Dr. Muret more than he had ever loved a grown man. When he spoke of him, he showed signs of suppressed excitement. Sometimes he even blushed. At night Father Schmidt dreamed of him. While saying mass, he fantasized about him, and when he heard his voice, he thought it was the voice of God.[8]

As for Anna, he loved her, too, even as he continued to love Dr. Muret. He had feelings for her from the first time he met her at St. Boniface in 1912. They became lovers after she nursed him through a period of illness. At first they had sex occasionally during the day in his room, then almost every night. In response to a question about the propriety of their relationship, Dr Jeliffe testified that Father Schmidt said:

One day, I wanted to find out what God thought about me and Anna. At night I brought her before the altar and I had intercourse with her on the altar itself. I was very much excited … I kept looking at the Host all the time. There was no change. Either God would speak or show a light or something, some sign He would have given to express His disapproval. But towards the end, He made it known to me she was to be sacrificed.[9]

In spite of God's command, Father Schmidt procrastinated. He took Anna to restaurants and plays. They met at Bronx Park at night and had sex there. On February 19, 1913, he married her in a ceremony he performed himself. He rented the Bradhurst Avenue apartment and visited her there at night. He also told her repeatedly that God had commanded him to sacrifice her. Finally, on September 2, 1913, following a visitation in which St. Elizabeth compelled him to follow through, he sacrificed his beloved wife.

On the night of the murder, Father Schmidt went to the Bradhurst Street apartment. There, he kissed his sleeping wife before cutting her throat almost through her neck. As she lay dying, he attempted intercourse with her. He mixed some of her blood with water and drank it as in saying mass. After that, he carried her to the bathroom where he dismembered her body as he had learned to do by watching pigs being slaughtered in Germany. Finally, he took the body parts to a vacant field near the apartment where he wrapped them in neat packages to which he added rocks for weight before disposing of them in the Hudson River. It took all night, Father Schmidt told Dr. Jellife, but he finished in time to get back to St. Joseph's just in time to officiate at the 7 A.M. mass.[11]

The testimony was so shocking and so graphic that a juror fainted. Spectators screamed and cursed. Police moved in to protect Father Schmidt from onlookers who seemed eager to take matters into their own hands. Perhaps the testimony had inflamed passions to the point that jurors would vote for the death penalty, or perhaps, as Koelble hoped, the testimony had made it perfectly clear that Father Schmidt was mentally unstable and almost certainly insane. But in the end, it didn't matter. The final two witnesses for the prosecution demolished any hopes Koelble and his client might have had.

Just before closing arguments were to begin, the prosecution called a Dr. Harold Hays to the witness stand. Hays was an examiner for the Postal Life Insurance Company. He could not recognize Anna from her picture, but he recognized Father Schmidt as the man whose wife he had examined in April 1913 so he could buy a $5,000 policy on her life. The final witness, Bertha Zech, said she had met Father Schmidt through Dr. Muret. On several occasions the three of them went to restaurants and plays together. At Schmidt's request she had posed as Anna so he could buy a life insurance policy as a surprise for his wife.[11]

To the jury that suggested premeditated murder, not insanity. When Judge Vernon Davis told jurors that in order to find Father Schmidt insane, they must find "he was laboring under such a defect of reason as to not know the nature and quality of the act he was doing and not to know that the act was wrong," Father Schmidt's fate was sealed.[12] The jury deliberated less than two hours before returning a verdict of guilty of murder in the first degree. The sentence was death in the electric chair.

While on death row at Sing Sing, Father Schmidt changed his story. At the time of her death, Anna was pregnant. She couldn't say she was married to a priest and she didn't want her child to suffer the stigma of illegitimacy she, herself, had suffered. Father Schmidt had been willing to leave the priesthood for her, but she didn't want that. She wanted an abortion. He had obtained the services of Dr. Muret and another doctor, Arnold Leo, but when they arrived at the Bradhurst Avenue apartment, they found Anna in bad shape. She had taken medicines to induce an abortion but had failed at it. The doctors tried to end her pregnancy, but Anna hemorrhaged and died. When neither doctor was willing to sign a death certificate, Father Schmidt agreed to protect them by disposing of the body and, if necessary, taking full responsibility for Anna's death.[13]

A new coroner's report confirmed that Anna had died of a botched abortion. Citing both faulty instructions to the jury and new evidence, Koelble filed an appeal, but to no avail. Judge Benjamin N. Cardozo agreed the instructions had been faulty. But in this case, that didn't matter. Father Schmidt's new story indicated the jury got it right. Father Schmidt was not legally insane. New evidence that could not have been known at the time of trial was the only grounds for appeal in New York at the time. The new evidence Koelble presented could have been known had Father Schmidt told the truth at trial. The verdict was upheld. Father Schmidt was to be executed for the murder of Anna Aumuller.

For his last meal, Father Schmidt ordered sauerbraten, string beans, mashed potatoes, cheesecake, and coffee. At 4 A.M. on Thursday, February 18, 1916, Father William Cashin, the prison chaplain, and Father Schmidt said mass together in Father Schmidt's cell. At 5:50 A.M., Father Schmidt entered the execution chamber. He was pronounced dead at 5:58 A.M.

On February 18, 1916, the *New York Evening Telegram* told its readers that "Hans Schmidt, the first Catholic priest ever to be executed in the United States, went to his death in the electric chair at Sing Sing prison today for the murder of Anna Aumuller."[14]

Dr. Muret was convicted of counterfeiting and served time in the federal penitentiary in Atlanta, Georgia. Joseph Wendling was paroled on January 25, 1935, pending deportation to his native France.

Almost 100 years later, Father Schmidt remains one of a handful of clergy convicted of murder. But in other ways, his case foreshadows the "Pedophile Priests" scandal described in Chapter 1. Like them, Father Schmidt had preyed on young people of both sexes, whom he identified and cultivated through information he obtained while performing his priestly duties. Like many of them, he had long been a problem priest. Instead of removing him from the clergy roster, or even seriously disciplining him, the Church let him move from one parish to another. Even when he was on trial for his crimes, the Church continued to support him. According to the January 23, 1914,

New York Times, the Church helped raise $10,000 for his defense in the Anna Aumuller case.[15]

A MONSTER AND/OR A MARTYR

To Time-Life publications and many of their readers, March 1964 pictures of Malcolm X holding an M1 Carbine illustrated the dangers posed by the radical wing of the civil rights movement that was sweeping the nation.[16] To others, it was a reminder of the danger that African Americans faced from those who would maintain segregation at any cost. But the picture also spoke to religious and political rifts within the African American community that threatened to derail their dream of equal rights in a still racially segregated America.

Malcolm X was an iconic figure on whom Americans, both white and black, projected their hopes and fears. Although he was never more than second-in-command within the Nation of Islam, Malcolm X was widely credited with increasing its membership from 500 in 1952 to 30,000 a decade later. He was responsible for bringing Cassius Clay into the fold, first as Cassius X and then under his Islamic name of Muhammad Ali (Chapter 6, "The Greatest"), but many of his recruits came from his proselytizing efforts in the nation's prisons, which then, as now, held many more African Americans than their proportion within the population would seem to warrant. He opened temples, including an influential one in Philadelphia, and headed his own.

In the 1950s and early 1960s, Malcolm X was the face and voice of the Nation of Islam. Unlike Nation of Islam leader Elijah Muhammad, who rarely spoke to the media, Malcolm X headed the Nation of Islam's Temple Number Seven on Lenox Avenue in Harlem where he had easy access to the media and the media to him. That the mainstream media branded him variously as a monster, a demagogue, and a criminal whose message outraged both traditional Muslims and respectable African Americans mattered little. Malcolm X was charismatic and articulate. The media could count on him to provide quotable quotes. He could count on the media to take his message to a broader audience.

That message was one of rage—a virulent blend of black pride and black nationalism. Blacks were, according to Muhammad's *Message to the Blackman in America,* "descendents of the Asian Black Nation and the tribe of Shabazz." Whites were devils, the product of a misguided breeding program. Separation from white society, its religion, and its political and economic system was mandatory if blacks were to regain their rightful place at the top of the social order.[17] If most blacks could not quite accept that message, many could empathize with the experiences that lay behind the rhetoric.

Malcolm X was born in Omaha, Nebraska, to Louise (Norton) and Earl Little, a Baptist minister and active advocate of Marcus Garvey and the

Universal Negro Improvement Association. The Little family left Omaha amid threats from the Ku Klux Klan, moving first to Milwaukee, Wisconsin, and then to Lansing, Michigan, where their home was mysteriously burned. When his father's body was found on streetcar tracks, the police labeled it a suicide, but Malcolm, like others in the African American community, believed he was murdered by white supremacists. The police could not explain to their satisfaction how someone could possibly bash in his own head before carefully lying down on the tracks.

As a child, Malcolm was embarrassed by and given the nickname "Red," for the reddish tinge to his hair that he inherited from a white man who raped his maternal grandmother. According to his autobiography, he dropped out of school after a teacher told him his dream of being a lawyer was "no realistic goal for a nigger."[18] After his mother had a nervous breakdown and was declared insane, Malcolm went to Boston to live with an older half sister, where he drifted aimlessly between menial jobs and petty crime. While serving eight years in the Massachusetts State Prison for larceny and breaking and entering, he both educated himself and learned about the Nation of Islam.

Once out of prison, Malcolm traveled to Chicago to meet Elijah Muhammad. Like others who joined the Nation of Islam, he took on the surname "X" to signify his rejection of a "slave name" with all it implied.

In 1952, Elijah Muhammad appointed Malcolm X to lead the Nation of Islam's Temple Number Eleven in Boston and then, after two years, to lead the Temple Number Seven in Harlem. But where once Malcolm X was Muhammad's favorite and heir-apparent, a decade later that was no longer true.

The break began in 1963 when Malcolm X found out that rumors that the Nation of Islam leader had engaged in adulterous affairs were true. The rift between the two men widened following Malcolm X's trip to Africa where he saw whites helping blacks and Muslims of all shades living and working together. After talking to and meeting with orthodox Muslims who encouraged him to learn more about the Islamic faith, he publicly announced his break with the Nation of Islam on March 8, 1964.

Malcolm X founded Muslim Mosque, Inc. on March 12, 1964. Then in April he made a pilgrimage to Mecca and formally converted to the Sunni branch of conventional Islam. As a Sunni Muslim, he took the name El-Hajj Malid El-Shabazz, although that name is rarely associated with him. Three months later, as head of his newly formed Organization of African-American Unity, he addressed the Organization of African Unity's first ordinary assembly in Cairo, Egypt, on July 17, 1964.

Malcolm X had posed with the gun for the March 1964 pictures to illustrate the danger he now faced from members of his former religion who were angered both by his revelation of Muhammad's adultery and by his rejection of the Nation of Islam's harsh, anti-white position for a more peaceful, cooperative one based on visions of pan-world unity. Violence was wrong, he now said, but he was willing to defend himself from the daily death threats he and his family were receiving. Those threats were very real.

Louis Farrakhan, one of Malcolm X's converts to the Nation of Islam who went on to become its leader, told followers that revealing Muhammad's adultery made Malcolm X "worthy of death."[19] In June 1964, the Nation of Islam successfully sued to gain possession of the house in Queens where Malcolm X lived with his family. On February 15, 1965, the night before a hearing to postpone their eviction, someone threw Molotov cocktails into the house and it burned to the ground. Malcolm and his family escaped unharmed. No one was ever prosecuted, but Malcolm X told authorities he thought it might be someone from the Nation of Islam.

A week later, just after Malcolm mounted the podium in the Audubon Ballroom in Manhattan to give a major speech, a scuffle broke out somewhere in the crowd of 400. As Malcolm X appealed for quiet, a man rushed forward and shot him in the chest with a sawed-off shotgun. As Malcolm X's horrified wife, Betty Shabazz, and their four children watched, two more men charged the podium firing handguns. Thirty-nine-year-old Malcolm X was pronounced dead on arrival at Columbia Presbyterian Hospital on February 21, 1965.

Malcolm's bodyguards managed to shoot one suspect, Talmadge Hayer, in the leg and hold him for police. Witnesses named Norman 3X Butler and Thomas 15X Johnson, both members of the Nation of Islam, as suspects, but they escaped.

Elijah Muhammad immediately went into hiding. Although suspected of being behind the assassination, he was never charged in connection with the crime. Hayer confessed and was convicted. Butler and Johnson were eventually caught, arrested, and convicted, but doubts about their role in the crime remain. Hayer said neither man was involved. The initial police report stating that two men were arrested and taken to the police station disappeared and has never been found. Therefore, many still wonder how two known enforcers for the Nation of Islam could have gotten past bodyguards at the Ballroom the night of the murder. To them it seems plausible that the assassination of Malcolm X might have been instigated by organized crime or even by the U.S. government. His efforts to rid Harlem of drugs, alcohol, and prostitution gave the mafia a reason to retaliate. The government might have wanted to silence him before his Organization of African-American Unity could make the nation's race problem an international issue; the government was known to keep files on civil rights activists and infiltrate their meetings.[20]

In its March 5 article on the assassination, *Time* told readers that Malcolm X was a disaster for the civil rights movement. His death was a logical consequence of quarrels among murderous thugs.[21]But a decade later, the magazine that had once seen him as dangerous had begun to list him as a "reconciler" of the races.[22] And if that view is not universally shared, over time Malcolm X has come to occupy a place in the pantheon of heroes of the civil rights movement just below that afforded the Rev. Martin Luther King and Rosa Parks. There are buildings, streets, and parks across America named for him. Nearly half a century after his death, the posthumously published *Autobiography of Malcolm X*, which he wrote with Alex Haley, is required reading in many high school and college classes. A radical and a reconciler in his own time, he was and remains an icon on which people project their hopes and fears.

THE FLAVOR-AID MASSACRE

Jim Jones's degree from Butler University in Indianapolis was in education. But he was a powerful preacher, and, in the civil rights era of the 1950s and 1960s, the congregations he led became the poster child for what the church should be. They were multiracial, socially active, and politically engaged. Theologically they were also somewhat eclectic, if not ecumenical.

After first serving a Methodist congregation in Indianapolis, Jones started his Peoples Temple by buying a building that had been a synagogue with funds that he raised by selling monkeys door-to-door for $29. Although he affiliated the Temple with the Disciples of Christ in 1960, the worship services he conducted on Sunday morning and the afternoon healing services were more generally Pentecostal. The Temple, which was located in a black area of the city, operated a free restaurant and provided other services for the city's poor people. The mayor rewarded Jones for the Temple's good works by naming him to the city's human rights commission.

Although the congregation was thriving, Indianapolis was not a comfortable city for a white pastor who led a multiracial congregation and who, with his white wife, had adopted children who were black and who were Asian. Interracial marriage was still illegal in Indiana. Indianapolis had been national headquarters for the Ku Klux Klan and the Klan still had local support.

Jones's uneasiness grew when, in 1961, he had a vision of the city being destroyed in a nuclear holocaust. After checking out a number of supposedly safe locations, Jones and about a hundred followers moved to Redwood Valley, California, in 1965. Over the next 15 years, his flock grew to an estimated 20,000 as Jones expanded his ministry, first to San Francisco and then to Los Angeles. Although Redwood Valley was officially Temple headquarters, the Peoples Temple that Jones set up on Geary Street in San Francisco in 1970 was its power base.

Like the Peoples Temple in Indianapolis, the one in San Francisco was a multiracial congregation located in a poor area of town where it operated a free dining hall for the city's indigent. In San Francisco, the Temple and its members also supported and staffed free clinics, a drug rehabilitation program, a child care center, carpentry shop, and a program offering legal aid to low income people. Jones and his followers could also be counted on to give money in support of a free press, to write letters in support of various political causes, and to get out the vote for favored candidates.

Political leaders courted Jones and he counted them among his friends. During the 1976 presidential election campaign, Jones appeared at a rally with Rosalynn Carter, the wife of Democratic presidential candidate Jimmy Carter; Walter Mondale, who was running for vice president on the Democratic ticket, invited Jones aboard his chartered airplane for a private chat. California Governor Jerry Brown, Los Angeles Mayor Tom Bradley, and San Francisco Mayor George Moscone were among the prominent elected officials who visited Peoples Temple. In December 1976, Moscone named Jones head of San Francisco's housing commission.

That led *New West* magazine to begin working on a story about Peoples Temple. In response, Jones, who once had channeled almost $10,000 to newspapers in support of press freedom, orchestrated a barrage of threatening letters and phone calls.[23] When the *San Francisco Examiner* carried a story about the letters and calls, it, too, was targeted. But the story also prompted former Temple members to call the magazine and the newspaper. A few of them agreed to let *New West* publish their names and their pictures, and on August 1, 1977, *New West* told their stories as part of its expose.[24]

At first, the defectors said, they had found Jones to be a warm, compassionate minister and the Temple a welcoming place, but the services they first attended and that the civic leaders saw were a sham. Members were expected to attend multiple services almost daily. Public humiliations and beatings were a part of them. The healings, they came to realize, were fakes. There were instances of cruelty at nursing homes and child care centers that the Temple operated. There were also very likely financial irregularities; the Temple was extremely wealthy. When they joined, some had sold everything, including their homes, and turned the money over to the Temple. Others had signed documents they later realized gave the Temple control of their property and, indeed, their lives. They would have left the Temple sooner, but they feared reprisals. Even now, they were taking a chance by speaking publicly. Peoples Temple, a Disciples of Christ congregation, had morphed into a dangerous cult—a new religion organized around a living, charismatic leader who claimed to be the deity.

As early as 1961, when Peoples Temple was still in Indianapolis, Jones had visited Father Divine, whose followers believed him to be the personification of God. In Philadelphia, Father Divine apparently convinced Jones that he was "The Man"—that he was God. After that, the man who had been known as Jimmy insisted that his flock call him "Father." The Bible, he claimed, was the "black man's idol." People should pay less attention to it and more to him. He would protect his people from a society that was planning a new holocaust to exterminate the black race. The *New West* article signaled the beginning of that campaign, Jones told his followers.[25] He had already bought land and established an agricultural village in Guyana. Now it was time for him and his flock to go there.

Nearly a thousand people followed their leader to Guyana where, together, they built Jonestown on a 27,000 acre tract on the edge of the jungle. Photos and glossy brochures that the Temple produced show a school, community dining hall, living quarters, and most prominently, Jones lovingly embracing members of his multiracial "Rainbow Family" of believers. But Temple members who stayed in California and outsiders who had relatives who had gone to Guyana began to ask questions.

After Robert Houston, an Associated Press photographer, told Leo Ryan, the Democratic Congressman from San Mateo, California, that Houston's son had been found dead just one day after he had defected from the Temple, Ryan decided to look into the matter.[26] Staff from the U.S. embassy in Guyana told him they had interviewed 75 cult members individually, none of whom wanted to leave. Ryan, unconvinced, decided to see for himself.[27]

On November 15, 1978, Ryan arrived in Jonestown on his own fact-finding mission. With him were several relatives of Temple members and eight journalists, including ones from NBC and *Time* magazine. Jonestown residents greeted the visitors warmly. They happily showed off their newly constructed combination school and assembly hall, a nursery, hospital, 10,000 volume library, and sawmill. At night they provided entertainment.

At first, no one professed to want to leave, but by the next day one member gave NBC correspondent Don Harris a note saying some people wanted to leave. Others began telling Ryan the same thing. Things began to turn ugly when Harris asked Jones about rumors that the colony was heavily armed, in part to guard against defections.

Angrily calling the allegation a bald-faced lie, Jones said people were free to come and go as they pleased. But as Ryan negotiated with him about taking some people back to the States, a cult member, Don Sly, attacked Ryan with a knife. As Jones sat passively, another cult member thwarted the attempt at murder. With families squabbling over whether they should stay or go, Jones told his followers not to worry because he would take care of everything.[28]

On the afternoon of November 18 as Ryan and his entourage were preparing to board Ryan's chartered plane and another one flown in to accommodate the 14 people who wanted to leave Jonestown, a tractor pulling a large trailer pulled up to the airstrip. The men in the trailer suddenly stood up and began shooting. So did Larry Layton, a defector who really was a "plant." When the shooting stopped, Ryan, one defector, and three journalists were dead. Ten people were wounded.

Those who survived managed to take off for Georgetown, Guyana, in the one airplane that escaped serious damage. There, while awaiting a larger plane to take them to the United States, the defectors nervously told more horror stories. Jones, they said, had told them the government of Guyana had given him authority to kill anyone who tried to leave. There were also "white nights" during which Jones would awaken everyone, harangue them for hours, and then order them to line up and drink a supposedly poisonous potion, only to be told after they had drunk it that it wasn't poisonous and that they had passed his "loyalty test."[29]

Two days later journalists and authorities from Guyana and the United States entered Jonestown where they found a grisly scene. Bodies, bloated and rotting in the jungle sun, were everywhere. Jones had died of a gunshot wound to his head. His body was found near his Jonestown throne. Some of his followers had been shot or strangled, but most had passed their final "loyalty test." They had drunk from huge vats of grape Flavor-Aid laced with cyanide.

When reporters and government authorities reached Jonestown, they found bodies everywhere. Almost a thousand followers of Jim Jones died from drinking cyanide-laced Flavor-Aid from vats like the one in the foreground. AP photo, Frank Johnson, pool.

In all, 913 cult members died; 79 who were at Jonestown on November 18, 1978, managed to survive. So did two of Jim Jones's sons, who were on the road with a Jonestown youth basketball team at the time.

Over the next few weeks, Robert Friedly, communications officer for the Disciples of Christ, found himself repeatedly explaining the connection between the denomination and Peoples Temple. Although the denomination had looked into some allegations about Jones's tactics that had come to its attention in 1974, the denomination had no provision for expelling a congregation.[30]

Questions also surfaced as to why the government hadn't responded in any meaningful way to citizen concerns about the Temple that were floating around even before the *New West* story. But the First Amendment's guarantee of religious freedom acts as a powerful protection against government action absent solid evidence of criminal activity. Defectors almost always tell atrocity tales about their former religion. As with Jonestown, some of these tales prove to be true. But with Jonestown, real evidence didn't come to light until after the massacre.

If the Disciples of Christ had been able to remove Peoples Temple from its congregation list, it would undoubtedly have saved itself some embarrassment. But doing that would not have kept Jones from operating his Peoples Temple. Nor would it have prevented the massacre.

Had the government launched a serious investigation when rumors about Peoples Temple first surfaced, it might have turned up evidence of criminal cruelty and fiscal improprieties, but it probably would not have changed the outcome. More likely it would have speeded up the date for the mass suicide.

The Jonestown massacre remains the largest religious mass suicide in American history, but in San Diego, on March 26, 1997, 39 members of Heaven's Gate committed suicide in peaceful anticipation of being transported to a "higher plane." In a country that promises religious freedom, there simply is no way to prevent a cult from springing up (Chapter 2, "The Kingdom, Money, Sex, and Maybe a Murder"; Chapter 7, "The Paiute Messiah"; Chapter 8, "Ballots and Bioterrorism") or to keep people from following their leader even unto death (Chapter 8, "Virgins and Guns").

DOMESTIC TERRORISTS

First the American Coalition of Life Activists (ACLA), an anti-abortion/pro-life organization, released a wanted-style poster offering a $5,000 reward for the "arrest, conviction and revocation of license to practice medicine" of a "Deadly Dozen" doctors who performed abortions. A year later, in 1996, its "Nuremburg Files" showed up on the Internet. Like the poster, the Nuremburg Files contained pictures, names, addresses, and other personal information about doctors who performed abortions. But unlike the posters, the names of doctors who had been injured in attacks on them were on gray backgrounds. The names of those who had been killed were crossed out.[31]

An Oregon chapter of Planned Parenthood, some of whose clinics provide legal abortions along with other medical services, considered the postings a clear threat, but at first its efforts to get an injunction to force the ACLA to remove the Nuremburg Files from the Internet were rebuffed in federal court. In 2000, however, the Court of Appeals for the Ninth Circuit agreed with Planned Parenthood. The Nuremburg Files weren't constitutionally protected political speech. They could be shut down and their creator forced to pay punitive damages to Planned Parenthood because the Files were a hit list—an invitation to kill.

The Ninth Circuit had good reason for concluding the Files posed a clear and immediate threat to those whose names were listed on the Web site. In the years since the United States Supreme Court issued its controversial *Roe v. Wade* decision legalizing abortion during the first trimester of a pregnancy, Roman Catholic and conservative Protestant opposition had become better organized. Protests and demonstrations had increased. They had also come to include more acts of civil disobedience.

In 1991, during the "Summer of Mercy" organized by Operation Rescue, thousands of pro-life activists staged six weeks of protests aimed at shutting down a Wichita, Kansas, abortion clinic owned and operated by George R. Tiller. Sit-ins and "rescues" during which protesters prevented people from entering the clinic by forcibly blocking access to it led to hundreds of arrests for disorderly conduct. The protestors' rhetoric labeling abortionists and the women seeking a legal abortion as murderers and baby killers also seemed to spark a wave of mayhem and murders directed at abortion clinics and the people who worked in them.

On March 10, 1993, Michael F. Griffin shot and killed Dr. David Gunn during an anti-abortion protest at the Ladies Center in Pensacola, Florida. During the year before that murder, Gunn had been the target of wanted-style posters distributed by Operation Rescue. Afterward, his successor at the clinic and his clinic escorts took to wearing bulletproof vests. But those vests did no good. On June 29, 1994, the Rev. Paul Jennings Hill fatally shot Dr. John Britton and his 74-year-old escort, James Barrett, in the head. Barrett's wife, June, was wounded but survived. Hill was ordained in 1968 as a minister of the conservative Presbyterian Church in America and had subsequently served as a minister in the Orthodox Presbyterian Church. More recently, he had pastored the independent Trinity Presbyterian Church in Valparaiso, Florida, before that congregation asked him to leave because of his advocacy of violence against abortion doctors. As a regular picketer at Dr. Britton's clinic, Hill routinely carried a sign saying abortionists are murderers who should be executed.[32]

On March 19, 1996, John C. Salvi III, a Roman Catholic, killed receptionist Shannon Lowney and wounded three others at a Planned Parenthood clinic in Brookline, Massachusetts. Ten minutes later at an abortion clinic a mile away, he killed receptionist Lee Ann Nichols and wounded two others. Although Salvi was most likely mentally ill at the time of the attack, he told the court that found him competent to stand trial that he was inspired to act by pamphlets from Human Life International and by the Rev. Pat Robertson's book *The New World Order.*

The murders were, of course, roundly criticized by pro-choice activists and women's rights organizations such as the National Association for Women and the Feminist Majority Foundation. But Griffin, Hill, and Salvi had their supporters. Demonstrators frequently showed up outside the jails where they were held to demand their release. When Rachelle Ranae "Shelley" Shannon was imprisoned for shooting and wounding Dr. George Tiller outside his Wichita clinic, Hill came to her defense. After he was arrested for the murder of Dr. Britton and his escort, she returned the favor by signing a petition on his behalf circulated by the Aryan Nation, which is part of the Christian Identity movement[33] (this chapter, "Another Domestic Terrorist"). Even after Roman Catholic Archbishop Oscar Lipscomb removed him from his duties as a priest, David Trosch remained an outspoken defender of what he considered justifiable homicide.[34]

Griffin, Hill, and Salvi were Christians who, like most of those who oppose abortion, believe that the Bible teaches that life begins at conception and killing an unborn child is murder. However, unlike most other abortion opponents, they also found warrant in the Bible for their claim that killing an abortion doctor to stop him from killing countless innocent babies is justifiable homicide.

Therefore, most churches and groups associated with the anti-abortion/pro-life movement took steps to disassociate themselves and their organizations from the killers. In the Hill case, for example, 14 pro-life organizations held a joint press conference in Washington, D.C., the day after the murder to say that their organizations saw nothing justifiable about murdering abortion doctors.[35] The American Center for Law and Justice, which represented Hill in a case stemming from his picketing as part of its mission to defend conservative Christians involved in religious freedom cases, announced it would not defend a killer who acted outside the mainstream of the pro-life movement.[36]

Even the Portland, Oregon, Advocates for Life Ministries (ALM), which once had supported Hill's claim that killing abortion doctors is justifiable homicide, backtracked a bit. In its statement, ALM called the murder of clinic workers unwarranted, but stopped just short of condemning the killing of an abortion provider.[37]

Roman Catholic Cardinals Bernard Law, Roger Mahoney, and John O'Connor repeatedly explained to the press and public that the ends do not justify the means. Committing murder to stop doctors from performing abortions undermines the pro-life position. More importantly, it is also contrary to Church teachings.[38]

Charles Schumer, a Democratic Representative from New York, called for the FBI to infiltrate pro-life groups.[39] President Bill Clinton referred to the clinic attacks as domestic terrorism. At his urging, Attorney General Janet Reno dispatched federal marshals to guard 18 clinics that appeared to be in the most immediate danger.[40]

In May 1994, Congress passed and President Clinton signed into law the Freedom of Access to Clinic Entrance Act that makes it a crime to block access to a medical facility and also provides a life sentence for anyone convicted of murdering an abortionist. In June 1994 in the case of *Madsen v. Women's Health Center*, the U.S. Supreme Court for the first time upheld the constitutionality of a state "bubble law" requiring protesters to stay a reasonable distance away from people entering or leaving an abortion clinic or other medical facility.

But neither condemnation nor laws serve as a deterrent to fanatics, especially ones who believe they are beholden to some higher law. Off-duty policeman Robert Sanderson died and nurse Emily Lyon was critically injured in the January 1997 bombing of a clinic in Birmingham, Alabama (this chapter, "Another Domestic Terrorist"). On October 23, 1998, James Charles Kopp fired a single shot through a rear window of Dr. Barnett Slepian's Amherst, New York, home, killing the doctor instantly as he sat at a table with his family. In addition to maintaining a private practice as an obstetrician-gynecologist, Dr. Slepian performed legal abortions at a clinic in Buffalo. Kopp was associated with the anti-abortion group The Lambs of Christ.

Although there were no more murders of abortion providers for over a decade, on Sunday morning, May 31, 2009, Dr. George R. Tiller, who long had been targeted by Operation Rescue for his willingness to perform late-term abortions, was murdered while serving as an usher at Reformation Lutheran Church in Wichita, Kansas. His killer was quickly identified as Scott Roeder, an anti-abortion activist who, though apparently not a member of the organization, had been in frequent contact with Operation Rescue.

In the years between 1998 and 2009 acts of vandalism and arson at abortion clinics remained relatively common. According to 2005 figures from the National Abortion Federation, since 1977 there have been at least 41 bombings, 173 arsons, 1,264 instances of vandalism, and 100 attacks with "stink bombs" containing the foul-smelling butyric acid. The earliest attacks occurred in Oregon in 1976; the most recent were attempted bombings in 2007 in Texas and Virginia.

Some of those attacks came from individuals whose motives had little to do with religion. Most of them, however, have come from those who are connected, in one way or another, with churches and religious-based organizations that are adamantly opposed to abortion. Many of those in the anti-abortion/ pro-life movement also are steadfastly opposed to granting any kind of civil rights to homosexuals.

Attacks on gays and lesbians are also fairly common, but to date hate crimes against them have not been linked to Christian activists the way violence against abortionists and abortion clinics has been tied to a tiny, radical fringe of the religious-based anti-abortion/pro-life movement. Hate speech, however, is another matter. The Rev. Fred Phelps of tiny, independent Westboro Baptist Church in Topeka, Kansas, opposes abortion, but it is his opposition to homosexuality that has made him both famous and infamous. Indeed, by 2006 his demonstrations replete with "God hates fags" signs at the funerals of homosexuals, even of those who died in military service in Afghanistan and Iraq, had become so distressing that 17 states and the federal government have enacted "bubble laws" limiting protests near funeral and burial sites.[41]

After the abortion murders committed by Hill and by Salvi, Archbishop Law called for those in the pro-life movement to tone down their rhetoric lest they be guilty of inciting violence.[42] That didn't happen. In the years before his death, Tiller was frequently called "baby killer" on television programs such as The O'Reilly Factor and even worse things on internet posting. Equally inflammatory rhetoric also spread into other religious-inspired demonstrations such as those of the Rev. Phelps. So the murders and mayhem that have been directed at abortion providers, their clinic staff, and their clinics serve as a reminder that words can do good. They can also encourage and legitimize violence.

MURDER FOR HIRE

The 911 call came in at 9:22 P.M. on Tuesday, November 1, 1994. Rabbi Fred Neulander had found his wife lying face down on the living room floor when he had returned to their Cherry Hill, New Jersey, home after teaching an evening class at Congregation M'Kor Shalom. She had apparently died from blows to her head.

Investigators thought it might have been a robbery gone awry. Carol Neulander sometimes brought large sums of money home with her before depositing receipts from her bakery, the Classic Cake Company. They also thought she might have known her assailant. There were no signs of forced entry and little indication that she had struggled with her assailant.

With little evidence to guide the investigation, rumors and speculation flourished. They grew even stronger four months later after Sheila Goodman, congregation M'Kor Shalom's president, called a special meeting to tell congregation members that the board had accepted their rabbi's resignation. In his letter of resignation, she said, the rabbi had cited the media frenzy surrounding his wife's murder, "information and disinformation" from the police, and "behavior I am not proud of" as his reasons for resigning.[42]

At first, many in the congregation were upset. Even though they had heard rumors that the rabbi had engaged in adulterous relations, they found it hard to understand why the board wasn't more supportive of the popular and charismatic rabbi who had built the congregation from a handful of members meeting in rented quarters to one of the largest and most influential Reform synagogues in South Jersey. After all, his letter also said, "Quite obviously I had nothing to do with my wife's death."[43]

The reason the synagogue board so readily accepted the rabbi's resignation became apparent as more details of his infidelity surfaced. Rabbi Neulander had had affairs with two women from his congregation. One of them was

Elaine Soncini, a popular talk show host on Philadelphia radio. Just before his wife's murder, she had pressured him to leave his wife so the two of them could be together. In August, she told the *Philadelphia Inquirer* newspaper that the rabbi had called her after the murder to discuss how they should describe their relationship to the congregation and the media.[44]

Two years later, the rabbi's friend Myron Levin told a grand jury looking into the case that the rabbi had once told him that he wished he could come home one night and find his wife dead in a pool of blood. He also had asked whether Levin could help arrange to have her killed.[45]

On September 10, 1998, Rabbi Neulander was charged with being an accomplice to murder, but remained free after posting $400,000 bail. The real break in the case came 18 months later when Leonard Jenoff, a private investigator, told *Philadelphia Inquirer* reporter Nancy Phillips that Rabbi Neulander had hired him and Paul Daniels, his roommate at the time, to kill Carol Neulander.[46]

While all of this was going on, there were two marriages and a romance. Elaine Soncini married the police officer who guarded her during the investigation. Rabbi Neulander officiated at Jenoff's wedding, which was held at the rabbi's home in the room where his wife was murdered; he ordered the wedding cake from the bakery she had founded. And the rabbi dated Miss Vicki, who had her 15 minutes of fame in 1969 when she married the ukulele-playing falsetto singer Tiny Tim on *The Tonight Show Starring Johnny Carson.*

On May 1, 2000, both Daniels and Jenoff were arrested. Daniels pleaded guilty to aggravated manslaughter and robbery. Jenoff pleaded guilty to the same charges; he also agreed to testify against Rabbi Neulander. On June 20, the charges against Rabbi Neulander were upgraded to capital murder, felony murder, and conspiracy. His bail was revoked, and he was sent to prison. With all of the hoopla surrounding the case, it took seven weeks to impanel an impartial jury. But finally on October 18, 2001, in New Jersey Superior Court in Camden County, the rabbi's trial began.

In court, Jenoff testified that the rabbi had instructed him to make the murder look as if robbery was the motive. The first time he and Daniels tried to follow through on the rabbi's instructions, he had posed as a repairman to gain entry to the house, but when he couldn't find Mrs. Neulander's purse, they left without killing her. However, they returned to the home on November 1 and carried out the plan. For their efforts, the rabbi had paid him $7,500 a few weeks before their first attempt at murder and another $7,500 afterward. He split both payments with Daniels. He also received some smaller payments before the rabbi hired him as a private investigator and began funneling money to him through his lawyer.

Attorneys for the defense argued that Jenoff's testimony should not be trusted. Jenoff admitted in court that he had faked CIA credentials and had forged a letter that made it look as if President Ronald Reagan had commended him for his work. Maybe it was that strategy. Maybe it was the media coverage; or maybe it was simply that the jurors found it hard to believe that a man of the cloth would hire hit men to kill his wife. Whatever the reason, the trial ended with a hung jury.

Judge Linda G. Baxter granted the defense's request for a change of venue to Monmouth County. There, however, the rabbi's luck ran out. On November 22, 2002, Rabbi Fred Neulander was convicted of arranging for the murder of his wife. His sentence was 30 years to life in prison. New Jersey law does not allow a convicted murderer to challenge the verdict or any of the state's evidence, so the rabbi will be in his mid-80s when he first becomes eligible to apply for parole.

In his final statement to the jury just before they began their deliberation, the rabbi professed his innocence and also his love for his wife. He also begged the jury to spare his life so he would have an opportunity to teach illiterate prisoners to read. But the rabbi's plea for clemency seemed hollow given the nature of the crime for which he was convicted.

As James Lynch, the first assistant prosecutor during the rabbi's first trial, said in his opening statement, Rabbi Neulander "was the architect of his own fate."[46] Divorcing his wife might have done some damage to his career, but his decision to have his wife murdered did even more damage. In ending her life, he destroyed his career. By hiring hit men, he and two other men ended up in prison—and citizens of New Jersey had to foot the costs associated with the investigation, trials, and incarcerations. The rabbi's story was, Lynch said, the story of a "successful man ... who fell guilty to his own needs, a man overwhelmed by lust, greed, arrogance."[47]

ANOTHER DOMESTIC TERRORIST

At 1:20 A.M. on Saturday, July 27, 1996, as Atlanta played host to the Summer Olympics, a homemade bomb went off in Centennial Olympic Park, killing spectator Alice Hawthorne and wounding 111 others, at least one of whom later died. Six months later, on January 16, 1997, there was a bombing in an Atlanta suburb at the Sandy Springs Professional Building that houses an abortion clinic. That attack caused some damage but no injuries or deaths, although two weeks later, on January 29, officer Robert Sanderson died and nurse Emily Lyons was critically injured in a bombing at the New Woman All Woman abortion clinic in Birmingham, Alabama. Also, on February 21, 1997, five people were injured in another bombing, this time at the Otherside Lounge, an Atlanta nightclub catering to homosexuals.

At first, police targeted Richard Jewell as the most likely suspect in the Centennial Park bombing. Although so many attacks in such close proximity to each other is highly unusual, the other attacks seemed unrelated. But neither first guess held up. After what turned out to be a law enforcement and media fiasco, Jewell turned out to be exactly what first reports said he was—a person at the scene of the crime who pointed police to the bag that had held the bomb and who also had immediately gone to the aid of victims of the attack. As for the connection among the cases, that began to become clearer when a witness told police he had seen a man leave the Birmingham clinic and get into a Nissan pickup truck with a North Carolina license plate. The license plate had been issued to Eric Rudolph. He was almost certainly the culprit in the Alabama bombing. Most likely, he was also the Atlanta bomber.

But by the time FBI agents found Rudolph's trailer home on Cane Creek in rural western North Carolina, he was gone. He had left so hastily that the door was open and the lights were still on. So the hunt for the serial bomber was on. Rudolph made the FBI's "Ten Most Wanted" list. Federal marshals scoured the Appalachian woods for him; police everywhere were on the lookout. In spite of a $1 million bounty for his capture, Rudolph remained on the lam for more than five years. When he was finally caught, it was more a matter of dumb luck than of all the hard work that had gone into hunting him down.

For years Rudolph had indeed been in North Carolina's Appalachian Mountains. Mostly he had lived off the land, but he had also made a bit of money growing and selling marijuana. On occasion, he had ventured into town to rummage for food in Dumpsters. That was how he was caught. On the night of May 3, 2003, Murphy, North Carolina, rookie policeman Jeff Postell spotted a man lurking behind a Sav-a-Lot grocery store, apprehended him without incident, and took him to the sheriff's office. At first, the man told officers he was Jerry Wilson, but when one of them thought the man looked familiar, he gave his real name, Eric Robert Rudolph.[48] In the days following his capture, he also confessed to the string of bombings.

Media reports quickly linked Rudolph to the Christian Identity movement.[49] Christian Identity is known more for its racism, anti-Semitism, and anti-government sentiment than for its apocalyptic version of Christianity. It is a form of the same British Israelism that in an earlier era undergirded Ku Klux Klan thinking. According to Christian Identity theology, white people of northern European descent are God's chosen people, and it is they who are called upon to rescue the Christian faith from the heretical notions preached by mainstream Christian churches. Among the most heretical of those beliefs is the one that identifies the Jews of today as the remnant of God's chosen people. In reality, according to Christian Identity doctrine, they comprise an international conspiracy of Jews intent on establishing one-world government, a New World Order. As a corollary of that belief, Christian Identity adherents oppose the United States government, which they believe is under the control of that Jewish cabal.

Although Rudolph repeatedly denied being a member of any Christian Identity group or even of having any real connection to one,[50] Christian Identity beliefs mixed together with a liberal sprinkling of neo-Nazi anti-Semitism and the virulent anti-government sentiments of Freemen philosophy clearly were an influence on his decision to carry out serial bombings in Atlanta and in Birmingham. Rudolph had learned about Christian Identity as a teen when he and his mother left their Carolina home to spend four months in 1984 at a Church of Israel compound in Schell City, Missouri, where the pastor, Dan Gayman, expounded on the tenets of Christian Identity doctrine.

In high school in North Carolina, Rudolph wrote a paper denying the holocaust ever happened—an idea he picked up from Gayman, from books such as *The Turner Diaries*, and perhaps from some of his neighbors in the woods of rural North Carolina. While living there, he spent hours with his neighbor Thomas Wayne Branham, who considered himself a Freeman, not subject to government law or jurisdiction, and especially not to that of a federal government intent on taxing people into submission as the first step toward establishing a one-world government.[51] Branham also gave him access to books that taught him both the bomb-making skills he used to commit his crimes and the survival techniques that helped him elude capture.

After he was apprehended, Rudolph told reporters he picked Atlanta for his attacks because of its large black population.[52] In a three-page letter he had sent anonymously to news organizations shortly after the bombings there, he referred to the Otherside Lounge as a "sodomite bar" and warned that anyone in or near "facilities that murder children may become victims of retribution." But he also wrote that his bombs had been "aimed at agents of the so-called federal government, i.e. A.T.F., F.B.I., Marshal's e.t.c. [sic]. We declare and will wage total war on the ungodly communist regime … and your legislative bureaucratic lackeys in Washington." The missive ended with, "Death to the New World Order."[53]

In an April 13, 2005, statement, Rudolph made his motives for the bombings even more explicit. He wrote:

> Even though the conception and purpose of the so-called Olympic movement is to promote the values of global socialism, as perfectly expressed in the song "Imagine" by John Lennon [Chapter 5, "More Popular than Jesus"], which was the theme of the 1996 Games even though the purpose of the Olympics is to promote these despicable ideals, the purpose of the attack on July 27 was to confound, anger and embarrass the Washington government in the eyes of the world for its abominable sanctioning of abortion on demand.[54]

Rudolph's words and his deeds made him a Christian Identity hero. The Aryan Nation in effect adopted him. His writing can often be found on its Web site along with commentary from Christian Identity and Freemen proponents who praise him for his support of their agenda and for having the courage to act on his convictions.

Although Rudolph's crimes are the best known, they are by no means the only ones committed by members of groups who were and who remain his staunchest supporters. In August 1982, for example, the Army of God was behind the kidnapping of Hector Zevallos, a doctor and clinic owner, and his wife, Josalee Jean. In June 2009, Stephen Tyrone Johns, a security guard at the United States Holocaust Memorial Museum in Washington, DC, was killed inside the museum by James Wennecker von Brunn who, like Rudolph, was a lone wolf with hard-core anti-Semitic and White Supremacist views.

Although von Brunn's rampage inside the Holocaust Museum was the work of a known anti-Semite who operated on the fringes of the Christian Identity movement, the most notorious attack on a Jew was the June 1984 murder of Alan Berg, a popular radio host in Denver, masterminded by David Lane, a member of The Order, the Christian Identity group that helped bankroll Gayman's Church of Israel. Their attempts to set up guarded, armed compounds around the nation from which they can safely wage what they consider a war against an illegitimate government have led to numerous incidents and confrontations. One of them occurred in 1992 at Ruby Ridge, Idaho, during which a government sharpshooter killed the wife and son of group leader Randy Weaver. Two years later, Timothy McVeigh said he detonated the bomb that killed 168 people in Oklahoma City because of the government's actions at Ruby Ridge and its 1993 siege at the Branch Davidian compound in Waco, Texas (Chapter 8, "Virgins and Guns").

When they occurred, the murder of Alan Berg and the confrontation at Ruby Ridge received their share of media attention. But those incidents, like the more notorious crimes of Eric Rudolph, seemed so beyond the pale that mainstream religious and political organizations have not gone out of their way to distance themselves from Rudolph or from the organizations that inspired him like they did when men who were tied, however loosely, to more mainstream anti-abortion/pro-life movements that killed doctors and staff members at abortion clinics (this chapter, "Domestic Terrorists"). In their silence, they failed to recognize and condemn the widespread racist, anti-Semitic and anti-government sentiment that made Rudolph something of a folk hero and "Run Rudolph Run" T-shirts hot sellers throughout Appalachia and beyond.

Those who oppose abortion and would condone the killing of abortionists are a tiny minority within the more mainstream opposition to abortion; those who would actually kill abortion doctors for religious reasons are an even tinier minority. Those who identify with movements like Christian Identity and condone its philosophy are probably more numerous, but they, too, are a minority. Because their targets are more numerous, they may be more dangerous. But even among Christian Identity members and supporters, more would probably condone violence than would actually kill except to defend their own life.

Still, in the days since 9/11, it has been easy to point to fanatical, Muslim terrorists as evidence that Islam is an inherently dangerous religion. But domestic terrorists like the more mainstream Christians who have targeted abortion providers, their staffs, and their clinics, and ones like Eric Rudolph, who find their rationalization in Christian Identity teachings, serve as reminders that any religion can inspire fanaticism of a kind that leads to mayhem and murder.

THE GOOD MOTHER

At their 1993 wedding, Andrea and Russell "Rusty" Yates made a point of telling their guests that they did not plan to use contraceptives. They would have as many children as nature allowed.[55] It was a pronouncement born of religious conviction.

Although raised in the Catholic faith, Andrea renounced it to embrace the teachings of Michael Peter Woroniecki, an itinerant evangelist who had been Rusty's mentor since 1984 when the two met during Rusty's student days at Auburn University. Rusty liked the part of Woroniecki's theology that said the man should be the head of the family and the wife's role was to be his helper and bear his children. Andrea found the preacher's "repent or burn" approach to understanding good and evil, sin and salvation, appealing. With her Catholic background, the part about shunning contraceptives and having many children also seemed right. For years she corresponded with Woroniecki and tried to enlist his help in converting her Catholic parents to her new understanding of what it meant to be a good Christian.[56]

Throughout the years of their marriage, Andrea did her best to be the kind of woman their spiritual guide said she should be. Three months after the wedding, Andrea was pregnant. The couple's first child, Noah, was born on February 26, 1994. Over the next six years they had four more children: John, Paul, Luke and Mary.

Rusty's job designing computer systems for NASA provided a comfortable living, and at first they had a nice four bedroom house. But when he wanted to simplify his life in accord with Woroniecki's teaching, Andrea moved with him into a small trailer and then into a 38-foot one her husband bought from Woroniecki. They lived in that trailer in a recreation-vehicle community in Florida while Rusty worked there on a NASA project. When that assignment ended and Rusty resumed working for NASA in Houston, they continued to live in the trailer. Finally, after Luke was born in 1999, Rusty bought a real house for his family in the Houston suburb of Clear Lake City.

Through those years, Andrea, who had been a nurse at the M.D. Anderson Cancer Center in Houston before she married Rusty, worked as a full-time stay-at-home mother. She baked, cooked, and sewed. She home-schooled the older children. Three nights a week the family had Bible study. By all accounts, she loved her children. She did her best to be the perfect wife and mother.

But at 9 A.M. on June 20, 2001, Andrea Yates dialed 911 and asked to have an ambulance sent to her home. Then she called her husband at work. "I finally did it," she told him. She asked him to come home and then hung up the phone. When he called back to ask what happened, she said, "It's the kids." Asked which of them, she replied, "All of them."[57]

Earlier that morning, Noah had begged his father to take him to work with him as Rusty sometimes did. But Rusty had a meeting, so he told Noah he would have to stay home with Mommy.[58] Shortly after Rusty left for his office at NASA, Andrea filled the bathtub. First she drowned Luke, then Paul, and then John. After each drowning, she placed the boys, still in their wet pajamas, on a bed. Then she drowned Mary. While her body was still in the tub, Andrea called Noah to come into the room. When he saw Mary face down in the water, he tried to run away, but Andrea caught him and managed to get him into the tub of water. Noah struggled, but she managed to drown him, too. Finally, she put Mary and Noah on the bed with their brothers and waited for the police and her husband.

When the police arrived, Andrea led them to her children. She killed them, she told the police, because the children "weren't developing properly." She had not been a good mother, she said. She had failed her children and they were doomed. The murder was, she said, a mother's final loving act of mercy.[59]

The murders may have been prompted by Andrea's acceptance of Woroniecki as her spiritual guide. Articles in his newspaper *Perilous Times* and a videotape he mailed to the family condemned the "husband goes to work, wife just exists, hypocritical Christian lifestyle." Parents, he said, should train their children so they could be saved by setting a godly example for them. That example required both parents to preach full-time on the streets. In letters written to Andrea, he castigated her for her "unrighteous standing before God." The role of women, he said, "is derived ... from the sin of Eve." Bad mothers create bad children.[60]

But the murders were really the end result of Andrea's long struggle with depression and psychosis. Interviews with Rusty following the murders and testimony in court by her family and her doctors indicated she probably suffered from depression and possibly also bipolar disorder as early as her teen years. Although no one knew it at the time, she had visions of a knife and of herself stabbing someone shortly after Noah was born. Before the birth of her fourth child, Luke, she was already beginning to feel overwhelmed.[61]

After Luke's birth in February 1977, Andrea developed severe postpartum depression with psychosis. She attempted suicide twice, and was hospitalized twice. On both occasions she was given emergency shots of the powerful antipsychotic drug Haldol. In the hospital she told her doctor that she wanted to kill herself because she was having visions and hearing voices telling her to hurt others.[62] Although she never fully cooperated with her therapist, by August she seemed to be on the road to recovery. On August 9, she was sent home with a handful of prescriptions, including one for Haldol, and a stern warning that any future pregnancies would almost certainly guarantee more episodes of psychotic depression.

At first Rusty and Andrea heeded that warning, but when after six months of outpatient therapy, she seemed better, Rusty stopped using condoms and Andrea again became pregnant. After Mary's birth on November 30, 2000,

Andrea's condition again began to deteriorate. On March 31, 2001, Rusty rushed her, against her will, to Devereux Texas Treatment Network where she was placed under the care of Dr. Mohammad Saeed. Although Andrea was generally uncooperative during her stay at Devereux, on April 12 Dr. Saeed transferred her from inpatient care to partial hospitalization. On April 18, he gave her a full discharge. Over the next month, her condition again deteriorated. She returned to Devereux and Dr. Saeed's care. On May 21, he again discharged her. On June 4, Dr. Saeed agreed to take her off Haldol. She stopped taking the drug on June 6. At a follow-up visit with Dr. Saeed on June 18, Rusty told the doctor that Andrea's condition was worsening. Dr Saeed, however, felt she was improving and refused to put her back on the Haldol that previously had stabilized her condition. Two days later Andrea killed her children.

Although a jury found Andrea Yates competent to stand trial, both the prosecution and her defense agreed she was mentally ill. But finding a defendant mentally ill is not tantamount to being able to prove he or she is legally insane. After John Hinckley's 1981 attempt to assassinate President Ronald Reagan, five states abolished the insanity defense. Most others, including Texas, changed state law. In Texas, to find a person "not guilty by reason of insanity," the law now required being able to show that, at the time of the crime, the defendant was unable to distinguish between right and wrong—to comprehend that his or her actions were illegal.

At her March 2002 trial, Andrea's defense lawyers set out to do just that. They introduced her lengthy psychiatric record. They presented evidence that mental illness ran in her family: a brother and a sister had been treated for depression; and, another brother was diagnosed with bipolar disorder. Rusty, other family members, and friends told of her steadily deteriorating state of mind. Professionals who treated her told of her delusions—the satanic voices and images—that led her to believe she must kill her children. Doctors who saw her while she was in jail testified that she believed she must kill her children. Only her execution for their murder would rescue her from the evil inside her, she told them. It would be a state-sanctioned execution through which then-Governor George W. Bush would release her from Satan's grasp. When she was executed, as she must be, she wanted to have the number 666, the mark of the Antichrist, on her scalp, and her hair fashioned into a crown of the kind Jesus will award those who are saved.

The testimony was powerful, but the prosecution undercut it with that of its star witness, Dr. Paul Dietz. Unlike most medical doctors who provide expert testimony in court cases, Dr. Dietz did not generally see patients. His specialty was providing expert testimony for prosecutors in high-profile cases: Susan Smith, who like Andrea Yates killed her children; John Hinckley; mass murderers Jeffrey Dahmer and Ted Kaczynski. He also served as a technical advisor for the television shows *Law & Order* and *Law & Order Criminal Intent*.

On the witness stand, Dr. Dietz pointed to the image of a knife Andrea had first seen following Noah's birth and other images and thoughts of killing as evidence that her crime was premeditated. The actual murder was, he said, a copy-cat crime inspired by a recent *Law & Order* episode in which a mother drowns her children. Although he made a point of telling the jury that he based his conclusions on the facts of the case, not personal opinion, he gave his own religious interpretation to her acts in a way that worked against the insanity defense.

Ignoring the fact that everyone who had come in contact with Andrea during the months before her trial described her demeanor as almost catatonic, he pointed to her blank expression and monosyllabic replies when she told the police that she had killed her children as evidence she was unfeeling, uncaring. Moreover, he said, she could not have loved them. If she had killed them as an act of love, she would have comforted them during the act by telling them they would soon be with Jesus. But most damning of all, she knew her act was wrong, he testified, because she was acting in response to satanic voices and not the voice of God.[63]

On March 16, 2002, the jury deliberated for only 40 minutes before finding Andrea Yates guilty of capital murder. The jury did, however, decline to impose the death sentence. Her sentence was life in prison.

When word surfaced that Dr. Dietz had based his testimony that Andrea Yates had committed a copy-cat crime on a nonexistent *Law and Order* episode, the Texas Court of Appeals remanded the case to the lower court for a new trial. On January 9, 2006, attorneys for Andrea Yates again entered her plea of not guilty by reason of insanity. On July 26, after deliberating for three days, the jury agreed that Andrea Yates was legally insane at the time she murdered her children.

Both verdicts and the case itself raised serious questions about the death penalty and about culpability. While many wondered if there should even be a death penalty if it could apply to people like Andrea Yates, others found the legal requirements for an insanity defense equally troubling. If a woman so clearly mentally ill could have been sentenced to death, as the jury's finding in her first trial showed could have happened, who, if anyone, would the insanity defense protect? Should it be modified? How?

Both the law as it was in 2001 when Andrea Yates killed her children, and any revised law, would still leave unanswered questions about who should be found responsible for a crime such as this one and who should not be found culpable. Although Andrea Yates did the actual killing, what of the doctor who released her from the hospital, took her off Haldol, and then said that she was doing well just two days before she killed her children? And what of the husband who, ignoring doctors' warnings, let her have a fifth child and then left her alone on the morning of June 20, 2001, when she was clearly agitated and barely functioning?

BTK

With each killing new waves of fear spread throughout the Wichita area. A serial killer was on the loose in their midst. The killings started on January 15, 1974, with the murder of four members of the Joseph Otero family. On April 4, Katherine Bright died. Over the next 16 years, the killer claimed five more victims: Shirley Vian Relford and Nancy Fox in 1977; Marine Hedge in 1985; Vicki Wegerle the next year; and Delores Davis on January 19, 1991.

After each murder, the killer taunted the police and the public in letters that provided details of the crime. With some letters there were poems about the victim or cryptic clues; others came in packages containing a driver's license or other small items taken from the scene of the crime. One message from the killer was found in an engineering book in the Wichita Public Library. A few went directly to the police; most, however, were addressed to the media—in letters to the *Wichita Eagle* newspaper and KAKE-TV, the killer demanded media attention. He also suggested that they call him "the BTK killer." The initials stood for his *modus operandi*: bind, torture, and kill.[64]

After the 1991 killing, nothing more was heard from BTK. People in Wichita began to breathe a bit easier—until March 2004 when BTK again began sending messages. The *Wichita Eagle* got a package from a Bill Thomas Killman that contained a photocopy of Vicki Wegerle's drivers license and photos of the crime scene. KAKE-TV got one containing a word puzzle. A package containing a chapter of a proposed book—"The BTK Story" that mimicked a 1999 Court TV story—was found taped to a street sign. Another message was enclosed in a cereal box placed in the bed of a truck at a Home Depot store. There were other messages—11 in all—sent between March 2004 and February 2005.[65]

BTK was a very competent, clever, and confident killer. But he wasn't very technologically savvy, and that led to his downfall. The message inside one of the cereal boxes he left around town instructed police to place a classified ad with the message "It'll be OK, Rex" in the local newspaper if it would be impossible to trace a computer disk to his computer.[66] The police placed the ad. On February 16, 2005, BTK sent a package containing a purple computer disk to Wichita FOX affiliate KSAS-TV. Meta-data embedded in a Microsoft Word document indicated the disk came from Christ Lutheran Church. The document had last been modified by someone named Dennis.

Surveillance photos from the Home Depot where BTK had put the cereal box in a truck told them what kind of vehicle he drove. A Google search provided Dennis's last name. That let police get a warrant to obtain a daughter's medical records. Tests showed a familial match between her DNA and semen found at one of the crime scenes.

The police had found BTK. BTK was Dennis Rader—life-long Wichita resident and married father of two adult children. Rader had spent four years in the U.S. Air Force. He had earned an associate's degree in electronics from Butler County Community College in El Dorado and a bachelor's degree in administration of justice from Wichita State University. In 2005, he was employed as a supervisor in the Park City, Kansas, Compliance Department that handled animal control, housing and zoning problems, and other minor complaints. But from 1974 until 1988, he had worked for ADT Security Services in jobs that would have shown him how to enter and leave homes without being detected.

For 35 years Dennis Rader had been a member of Christ Lutheran Church where his wife's family were charter members and she sang in the choir. He led a Scout troop and was an usher. He was president of the church council in 2005. On February 27, 2005, he was also scheduled to count the offering. But on February 25, police arrested him.

The Park City Council terminated Rader's employment on March 2. On July 27, he pled guilty to the 10 murders with which he was charged. The same day, Sedgwick County District Judge Eric Yost waived the usual waiting period to grant Rader's wife of 34 years an immediate divorce. On August 18, Rader was given 10 consecutive life sentences, one for each victim. At the time of the killings, Kansas had no death penalty, but Rader will not be eligible for parole for 175 years.

Rader's family did not attend his court hearings. Neither have they visited him in jail, but the Rev. Michael G. Clark, pastor of Christ Lutheran, did attend the trial and has visited Rader occasionally in prison.

As Pastor Clark told *The Lutheran* magazine, the important thing is how we respond to evil.[67] While the whole episode has been stressful for him, his congregation, Rader's family, and for all of Wichita, he said, it also has led people to think seriously and to have some good conversations about the nature of good and evil.[68] There is a myth that all serial killers are antisocial or else they are loners. But often that is not the case. BTK was in most respects just like the people in the community whom he terrorized for more than 30 years. Sometimes a person who does much that is good also does very bad things.

FOR FURTHER READING

BTK archive. 2007. *Wichita Eagle.* Retrieved May 10, 2007, from http://www.kansas.com/ 215.
Clinic killings. 1995, January 27. *Commonweal,* pp. 3–4.
Denno, Deborah W. 2003. Who is Andrea Yates? A short story about insanity. *Duke Journal of Gender Law, and Policy* 10(1): 1–84.
Gado, Mark. 2006. *Killer Priest.* Westport, CT: Praeger.
Geselman, Anne Belli, and Lynette Clemetson. 2002, March 25. A crazy system. *Newsweek,* p. 30.

Hanley, Robert. 2002, November 23. Rabbi gets jail, not death, for hired murder of wife. *New York Times*, pp. A1, B5.

Kennedy, John W. 1994, September 12. Killings distort pro-life message. *Christianity Today*, pp. 80–81.

Kilduff, Marshall, and Phil Tracy. 1977, August 1. Inside Peoples Temple. *New West*, pp. 30–38.

Lentz, Richard. 1993. The incorporation of Malcolm X. *American Journalism* 10(3): 38–69.

Lincoln, C. Eric. 1965, March 5. The meaning of Malcolm X. *Christian Century*. pp. 431–433.

Loomis, James. 1965, February 27. Death of Malcolm X. *New York Times*, p. 24.

McCabe, Nancy. 2005, October 17. A bogeyman with supernatural powers. *Newsweek*, p. 26.

Nightmare in Jonestown. 1987, December 4. *Time*, pp. 16–21.

Peterson, Iver. 2001, November 16. Trial begins for a rabbi in New Jersey accused in his wife's killing in 1994. *New York Times*, pp. D1, D7.

Roche, Timothy. 2002, January 28. The Yates odyssey. *Time*, pp. 42–50.

Scotchmer, Paul, with Edward Plowman. 1978, December 15. Jim Jones: Man who would be "God." *Christianity Today*, pp. 38–40.

Sevig, Julie B. 2005, May. Images of hope: Congregation echoes pastor. *The Lutheran*. Retrieved May 10, 2007, from http://www.thelutheran.org/article/article.cfm?article_id=5092&key=25928462.

Sevig, Julie B. 2006, February. Beyond BTK—Wichita pastor: Blessings amid the "muck and mire." *The Lutheran*. Retrieved May 10, 2007, from http://www.thelutheran.org/article/article.cfm?article_id=5723&key=32752727.

Southwick, Albert B. 1963, June 5. Malcolm X: Charismatic demagogue. *Christian Century*, pp. 740–741.

Springer, John. 2003, January 18. Rabbi gets life in prison, still professes innocence in wife's slaying. Court TV. Retrieved August 16, 2007, from http://www.courttv.com/trials/neulander/sentencing_ctv.html.

Szegedy-Maszak, Marianne. 2002, March 18. Mothers and murder. *U.S. News & World Report*, p. 23.

The violent end of Malcolm X. 1965, March 5. *Life*, pp. 26–31.

Wilkinson, Peter. 2003, July 10. The making of a maniac. *Rolling Stone*, pp. 31–32, 34.

Part II

Scandals of Conscience: Challenges to Secular Custom and Law

Chapter 5

BLASPHEMY AND ITS PROGENY

When James Madison drafted the religion clauses of the First Amendment, he used as a model the law establishing religious freedom in Virginia written by his friend, Thomas Jefferson. Of that law, Jefferson wrote in his *Autobiography*:

> Where the preamble declares, that coercion is a departure from the plan of the holy author of our religion, an amendment was proposed, by inserting the word "Jesus Christ," so that it should read, "a departure from the plan of Jesus Christ, the holy author of our religion"; the insertion was rejected by a great majority, in proof that they meant to comprehend, within the mantle of its protection, the Jew and the Gentile, the Christian and Mahometan, the Hindoo, and Infidel of every denomination.[1]

But as Jefferson's words suggest, some found the idea of protecting those who were not Christian troubling.

Even though Jefferson, along with Madison, drafted the laws that protected their own right to practice religion as they saw fit, there were those who found Jefferson's ideas about religious freedom, as well as his own approach to religion, scandalous. When as vice president he traveled home to Monticello from a dinner in Fredericksburg, Virginia, on the Sabbath, his political opponents deemed it sacrilegious and branded him an atheist. When he wrote in his *Notes on the State of Virginia*, "It does me no injury for my neighbour to say there are twenty gods, or no god. It neither picks my pocket nor breaks my leg," then, as now, many found his opinion scandalous.[2]

To them, the First Amendment meant simply that the federal government could not favor one Christian denomination over another. People could freely choose what kind of Christian they would be, but the freedom of religion they enjoyed need not extend to other religions. Their country was, and was forever meant to be, a Christian nation—and for over 150 years, courts agreed.

The first section in this chapter tells the story of a man whose conviction under New York law for blaspheming the Christian god was upheld by the

During his lifetime Thomas Jefferson's opinions about religious freedom were controversial, but over the centuries his writings have shaped both public opinion and court decisions about the First Amendment's Free Exercise and Establishment clauses. Library of Congress, photograph of a mural by Constantino Brumidi in the United States Capitol.

state's Supreme Court on the grounds that "We are a Christian nation." At the time of that case, the Bill of Rights, including the First Amendment, applied only to the federal government. States were free to limit basic rights in any way they saw fit. That changed in 1868 with passage of the Fourteenth Amendment, but even with its adoption it took more than 50 years before courts began to hold state and local governments to Constitutional standards. On the matter of blasphemy and the closely allied offenses of profanity and sacrilege, change came only in 1952, when New York rescinded permission for public showings of a scandalous movie. That movie, *The Miracle*, is the subject of the second section in this chapter.

Since then, all religions and no religion have generally been treated as equal under the First Amendment. In courts of law, no religion is automatically privileged and none is automatically disfavored. But things are different in the court of public opinion.

In the last half century as the United States has become religiously more diverse, religious minorities have been more inclined to speak out in defense of themselves and their religion. During 2007 and 2008, for example, Muslims filed seven times as many complaints with the federal government about religious discrimination as did Christians. Muslims and other minorities have also, from time to time, complained about stereotypical and sacrilegious treatment: Hindus over the portrayal of Krishna as a fictional character in an episode of the television show *Xena, Warrior Princess*; Jews over the movie *The Passion of the Christ*; and Muslims most recently over the use of the derogatory term "raghead" as the title for a movie. Sometimes their complaints meet with sympathy; occasionally, they lead to apologies and a change in a script or media policy. But as with the fatwa placed on the author Salman Rushdie for his book *The Satanic Verses* and the more recent protests by Muslims about cartoons published in Danish newspapers that poked fun at Islam and its founder, Americans are inclined to dismiss the complainers as thin-skinned—to find their protests at least as scandalous as the message the complainers found offensive. But when the target is Christianity, it's a different matter as the remaining sections in this chapter show.

"More Popular than Jesus" tells the story of a musician whose offhand comment about Jesus led to boycotts, while "The Too Candid Candidate" tells of a presidential candidate who found himself the center of a furor, not for his religious beliefs, but for how and where he said them. The last two sections deal with religious images—images in a rock video that led to threatened boycotts and a cancelled contract, and in fine art that sparked a public debate over government funding for the arts and humanities.

WE ARE A CHRISTIAN NATION

No newspaper covered the story. The court record is maddeningly fragmentary. Even the defendant's first name has been lost with the passage of time. But this much we do know: the 1811 New York blasphemy case of *People v. Ruggles* shaped American law for well over 100 years.

Mr. Ruggles was neither the first American nor the last to voice similar sentiments, but the many people in Salem, New York, who heard him say, "Jesus Christ was a bastard, and his mother must be a whore" were outraged.[3] For his words, Ruggles was arrested and charged with the crime of blasphemy. At trial, Judge Ambrose Spencer found him guilty, sentenced him to three months in jail, and ordered him to pay a fine of $500, which in 1811 was an enormous amount.

On appeal to New York's highest court, John L. Wendell, acting as Ruggles's attorney, pointed out that prohibitions against licentiousness applied to behavior, not to words. New York had no law making blasphemy a crime. Although Wendell admitted that English common law made blasphemy a crime, New York followed that law only to the extent it was consistent with state law. New York's constitution promised freedom of religion and freedom of speech to everyone. "*Judaism and Mahometanism* [ital. in original] may be preached here without any legal animadversion," Wendell argued. "For aught that appears, the prisoner may have been a *Jew*, a *Mahometan*, or a *Socinian;* and if so, he had a right by the constitution, to declare his opinions."[4] Therefore, there was no legal basis for finding Ruggles guilty of any crime, and most certainly not for the "crime" of blasphemy.

Nevertheless, Chief Justice James Kent, who heard the case, found a way. After citing precedents from English blasphemy cases, Kent concluded that the English common law of blasphemy should apply because, in his opinion, the offense existed independently of an establishment of religion. "There is nothing in our law which has prevented the application or the necessity of this part of the common law. We stand equally in need, now as formerly, of all that moral discipline and of those principles of virtue, which help to bind society together," he continued. Because most people in New York accept the basic doctrines of the Christian faith, "scandalize[ing] the author of these doctrines … is a gross violation of decency and good order," Chief Justice Kent wrote.[5] That Ruggles might have been, as his attorney suggested, an adherent of some other religion, did not impress him. Although New York, unlike England, does not have an established religion, "We are a Christian people, and the morality of the country is deeply ingrafted upon Christianity, and not upon the doctrines or worship of these imposters," Kent opined.[6]

The conviction and sentence were upheld. Ruggles was guilty of the crime of blasphemy. But the decision did not end the controversy.

During an 1821 convention called to hammer out a new constitution for the state of New York, Erastus Root spoke forcefully against the *Ruggles* decision. Noting that the sheriff of New York is a Jew who, because of that case "is guilty of blasphemy every time he enters the synagogue," as would be a "Musselman" for reading the Koran, he proposed adding a statement that the "judiciary shall not declare any particular religion to be the law of the land," to the constitutional guarantee of religious freedom.[7] Kent, in his current position as chancellor of the state, countered that *Ruggles* did not establish a religion; it merely acknowledged that Christianity is the religion of the people and the basis of morality. In response to what Kent perceived to be an unwarranted attack on the judiciary, Root amended his motion so it read: "It shall not be declared or adjudged that any particular religion is the law of the land."[8]

In that form, the amendment passed 62 to 26, with Kent voting with the majority. But 12 days later, Ambrose Spencer, the trial judge in the *Ruggles* case who succeeded Kent as chief justice, proposed deleting Root's clause from the final version. Martin Van Buren, who later became president, argued against deleting the clause. Kent contended that Van Buren, like Root, misunderstood *Ruggles*. Although "the duties and injunction of the Christian religion" are interwoven with the law of the land and part and parcel of the common law," people could express contrary religious beliefs. Blasphemy, Kent now argued, became a crime only if the attack on Christianity offended public morals or disturbed public order.[9] Spencer countered that Christianity is the established law of the land; religious freedom applies equally to all Christian sects, but it need not apply to other religions. "Are we prepared to send forth to the people a provision in our constitution, that shall suffer any man to blaspheme, in the most malicious manner, his God, and the religion of the Redeemer of the world?" he asked.[10] Rufus King, one of the framers of the Constitution of the United States, sided with Spencer. After much debate, Kent ultimately supported Spencer's motion to delete Root's clause from the constitution. By a 74 to 41 vote the convention adopted Spencer's motion, thereby nullifying its earlier vote for Root's resolution. *People v. Ruggles* remained the law.

Technically New York law applies only in New York, but the decision of the New York constitutional convention gave added weight to the New York Supreme Court opinion crafted by James Kent, who is generally recognized as one of the most important legal scholars of his day. Blaspheming Christianity and the Christian God—but not other religions and their gods—remained a punishable offense until 1952 when the United States Supreme Court ruled that laws against blasphemy and the related offense of sacrilege are unconstitutional (this chapter, "*The Miracle*"). Although blasphemy cases have always been relatively rare in the United States, *People v. Ruggles* influenced both federal law and the law in most other states for 150 years. Even today, people who believe the United States was meant to be a Christian nation routinely cite Judge Kent's opinion in the *Ruggles* case and a similar ruling from a Massachusetts court (Chapter 6, "Satan's Hoary-headed Apostle") to buttress their claim.

THE MIRACLE

The Supreme Court of the United States has never heard a blasphemy case, but in 1952 it did hear the case of the movie *The Miracle*, which was censored in New York on grounds that it was sacrilegious.

The movie, made in Italy by the Italian director Roberto Rosselini and starring Anna Magnani, gave dramatic form to sentiments similar to those that garnered Mr. Ruggles a fine of $500 in 1811 (this chapter, "We Are a Christian Nation"). The movie told the story of a young, emotionally disturbed peasant girl who meets a stranger who rapes her. Pregnant with his child, she believes the stranger to be St. Joseph. Taunted by villagers, she flees into the countryside where she lives alone in a cave until finally making her way to an empty church in time to give birth to a son whom she believes to be a miracle, conceived without sin.

In Italy, which had religious censorship, the Cinematographic Centre, a Vatican censorship agency, said the movie "constitutes an abominable profanation from religious and moral viewpoints."[11] But the film was not censored. Instead, it was freely shown in Italy, apparently without incident. When the movie opened in Paris, however, it was greeted by protesters carrying angry signs declaring "Don't Be a Communist," "Don't Enter the Cesspool," and "This Picture Is an Insult to Every Decent Woman and Her Mother."

As the result of a 1915 U.S. Supreme Court ruling in the case of *Mutual Film Corp. v. Industrial Commission* that movies are purely an entertainment business unworthy of First Amendment protection, film did not have the same guarantees of freedom of speech and press that print and broadcast media enjoyed. Although there was no federal censorship, many states, including New York, did have official state agencies that acted as censors.

On two occasions before *The Miracle* was shown, the Motion Picture Division of the New York Department of Education's Board of Regents issued the license necessary for its public showing. An English subtitled version opened on December 12, 1950, at the Paris Theater in New York City as part of a trilogy titled *Ways of Love* that also included Jean Renoir's *A Day in the Country* and Marcel Pagnol's *Jofroi*.

As in Rome, movie critics generally gave *The Miracle* favorable reviews. The trilogy was voted the best foreign-language film of 1950. Much of the public disagreed. The Board of Regents received hundreds of letters, most of them protesting the film. The National Legion of Decency, a private Catholic organization that advocated film censorship and was instrumental in helping shape the Production Code under which the Hollywood movie industry operated and which forbade the ridicule of religion among other things, denounced the film as "a sacrilegious and blasphemous mockery of Christian religious truth."[12] On December 23, Edward T. McCaffrey, Commissioner of Licenses for New York City, declared the film "officially and personally blasphemous" and ordered it withdrawn at the risk of suspension of the theater's license to operate.[13]

Although the New York Supreme Court quickly ruled that the city did not have censorship power, His Eminence, Francis Cardinal Spellman, joined the fray when, on Sunday, January 7, 1951, a message from him condemning the picture and calling on "all right thinking citizens" to unite to tighten censorship laws was read at all masses in St. Patrick's Cathedral in New York City.[14]

Most Catholics sided with the National League of Decency and Cardinal Spellman, but some did not. The National Board of Review, a national Catholic lay organization operating under the slogan "Selection Not Censorship," recommended the film as particularly worth seeing.[15] In a March 16, 1951, article in the influential lay-edited Catholic magazine *Commonweal*, University of Notre Dame professor William P. Clancy contended that "the film is not obviously blasphemous or obscene, either in its intention or execution."[16] The magazine itself questioned the appropriateness of making religious teachings the arbiter of what the government will allow to be said about religion and religious teachings.[17]

But in the wake of the controversy, the Board of Regents appointed a committee to review the decision of the Motion Picture Commission to license showing of the movie. After viewing the movie, the committee declared it "sacrilegious." On February 16, 1951, the Board of Regents rescinded the license to show *The Miracle* in accord with a provision of state statute authorizing denial of a license if a "film or a part thereof is obscene, indecent, immoral, inhuman, sacrilegious, or is of such a character that its exhibition would tend to corrupt morals or incite a crime."[18]

After the Board of Regents' Appellate Division upheld that decision, the movie's American distributor, Joseph Burstyn, took the case to court where he argued both that movies should be protected by the First Amendment and that censoring a movie for "sacrilege" violated state and federal constitutional guarantees of religious freedom. Basing its ruling primarily on the 1915 *Mutual Film* case and state law, New York's highest court rejected Burstyn's argument. Movies, the court said, do not have First Amendment protection; state law allows banning of any motion picture "that may fairly be deemed sacrilegious to the adherents of any religious group" because sacrilege "is directly related to public peace and order."[19]

Although the movie industry had always contended that movies should be afforded the same constitutional protection as other media, it chose not to fight for that protection for fear that a loss before the Supreme Court would lead to federal censorship on top of the state efforts that were already costing $2 million in state censorship board charges. Fighting a case involving an allegedly sacrilegious movie, especially one such as *The Miracle*, seemed particularly dangerous. Sensational media coverage of an affair between the movie's divorced and Catholic producer, Roberto Rosselini, and the married Swedish movie star Ingrid Bergman had given U.S. Senator Edwin Johnson of Colorado, head of the powerful Interstate Commerce Committee, all the ammunition he needed to introduce a bill calling for federal censorship of motion pictures and a licensing system for actors, producers, and directors that would have taken into account their moral qualifications.

But Burstyn persevered. In 1811, when Mr. Ruggles was convicted of blasphemy, the First Amendment applied only to the federal government, but with the passage of the Fourteenth Amendment to the U.S. Constitution, the U.S. Supreme Court gained the authority to require states to provide the same level of individual rights that the Bill of Rights required of the federal government. Therefore, on April 24, 1952, the Supreme Court heard arguments in the case of *Joseph Burstyn, Inc. v. Wilson, Commissioner of Education of New York*. On May 26, 1952, it issued an opinion overturning both its own earlier decision regarding motion pictures and also the ruling of New York's highest court on the matter of sacrilege.

In his unanimous opinion for the court, Justice Tom C. Clark now wrote:

> The importance of motion pictures as an organ of public opinion is not
> lessened by the fact that they are designed to entertain as well as to
> inform….
>   [W]e conclude that expression by means of motion pictures is included
> within the free speech and free press guaranty of the First and Fourteenth
> Amendments. To the extent that language in the opinion in Mutual Film
> Corp. v. Industrial Comm'n, supra, is out of harmony with the views here
> set forth, we no longer adhere to it.[20]

On the matter of New York's prohibition on sacrilege, the court concluded
that the definition given to it was both vague and over-inclusive. New York's
contention that the statutory provision means that

> no religion, as that word is understood by the ordinary, reasonable person,
> shall be treated with contempt, mockery, scorn and ridicule … is far from
> the kind of narrow exception to freedom of expression which a state may
> carve out…. In seeking to apply the broad and all-inclusive definition of
> "sacrilegious" given by the New York courts, the censor is set adrift upon a
> boundless sea amid a myriad of conflicting currents of religious views, with
> no charts but those provided by the most vocal and powerful orthodoxies.[21]

In a concurring opinion joined by Justices Robert H. Jackson and Harold
Hitz Burton, Justice Felix Frankfurter traced the history of the case before cas-
tigating New York for basing its ruling on a vague term and, in the process
defining *sacrilege* as if it were synonymous with the different, but equally
malleable, term *blasphemy*. To make the point abundantly clear, Frankfurter
attached an eight-page Appendix that provided definitions of *profanity, blasphemy,* and *sacrilege* culled from standard American and English legal references dating back to 1651.[22]

Although that Appendix does not have the force of law, the Appendix in
combination with the court's unanimous ruling did have the effect of making
it quite clear that the Supreme Court would uphold profanity convictions only
in narrow circumstances where the allegedly profane words are a clear threat
to peace. With the narrow exception of movies judged also to be legally
obscene, it would not uphold any kind of censorship for blasphemy or
sacrilege.

The Miracle was the last movie to be censored because it offended religious
sensibilities. Where some point to the case of *The Miracle* as an early example
of what they see as a "godless court" that leaps at any chance to undermine
religion, others find in it an early example of a court intent on protecting individual rights against the tyranny of the majority.

Controversies surrounding movies and other art forms that are allegedly blasphemous or sacrilegious remain common, but battles today are generally fought in the court of public opinion instead of in a court of law. Although protests by the Roman Catholic Church and orthodox rabbis about the Monty Python film *Life of Brian* and by conservative Protestants about *Oh, God!* starring George Burns and John Denver had little effect, sometimes protests and threatened boycotts work. Controversy caused General Motors to withdraw its sponsorship of a television showing of Franco Zeffirelli's six-hour movie *Jesus of Nazareth*, and some theaters canceled scheduled showings of *The Last Temptation of Christ*. Other times complaints and the attendant controversy turn a case of alleged blasphemy into gold as happened with Mel Gibson's *The Passion of the Christ* and with both Dan Brown's novel *The Da Vinci Code*, which became a best seller, and the movie of the same name, which was a box office hit.

MORE POPULAR THAN JESUS

American record companies and radio stations initially saw nothing special about them. Music critics said they were just a fad. But young people adored them. A crowd estimated at 3,000 greeted them when they landed at Kennedy International Airport on February 7, 1964, on their first trip to the United States. Fan reaction to their first live American television performance on the *Ed Sullivan Show* confirmed it—Beatlemania was sweeping the country.

George Harrison, John Lennon, Paul McCartney, and Ringo Starr—the loveable "mop tops" with their funny haircuts and funnier clothes—were enchanting and endearing. Their music, their lifestyle, and their views on anything and everything spoke to and for a generation. But in an era marked by rapid cultural, social, and political change, they were also a lightning rod for controversy. In those controversies, John Lennon often found himself front and center stage.

An early comment by Lennon that Jews control the music industry got some attention for its anti-Semitic overtones. After the Beatles broke up, Lennon's involvement in anti-Vietnam War protests got more publicity, much of it negative. The "bed-ins" for peace he and wife Yoko Ono conducted in 1969 garnered reams of sensational media attention. His involvement in protests scheduled to coincide with the 1972 presidential election led the administration of President Richard Nixon to begin proceedings to have Lennon deported, but ultimately nothing came of that attempt to silence him, and he received his Green Card authorizing him to continue living and working in the United States.

Lennon's 1971 song "Imagine" became one of the unofficial anthems of the peace movement. In the context of the antiwar sentiment of the times, few chose to criticize him when, in song, he asked people to imagine a world without nations or religions "to kill or die for." But five years earlier, in

August 1966, his musings on religion and culture almost derailed the Beatles' 14-city American tour and came close to wrecking their career.

In a story published in the London *Evening Standard* on March 4, 1966, friend and journalist Maureen Cleave quoted Lennon as saying:

> Christianity will go. It will vanish and shrink. I don't know what will go first, rock 'n' roll or Christianity. We're more popular than Jesus now. Jesus was all right, but his disciples were thick and ordinary. It's them twisting it that ruins it for me.[23]

At first neither the original article nor the few American newspaper stories quoting it attracted much attention. But five months later, the "more popular than Jesus" quote was printed on the cover of *Dateline*, an American teen magazine, and ignited a wave of protest. First, a radio station in Birmingham, Alabama, suggested burning Beatles records. Then Tommy Charles, manager of WAQY in Birmingham banned playing their records on his radio station. From there, the movement to ban or burn Beatles music spread throughout the Bible Belt and from there to Idaho and even to Spain and South Africa. The Grand Dragon of the South Carolina Ku Klux Klan burned a Beatles record on a cross. Politicians jumped into the fray. Citing a "duty to protect Memphians against the Beatles' use of the public coliseum to ridicule anyone's religion," Mayor William Ingram Jr., of Memphis, Tennessee, said they could not perform in the facility during their American tour.[24]

A statement from Beatles manager Brian Epstein saying that "John is deeply concerned and regrets that people with certain religious beliefs should have been offended in any way" did little to quiet the uproar.[25] In England, fans, fearing for the Beatles' safety, implored them to cancel their tour. Lennon, himself, said he had misgivings about the trip. In its August 23 issue, *Newsweek* commented that "for a time, it looked indeed as if there might be a jihad," but Lennon managed to defuse the situation when, on August 11 at a press conference in Chicago, he explained that he hadn't meant the Beatles were better than Jesus. He had been commenting on the interests of British youth.[26]

Although the Southern Baptist Convention refused to accept Lennon's explanation, the Vatican did. *Commonweal* magazine told its Catholic readers that Lennon's message hadn't been any different than what clergy had been saying for years about young people's affinity for popular culture.[27] Secular magazines joined in with a similar message.[28] Things quieted down. The tour proceeded as planned. "Yellow Submarine," the Beatles' newest release, went to the top of the charts. The *Chicago Evening News* summed up the flap with the words "Beatles mosey on, richer than ever."[29]

But it was the last time the Beatles toured as a group. In a 2005 article for the London *Telegraph*, Maureen Cleave, whose reporting initiated the scandal, quoted Lennon as thanking the flap over his comments about Jesus for ending the Beatles' days on the road.[30] Whether or not the offending quote really was responsible for the end of the Beatles as a touring band, this much remains certain, Lennon's words weren't far from the truth.

In 1977, the Beatles won BRIT awards as best British group of the past 25 years and for their outstanding contribution to music during the past 25 years. Their album *Sgt. Pepper's Lonely Hearts Club Band* got the BRIT award as the best album of the past 25 years. They won another BRIT for outstanding contribution to music in 1983. In 1988, in their first year of eligibility, they were inducted into the Rock and Roll Hall of Fame in Cleveland, Ohio. In 2004, *Rolling Stone* magazine ranked the Beatles as Number 1 on its list of 100 Greatest Artists of All Time.

On the night of December 8, 1980, radio and television stations broke in to their regularly scheduled programming to announce that Mark David Chapman had shot and killed John Lennon outside the Dakota apartment

A woman pays tribute to John Lennon on December 8, 2005, the 25th anniversary of his death, by placing a holly bough on the "Imagine" mosaic in Central Park's Strawberry Fields. AP photo, Richard Drew.

building in New York City where Lennon lived with his wife, Yoko Ono, and son, Sean. The Dakota quickly became a shrine to Lennon as people flocked there to leave mementos, sing Lennon songs, burn candles, and pray. On December 14, in response to a request from Yoko Ono, people around the world paused for 10 minutes of silence in honor of Lennon—an estimated 100,000 of them in New York City's Central Park. Central Park is now the site of Strawberry Fields, a memorial garden named for the Beatles' 1967 song "Strawberry Fields Forever," where people still hold vigils in memory of Lennon each year on the anniversaries of his birth and his death.

In 1982, John Lennon won a BRIT as a solo artist for his outstanding contribution to music. In 1991, he received a Grammy for lifetime achievement. In 1994, he was inducted into the Rock and Roll Hall of Fame as a solo artist.

THE TOO CANDID CANDIDATE

He seemed to come out of nowhere. He had name recognition by only 2 percent when he began his campaign to become president of the United States. But then he won the New Hampshire primary and the Iowa caucuses. Suddenly, James Earl "Jimmy" Carter seemed to be the perfect candidate.

Carter had done military service aboard a submarine. He was a farmer and successful businessman, having turned a struggling family farm in Plains, Georgia, into a thriving enterprise. He had political experience, albeit at the state level as senator and governor in Georgia. That was the advantage. To a nation traumatized first by the Vietnam War and then by the Watergate scandal that culminated with the resignation of President Richard Nixon, "The Man from Plains," as Carter styled himself, ran as an outsider who would provide a moral compass for a nation seemingly adrift. That his moral compass was firmly grounded in his religious faith seemed refreshing, if a bit quaint.

Although the U.S. Constitution makes it very clear that there is to be no religious test for holding office, American citizens have always imposed their own informal religious test. John F. Kennedy became the first Roman Catholic president only by assuring voters that he was not so religious that he would defer to the Pope should a conflict ever arise between the demands of his Church and his duty to the Constitution and laws of his country. The message of the 1960 election seemed clear. Americans would prefer their president to be Christian of the mainstream Protestant variety. But whatever their faith, the president should be religious, but not too religious.

Carter, however, never quite got that message. He publicly called himself a "born again Christian." The language of his evangelical Protestant faith frequently crept into interviews and speeches in ways that both baffled and bothered almost everyone.

For half a century, since the 1925 trial in Tennessee of John Scopes for teaching about evolution in his high school biology class, conservative

Protestantism had received little public attention. In 1976, the television ministries of the Revs. Jerry Falwell and Pat Robertson were in their infancy. As a result, few outside the conservative Protestant tradition could distinguish between a moderate, evangelical Southern Baptist like Carter and the more authoritarian and fundamentalist strains that might want to impose their religion on others. But even those who shared Carter's faith had questions. While many evangelicals thought it would be good to have one of their own in a position of power, some conservative Protestants wondered whether he was really one of them. Where they had been brought up to believe they should refrain from political involvement and other secular pursuits, he was pursuing a position of worldly power that might lead him astray. In pursuing that position, he also seemed more concerned about peace and justice issues than matters of individual and sexual morality that they considered more pressing problems.

As a result, Carter found himself spending much of his time trying to hold on to his conservative Protestant southern base while reassuring Jews and Catholics that he would not try to impose his beliefs on anyone or turn them into public policy. His firm belief that he had been saved did not mean he thought he was always right or that he was somehow better than everyone. As a Baptist in the tradition of Roger Williams, the founder of Rhode Island as a refuge from the established religions of Massachusetts and other states, he believed firmly in the separation of church and state and in religious freedom for everyone.

It was a tough message to get across to a public unaccustomed to public displays of religiosity. Carter's attempts to explain himself and his faith, which often seemed too complex and too preachy, diverted attention from his positions on more pressing domestic and international issues. Sometimes they also seemed scandalous, as happened in the case of an article about him that Robert Scheer wrote for the November issue of *Playboy*.

Over the course of four months during the summer of 1976, Scheer engaged Carter in lengthy conversations during which the candidate gave detailed and quite candid answers to the reporter's questions. The article distilled from those conversations began conventionally enough with the reporter's assessment of the candidate followed by detailed information on Carter's opinions on major issues such as Vietnam, taxes, and civil rights. But as was common with a candidate who had an almost uncanny knack to turn every speech and every interview into a Sunday school lesson, religion kept getting woven in. At the end, it became THE theme.

After the last interview had officially ended, Scheer tossed out a comment inviting Carter to respond to those who might be uneasy about his having agreed to an article for *Playboy* and others who might be "uneasy about your religious beliefs, who wonder if you're going to make a rigid, unbending President." Taking Matthew 5:28, from the Sermon on the Mount, as his text, Carter launched into the sermon that became the article's blockbuster ending:

> I try not to commit a deliberate sin. I recognize that I'm going to do it anyhow, because I'm human.... Christ set some impossible standards for us. Christ said, "I tell you that anyone who looks on a woman with lust has in his heart already committed adultery."
>
> I've looked on a lot of women with lust. I've committed adultery in my heart many times. This is something that God recognizes I will do ... and God forgives me for it. But that doesn't mean that I condemn someone who not only looks on a woman with lust but who leaves his wife and shacks up with somebody....
>
> Christ says, Don't consider yourself better than someone else because one guy screws a whole bunch of women while the other guy is loyal to his wife.[32]

Knowing Carter's words would create a sensation, *Playboy* alerted the *New York Times*, Associated Press, and the *Today* show a month before the magazine hit the news stands.[33] It quickly became apparent that Carter's comments to *Playboy* were not an aberration. In an interview with Norman Mailer for an article for the *Times'* Sunday magazine, Carter had said the same thing except he had used the word *fuck* instead of *screw*. Probably unwilling to detract from its own forthcoming story, but also reluctant to create an issue by pulling quotes about sex out of an unpublished story, and even more reluctant to print Carter's salty language, the *Times* held off for a bit. When it did report on the *Playboy* article, it said only that Carter had used a vulgarism. In its own article by Mailer, it replaced the word *fuck* with a dash.[34]

But that didn't really matter much. It was the part about having committed lust in his heart that caused the sensation. The quote showed up in newspaper headlines across the country and quickly became fodder for political cartoons and stand-up comedians. Politicians from both parties labeled Carter as naïve; Democrats worried that his staff's failure to take advantage of its opportunity to approve the article before publication indicated a sloppiness that would carry over into a Carter presidency.

Mainline Protestant leaders and some Catholic theologians applauded Carter for his sound theology, but they, too, worried that he was too candid for his own good and for that of his country. But many of his fellow conservative Protestants were less understanding. His salty language and his too candid comments about sex embarrassed them. Even worse, granting an interview to *Playboy* seemed to them akin to endorsing a magazine they considered sinful and downright pornographic, if not obscene. For that, many never quite forgave him.

Over the course of the campaign, the double-digit lead in opinion polls Carter had once enjoyed over Gerald Ford, the incumbent president and

Republican nominee for reelection, had steadily declined, but it fell even more sharply in the wake of the furor over the *Playboy* interview. Limping to the finish line, Carter won the election with just 50.1 percent of the popular vote. The vote in the Electoral College was 297 for Carter to 240 for Ford. Four years later, aided by the organizational skills of the Rev. Jerry Falwell's Moral Majority, conservative Protestants switched their vote from their fellow evangelical to Ronald Reagan. In the 1980 election, Carter carried only three states.

THE COLA CONTROVERSY

The latest round in the long-running battle for supremacy in the $43.2 billion U.S. soft drink market began in mid-January 1989 when the Coca-Cola Company announced plans to try to push regular Pepsi out of its second-place slot with an ad campaign for Diet Coke featuring National Hockey League icon Wayne Gretzky, actor Don Johnson of *Miami Vice* fame, and supermodel Elle MacPherson. Pepsi responded by signing pop music star and actress Madonna to a $5 million contract that gave Pepsi final say on the commercials, but no control over Madonna's stage performances or rock videos for the same songs used in Pepsi commercials.

For Madonna, it was a great deal. Not only did she get money and sponsorship for a 1990 concert tour, but the first commercial featuring the title track from her *Like a Prayer* album would provide free advance publicity for the song and the album, which would be released a week later. But for Pepsi, the deal was more risky.

Ever since Madonna had burst on the pop music scene six years earlier, her trademark mixing of sexuality and religious symbolism had made her a lightning rod for controversy. Never mind that her parents named her Madonna Louise Ciccone. That she performed as Madonna served only to confirm many people's impression of her as a blasphemous slut.

In the early years, parents fretted when their preteen daughters begged to go to her concerts wearing "Madonna wannabe" costumes of short, tight skirts and navel-baring undershirt tops accessorized with a "Boy Toy" belt and crucifixes as jewelry, which many religious people, both Catholic and Protestant, deemed sacrilegious. In 1986, they complained that the story of a young, unmarried girl confessing to her father that she is pregnant and planning to keep her baby told in her hit song "Papa Don't Preach" legitimized teen sex. During her 1987 *Who's That Girl* tour in Italy, the Vatican denounced Madonna when she performed the song with a picture of the Pope, whom Italians often call "Papa," as a backdrop.

But for all the controversy, Madonna definitely had star power. Her albums always went platinum; her concerts were always sold out. She definitely was popular with Pepsi's target market. In the last year or so, much of the controversy surrounding her had died down. Signing her to a multi-commercial contract seemed like a good idea.

Amid much advance publicity, the two-minute "Like a Prayer" Pepsi commercial aired on March 2, 1989, during *The Cosby Show* in the United States and on ITV in the United Kingdom during a commercial break in *The Bill*. That version showed Madonna drinking a Pepsi while watching a home movie of a celebration for her eighth birthday.

Madonna's MTV video was very different. Framed as a morality play cautioning against making snap race-based judgments about guilt, the video begins with Madonna witnessing the stabbing of a white woman by a white thug and the arrest for the crime of a black man who has come to the victim's aid. Concluding scenes show the video cast taking a bow on stage and Madonna singing the chorus in front of a field of burning crosses after she has gone to the jail where she secures the black man's release by telling the police what she has seen. In between, Madonna takes refuge in a church where she encounters a statue of a saint who looks remarkably like the black man arrested for the murder. The statue of the saint comes to life; he briefly and gently kisses Madonna who is lying on a pew. She then arises, receives stigmata on her palms while handling a knife like the murder weapon, and dances ecstatically with the church's black choir.

The uproar was immediate. As usual some people faulted Madonna's dress. Throughout the video she wears a black slip dress with spaghetti straps that slide provocatively off her shoulders. But it was the religious symbolism, particularly the scenes inside the church, that really upset people. Instead of understanding the encounter with the saint as a visual portrayal of God's power to come to people and inspire and embolden them to do the right thing, they interpreted it literally as a sex scene. Although the saint in the video is generally identified as St. Martin de Porres, some thought Madonna was having sex with Jesus. Many Catholics found the portrayal of Madonna receiving stigmata offensive. Others took the scene with the burning crosses as further evidence of Madonna's disregard for sacred Christian symbols.

Once again Catholics denounced Madonna for her "blasphemous" mixture of sex and Catholic symbolism.[37] The Rev. Donald Wildmon, the Methodist minister and president of the 380,000-member American Family Association, threatened to call a boycott against Pepsi.[38]

Initially Pepsi stood behind the ad campaign. But when the outcry showed little sign of abating and it became clear people were mixing up Madonna's MTV video with the soft drink commercial, Pepsi pulled the plug. On April 4, 1989, Pepsi announced the cancellation of its commercial deal with Madonna. The "Like a Prayer" commercial, which had aired only once in the United States and once overseas, would not be shown again.

Although Madonna got to keep her $5 million because Pepsi broke a contract that clearly had given her creative control over the MTV video, the episode raised concern among artists about the wisdom of entering into contracts that would allow, or give the appearance of allowing, corporate control over art. Once again, the episode also raised questions about the wisdom and effectiveness of protests and threatened boycotts (this chapter, "More Popular than Jesus"). The protests did force Pepsi to cancel the commercial and break its contract with Madonna, but the scandal had little effect on Pepsi's bottom line. Neither did it hurt Madonna.

"Like a Prayer" debuted at #11 on the *Billboard* Hot 100 chart. Fueled partly by the controversy, it rose to #1 within three weeks and held that spot for more than a month. In 2005, the video topped MTV's list of "100 Videos That Broke the Rules." In 2007, MTV viewers voted it "The Most Groundbreaking Video of All Time." Critics generally consider *Like a Prayer* and the 1998 *Ray of Light,* both of which went platinum, to be Madonna's best albums. *Rolling Stone* ranked her #36 on its 2004 list of the "100 Greatest Artists of All Time." In 2008, Madonna was elected to the Rock and Roll Hall of Fame in Cleveland, Ohio.

THE FUNDING FLAP

Usually it's popular media fare that upsets people, especially when it's entertainment accessible to and popular with children, teens, and young adults. But this time it was fine art. The artist at the center of the controversy was Andres Serrano, the son of a Honduran father and Afro-Cuban mother who grew up Catholic in an Italian neighborhood in Brooklyn. As an artist, he made a name for himself by producing special effects with lighting and bodily fluids in fine art photographs he made using conventional photographic techniques without any digital manipulation.

The work in question won the Southeastern Center for Contemporary Art's visual arts competition. Like other works in the series that made Serrano famous, his 1987 image of a cheap plastic crucifix floating in a shimmering golden liquid would have attracted little attention outside the art world had it not been for the photo's title and for program notes explaining its provenance. The title: "Piss Christ." The shimmering golden liquid: the artist's urine.

As part of a multicity touring exhibit during 1988 for which the Southeastern Center for Contemporary Art received $75,000 from the National Endowment for the Arts (NEA), and each of the artists in the show received a $15,000 award, the work attracted little attention—at least not until the spring of 1989.

The first real public attention to the offending art work came through publications of the Rev. Sun Myung Moon's Unification Church—the *Washington Times,* the *New York Tribune,* and *Insight* magazine.[37] Then someone who had seen the Serrano photo in a show at the Virginia Museum of Fine Arts, or perhaps just heard of it, alerted the Rev. Donald Wildmon, head of the American Family Association (AFA).[38]

It had been two years since boycotts and threatened boycotts led by religious and political conservatives had managed to stop some showings of the movie *The Last Temptation of Christ* with its dream sequence in which Jesus imagines a married life with Mary Magdalene. Now, "Piss Christ" provided the perfect excuse for Wildmon to launch another crusade to protect the country from moral decay, especially because there were also pending obscenity cases against the rap group 2 Live Crew for their *As Nasty As They Wanna Be* album and Dennis Barrie, director of the Cincinnati Contemporary Arts Center, for an exhibit of Robert Mapplethorpe fine art photographs, some of them with homoerotic and sadomasochistic themes.

But instead of calling for a crusade to protect true religion from blasphemy and sacrilege, Wildmon mobilized his American Family Association by raising questions: Should the government be spending your money to fund art? If it is going to fund art, why should the government spend your money on "trash" when it could be spending it on "good" art?[39]

Although the amount of money involved was small, framing the issue as one of fiscal prudence and propriety garnered support the AFA might otherwise not have received so readily. Televangelist M. G. "Pat" Robertson's Christian Coalition launched a $200,000 advertising campaign daring Congress to "make my day" by authorizing renewed funding for the NEA; 17 conservative religious and political groups joined the AFA in a coalition known as Taxpayers for Accountability in Government (TAG). Members of TAG organizations swamped members of Congress with letters and postcards demanding an end to funding for the NEA because of its irresponsible financing of "obscene and sacrilegious art."[40]

Congress got the message. In May 1989, Congress, led by Republican Senators Jesse Helms of North Carolina and Alphonse D'Amato of New York, scheduled full-scale hearings instead of its usually routine five-year review of NEA funding. At the hearings, the recently appointed NEA chairman, John Frohmeyer, attempted to mollify critics by patiently explaining that respected members of the art profession judged applications for NEA grants solely on artistic merit. The grants in question were awarded under the tenure of his predecessor using standard, approved processes. With a budget of more than $1.6 million, the NEA had made more than 85,000 grants. Including the Serrano one, only three grants totaling less than $50,000 went to support works that anyone had considered controversial.

Serrano tried to explain that he often made photographs with religious themes. Many of them were expressions of his Catholic faith; in others, he wrestled with his sometimes ambivalent feelings about the teachings and practices of the Roman Catholic Church, or explored personal feelings about religion in general. "Piss Christ" was that kind of work. It wasn't meant to denigrate the Savior. It was his commentary on what has happened to Christ and his true message in a secular age.[41]

While many Christians found "Piss Christ" blasphemous and wanted an end to NEA funding because of it, some lent their support. In a June 18, 1990, article in *Time*, Ed Knippers, a Christian painter and editor of *Christians in Visual Arts Newsletter*, pointed out that rules rarely work as intended. Saying that the appropriate response to objectionable art is to greet it with a yawn, he recommended both continued NEA funding with no criteria for grants other than artistic merit and increased funding by Christians for fellow Christian artists.[42]

In a televised interview, noted art historian and critic Sister Wendy Beckett, a member of the Sisters of Notre Dame de Namur who lives as a Consecrated Virgin of the Catholic Church at a Carmelite monastery in England, told Bill Moyers that the work clearly had artistic merit. Like the artist, she regarded the photograph as a commentary on the way contemporary society regards Christ and the values he represents.[43]

But Senator Helms wasn't impressed. When the House subcommittee in charge of the NEA budget showed little inclination to eliminate or even reduce the agency's budget, Helms introduced an amendment to the Senate's version of the funding bill that called for a prohibition on funding for "obscene or indecent" art or for "material which denigrates the objects or beliefs of the adherents of a particular religion or non-religion."[44] Exasperated, Sidney Yates, the Democratic Representative from Illinois who was in charge of the House subcommittee overseeing the NEA budget, remarked, "We've had a tradition of artistic freedom in this country. The communists tell their artists what to do with their art. We don't."[45]

With the House and Senate so far apart on the issue, the debate over what to do about the NEA dragged on for almost a year. In the end, Congress did pass a bill establishing an Independent Commission to review the grant-making process, but the bill also gave the NEA a 1990 budget of $171,225,000—an increase of almost $2 million over the 1989 level—and authorized continuing funding through 1993.

However, five years later Republican victories in the 1994 congressional elections combined with President Bill Clinton's push for a balanced federal budget produced what the American Family Association and TAG had not been able to accomplish. In 1995, Congress slashed the NEA budget to just $99.5 million for 1996. It also prohibited the NEA from awarding grants to individual artists and imposed prohibitions on funding works that do not comply with "general standards of decency and respect for the diverse beliefs and values of the American public."

When the furor over "Piss Christ" died down, Congress began giving the NEA annual budget increases. But even though the budget remains lower than it once was and the decency guidelines remain in place, there is little reason to believe artists or art galleries are engaging in self-censorship in order to obtain government grants or avoid controversy.

Since 1989 when the controversy over federal funding for the arts began, galleries around the country have continued to include "Piss Christ" in exhibits. Artists, including Andres Serrano, have continued to make religiously themed art, some of it quite controversial. In 1999, for example, Chris Ofili, a British artist of Nigerian descent, found himself at the center of controversy, first by referencing Nigerian rituals in his painting "The Holy Virgin Mary," which showed Mary surrounded by cherubim and seraphim and with a smear of elephant dung on her breast, and then when it became known that the respected Tate Gallery had violated its own rules by buying Ofili works even though he was a member of its board of directors.

While the practical, long-term effect of the 1995 legislation on art and artists seems minimal, the debate over whether the government should fund art is a legitimate one. So, too, is debate over standards for awarding grants. But funding rules that require taking into account both "general standard of decency" and "respect for the diverse beliefs and values" raise their own questions about public opinion and the tyranny of the majority versus artistic merit and minority interests.

In its ruling in the case of *NEA v. Finley*, challenging the 1995 legislation, the Supreme Court broke no new legal ground when it pointed out that a refusal to fund is not synonymous with censorship; while the First Amendment guarantees freedom of speech, press, and religion, there simply is no First Amendment right to receive government money to fund people engaging in those protected rights. But the Court also ignored its own ruling that found the New York law that was at the center of *The Miracle* case unconstitutionally vague and overbroad, when it ruled that the similarly worded decency standard in the 1995 NEA legislation is constitutional.

The Congress that passed the 1995 bill with its decency standard was more Republican and more conservative than the Congress that rejected a similar provision in 1992. So, too, the justices on the Supreme Court who heard the 1998 case of *NEA v. Finley* were very different from the ones who heard the 1942 case of *Burstyn v. Wilson*. The lasting legacy of the "Piss Christ" controversy may lie in its illustration of the impact of political climate on law.

FOR FURTHER READING

Blues for the Beatles. 1966, August 23. *Newsweek*, p. 94.

Fisher, Carrie. 1991, June 27. True confessions: The *Rolling Stone* interview with Madonna, part two. *Rolling Stone*, pp. 45–49, 78.

Gelman, David. 1976, October 4. The great *Playboy* furor. *Newsweek*, pp. 70–71.

Hein, Marjorie. 2005. The "Miracle" of *Burstyn v. Wilson*. In Joseph Russomanno, ed., *Defending the First: Commentary on First Amendment issues and cases*. Mahwah, NJ: Lawrence Erlbaum, pp. 61–84.

Hochman, Steve. 1989, February 18. Madonna poised for big media blitz. *Los Angeles Times*, Sec. 5, pp. 1, 7.

Lawton, Kim A. 1990, June 18. Taking aim at art. *Christianity Today*, pp. 52–55.
Levy, Leonard W. 1993. *Blasphemy: Verbal offense against the sacred, from Moses to Salman Rushdie*. Chapel Hill: University of North Carolina Press, pp. 400–406, 525–527.
Lippard, Lucy R. 1990, April. The spirit and the letter. *Art in America*, pp. 230, 238–245.
Mathews, Tom. 1990, July 2. Fine art or foul? *Newsweek*, pp. 46–51.
Scheer, Robert. 1976, November. *Playboy* interview: Jimmy Carter. *Playboy*, pp. 63–86.
Talk of the town. 1966, August 27. *New Yorker*, pp. 21–22.
Walters, Fred. 1952, August. The Supreme Court ruling on *The Miracle* and *Pinky* gives censorship a punch in the nose. *Theater Arts*, pp. 74–77.
Week by week: *The Miracle* decision. 1952, June 13. *Commonweal*, pp. 235–236.
Woodward, Kenneth L. 1976, June 7. Carter's cross to bear. *Newsweek*, p. 56.

Chapter 6

RELIGIO–POLITICAL HERESY

Each religion carries with it certain beliefs about what people owe to their god and to their country, and, as a corollary, what positions they should take on political, social, and economic issues in order to please their god. But in the United States, people practice many different religions; even within the Christian majority, interpretations and emphases vary. Out of these differences, political battles and culture wars are born.

Struggles of that kind to shape America are nothing new. In 1800, as war between England and France loomed, the presidential election campaign of 1800 turned into one of the dirtiest on record. John Adams and the Federalists simultaneously labeled Thomas Jefferson as a closet papist for siding with the French, and also as an atheist who would close all the churches; Jeffersonian anti-Federalists accused John Adams and the Federalists, who supported England, of planning to establish a single, national religion. In 1928, any chance the Democratic candidate Al Smith might have had to become president disappeared when, like most Catholics, he opposed prohibition. John F. Kennedy became president only after he managed to reassure conservative Protestants that his Catholic faith did not mean he would take orders from the Pope. Religion has been a theme in every election since 1976 as conservative Protestants and many Catholics became single-issue anti-abortion/pro-life voters.

But as divisive along religious lines as those elections may have been, in all of them there was significant support for each candidate and for his issue positions. Religio-political heresies emerge only when a person or a group says or does something for religious reasons that is well outside mainstream opinion on political, social, or economic matters. Scandals of this type are the subject of this chapter.

"Satan's Hoary-headed Apostle" tells of a man who was convicted of blasphemy in nineteenth-century Massachusetts. The real outrage, however, was not directed at his religious views, but at the positions he took on social issues that remain divisive ones even today. "The Father of Hate Radio" is about a Catholic priest whose popular radio broadcasts during World War II increasingly seemed a threat to national interests, while "The Radical Priests" is about religion-based opposition during and since Vietnam. Like "The Radical Priests," "God Damn America" tells of a pastor's condemnation of racism and international foreign policy in the context of the 2008 presidential election campaign. "Soldiers of the Lord" and "The Greatest" are about members of unpopular religions who stood up for what they believed and, in spite of overwhelmingly negative public opinion, ultimately prevailed. "The Monument," however, tells the story of a twenty-first-century judge who believes, as did the judge in "Satan's Hoary-headed Apostle," that "We are a Christian nation."

SATAN'S HOARY-HEADED APOSTLE

An article about Abner Kneeland posted online at the Unitarian-Universalist Association Web site describes him as "the most controversial character ever ordained to the Universalist ministry."[1] Initially a Baptist lay preacher, Kneeland was ordained to the Universalist ministry in 1804 and served congregations in four states for nearly 25 years, until his increasing skepticism about revealed religion led him to renounce Christianity. Automatically disfellowshipped by the New England Universalist General Convention, Kneeland moved to Boston where more than two thousand people flocked to his Sunday and Wednesday lectures for the First Society of Free Enquirers at the Federal Street Theater. Similar numbers subscribed to his newspaper, the *Boston Investigator*.

Articles published in that newspaper led to a series of five trials that excited the people of Massachusetts for nearly a decade. Although Kneeland was charged under a Massachusetts law making it a crime "willfully to blaspheme the holy name of God" by denying his existence or denigrating conventional Trinitarian Christian beliefs, evidence suggests his real offense may have been preaching social and political views that were well ahead of their time.

At a time when most of the Massachusetts establishment, including the prosecuting attorney, the judges, and most jurors who heard his case, were Whigs, Kneeland was a Jacksonian Democrat who characterized the rich as tyrants, railed against high prices and property laws, and called for a union of farmers and workingmen. As a Free Thinker, he was friends with the controversial communitarians Frances Wright and Robert Owen and shared many of their social views. Worse yet, he undermined the sacredness of marriage by claiming it should be entered into freely by a man and woman who loved each other and shared equally in its benefits and responsibilities. Not only did he oppose laws restricting marriage and other relationships between the races, but he also taught that married women should be able to retain their maiden name if they so chose, own property, keep bank accounts in their name alone, and have the same right to file for divorce as their husbands. He also provided women with the information on female reproductive anatomy and contraception he believed they needed as equal and equally responsible partners in marital relations.[3]

The indictment against Kneeland listed three counts of blasphemy. Two of them, stemming from reprints of articles from the New York *Free Inquiry* questioning the virgin birth and ridiculing prayer, played little role in the case that centered on publication of a letter written by Kneeland to Thomas Whitmore, the editor of the *Universalist Trumpet*.[4] In the offending passage that became the focal point of the case, Kneeland described his theological differences with his former church:

> Universalists believe in a god which I do not; but believe that their god, with all his moral attributes (aside from nature itself) is nothing more than a chimera of their own imagination.[5]

As the case wended its way through the court system, articles by the Unitarian humanitarian Samuel Gridley Howe published in December 1834 and January 1835 warned readers of the *New England Magazine* that atheism was infesting their community through the blasphemy and abhorrent social and political views propagated by this "hoary-headed apostle of Satan."[6] John Barton Denby, a former Jacksonian who had returned to the Whig fold, published claims that "nineteen-twentieth" of the attendees at Kneeland's "infidel orgies" at the Federal Street Theater were radical Jacksonians.[7]

In court, the Whig prosecuting attorney, Samuel D. Parker, played up those same themes, consistently portraying Kneeland as willfully intent on spreading the pernicious doctrine of atheism through blasphemous utterances intended to undermine social and moral order. This "peddler of obscenity," he warned, was teaching people how to have illicit intercourse "with safety and without discovery." If Kneeland were acquitted, he warned, "marriages [will be] dissolved, prostitution made easy and safe, moral and religious restraints removed, property invaded and the foundations of society broken up, and property made common." Pointing out to the jury that the *Investigator* had a large circulation among the young and the poor because of its low price, he further asserted that Kneeland's strategy included using it "with a view first to demoralize them, and then to make them apt instruments to root up the foundations of society and make all property common, and all women as common as brutes."[8]

First through his attorney Andrew Dunlap, who was active in the Massachusetts Democratic Party, and then as his own attorney during the final appeal before the highest court in Massachusetts, Kneeland defended himself as best he could. He pointed to grammar and punctuation in the offending article and to sentiments in it that the court seemed to ignore. There was no comma between *God* and *which* in the statement in question; he had, therefore, not denied the existence of God. He had merely said he did not believe in the Universalists' God as was his right under state law. Far from being an atheist, as the prosecutor contended, the article clearly stated that he was not an atheist. In it, he wrote:

> I believe … that God and Nature, so far as we can attach any rational idea to either, are synonymous terms. Hence, I am not an atheist, but a pantheist; that is, instead of believing there is no God, I believe that in the abstract, all is God; … it is in God we live, move, and have our being.[9]

He also raised concerns about the court's interpretation of state constitutional guarantees of freedom of religion and press, but to no avail.

Two appeals ended with hung juries when the lone Democrats on the juries refused to vote for conviction; however, the prosecutor's warnings ultimately had the intended effect. At a fourth trial in November 1835, Kneeland was convicted of blasphemy and sentenced to 60 days in jail. In April of 1838, two full years after Massachusetts's highest court heard the appeal, Chief Justice Lemuel Shaw, a Whig and a Unitarian, finally handed down a verdict upholding the conviction and jail term. The only dissent came from Marcus Morton, the sole Jacksonian Democrat on the court.

William Ellery Channing circulated a petition calling for a pardon. Ralph Waldo Emerson, William Lloyd Garrison, and Bronson Alcott were among the noteworthy people who signed it. But a counterpetition signed by many Universalists, clergy from other churches, and many political leaders got more signatures.[10] The case of *Commonwealth v. Kneeland* joined the *Ruggles* case (Chapter 5, "We Are a Christian Nation") in shaping blasphemy law for more than a century (Chapter 5, "The Miracle"). Along with *Ruggles*, it is still cited by those who believe the First Amendment was meant only to protect Christians and Christianity from government interference.

Although Kneeland was the only person jailed for the offense of blasphemy in Massachusetts, and the last one convicted for that crime, he was neither the last nor the only one jailed for expounding the social and political views that exacerbated his case. Between 1877 and 1890, Ezra Heywood, a former Congregationalist minister who, like Kneeland had become a Free Thinker and gravitated into the Free Love movement that advocated views similar to Kneeland's, was arrested five times, and convicted and jailed three times for mailing publications containing information about anatomy, reproduction, and birth control, and a birth control device he dubbed "the Comstock syringe," all of which were defined as obscene under terms of the restrictive 1873 Comstock Act.

This was not an isolated case. During the last half of the nineteenth century and well into the twentieth century, arrests, convictions, and jail terms were a common fate for those providing information on sex and/or contraception that offended religious and political conservatives.

In 1957, the U.S. Supreme Court liberalized the definition of obscenity so it applied only to material that, taken as a whole, appeals to the prurient interests of normal, average people, but contraception and information about it remained illegal in many states until the Supreme Court struck down Connecticut's law outlawing contraception in the 1964 case of *Griswold v. Connecticut*. The federal government still generally restricts distribution of condoms, even as part of programs intended to prevent the spread of AIDS; private insurers who will pay for prescriptions to treat male erectile dysfunction often will not cover birth control prescriptions. Few issues will incite passions as quickly as the question of how much information about anatomy, reproduction, and contraception to include in sex education curricula in public schools.

THE FATHER OF HATE RADIO

For 40 years, between 1926 and 1966, Father Charles Coughlin was the parish priest at the Shrine of the Little Flower Church in Royal Oak, Michigan, but it was radio that brought him fame. It was also radio that made him infamous.

Father Coughlin began his radio career October 17, 1926, on local stations as a way to garner support for his tiny, impoverished parish and to raise money to repair damages incurred when fire from a cross the Ku Klux Klan burned in the churchyard spread to the church itself. The programs became so popular that in 1930 CBS picked them up for broadcast nationwide, but over time they became increasingly political.

An early supporter of Franklin Delano Roosevelt, Father Coughlin played on people's fears by blaming the administration of President Herbert Hoover for the nation's economic woes. He also used his broadcasts to campaign for Roosevelt, using slogans such as "Roosevelt or Ruin" and "The New Deal Is Christ's Deal" that helped Roosevelt win the 1932 election.[11]

But when Roosevelt did not reward Father Coughlin by appointing him to a position within his administration and ignored Coughlin's ideas for economic reform, Coughlin turned against Roosevelt, branding him a "liar," and simultaneously as a "tool of capitalists" and a "communist." His messages also became virulently anti-Semitic.[12]

At the peak of Father Coughlin's popularity, in the early 1930s, an estimated 40 million listeners tuned in; 80,000 wrote to him each week. But as the world moved inexorably toward war, his vehement outbursts against Roosevelt and his capitalist, communist, and Jewish co-conspirators increasingly became viewed as dangerous. Both his virulent anti-government and anti-Semitic rhetoric also proved an embarrassment to Catholics. But at first their efforts to get the Church to silence him met with little success.

The Vatican had no authority to stop Father Coughlin so long as he maintained the support of his bishop, Michael Gallagher. Father Coughlin maintained that support until 1937 when Gallagher died and was replaced by the much-less-supportive Edward Mooney. He lost even more support the next year when just two weeks after Kristallnacht he told his listeners that the Jews deserved their fate because they were persecuted only after having first persecuted Christians.[13] Kristallnacht—November 9, 1938, "the night of broken glass"—saw Jewish homes, businesses, and synagogues in Germany destroyed, nearly 100 Jews murdered, and thousands more rounded up and deported to concentration camps.

Still, Father Coughlin managed to stay on the air until 1939, when the Code Committee of the National Association of Broadcasters adopted new rules severely curtailing the sale of air time to spokesmen for controversial issues. After that, radio stations in New York and Chicago refused to continue carrying his broadcasts.

Cut off from his large radio audience, Father Coughlin turned to print media. He reprinted the *Protocols of the Elders of Zion*, which scholars agree is a fictional piece of anti-Semitic propaganda, in *Social Justice*, the newspaper of his National Union of Social Justice. He wrote editorials paraphrasing speeches and writings of Nazi leaders or that were taken verbatim from them.

Although the government has less authority over print media than it has over broadcasting, it was not powerless against Coughlin's alleged treason. In 1942, a federal grand jury indicted Father Coughlin under terms of the Espionage Act of 1917 for activities undermining the war effort against Nazi Germany. He lost his second-class mailing permit and with it the ability to raise funds. His bishop ordered him to give up his political activities and return full time to the parish ministry.

Father Coughlin died in 1979 at the age of 88 in Bloomfield Hills, Michigan. With the passage of time, memory of him has faded, but the legacy of this "father of hate radio" lives on.[14] His kind of anti-Semitism has not gone away. Today it can be found on the Internet and in programs on small radio stations, many of which are the creations of various branches of the neo-Nazi and Christian Identity movements (Chapter 4, "Another Domestic Terrorist").

Anti-Semitism of a less virulent, but still troubling, kind also pops up from time to time in outbursts from individuals in ways that do more to discredit the speaker than to harm the target. In February 1984 any hope the Rev. Jesse Jackson may have had of becoming the presidential candidate on the Democratic ticket were dashed when *Washington Post* reporter Milton Coleman revealed that the Rev. Jackson had called Jews "Hymies" and referred to New York as "Hymietown."[15]

Nation of Islam leader Louis Farrakhan quickly came to Jackson's defense. However, his support was no help. His comments succeeded primarily in reviving memories of earlier inflammatory statements about white people and Jews that had made Black Muslims seem dangerous during the late 1960s and early 1970s when many white Christian and Jewish clergy and laypeople were working alongside black Christians to end desegregation and secure full civil rights for African Americans (Chapter 4, "A Monster and/or a Martyr").[16]

After Mel Gibson's July 28, 2006, arrest for speeding and suspicion of drunk driving, police reports surfaced indicating he had been abusive to the arresting officers. News that Gibson had asked the officers if they were Jewish and told them "Fucking Jews are responsible for all the wars in the world" created a mini-scandal, coming as the incident did so soon after the release of his movie *The Passion of the Christ*, which some Christians and Jews considered anti-Semitic.[17]

SOLDIERS OF THE LORD

Lillian Gobitas promised herself that she would do it because "God hate's hypocrites."[18]

She was a good girl, an "A" student, president of her seventh grade class, and well-liked by teachers and classmates. But she was also afraid of losing everything she had worked so hard for, and so she procrastinated. Then her younger brother, William, announced he had done it. That gave her the courage to do it, too. The next day, October 23, 1935, Lillian remained seated and silent when her classmates stood up and recited the Pledge of Allegiance.

Lillian's fears about acting on her beliefs were well founded. During the 1930s and 1940s, Jehovah's Witnesses were the most hated group in the United States and, indeed, throughout much of the Western world. Their literal, apocalyptic interpretation of the Bible placed them outside mainstream Christianity. Their door-to-door proselytizing was annoying. Their practice of using phonograph recordings that blared their beliefs disturbed the peace. It could also seem downright threatening when the messages attacked both secular government and other religions, especially Catholicism, as Satanic rackets. Many Jehovah's Witnesses refused military service on the grounds that as "ministers of the Lord" they were entitled to the clergy exemption. Now their children were refusing to give due respect to the nation and its flag. They were downright un-American—probably part of a dangerous Fifth Column that was propagandizing in league with Hitler and his minions.

Although Jehovah's Witnesses generally considered all secular governments to be Satanic rackets, they never meant any disrespect for the flag or for the nation and the government it represents. The idea for boycotting the Pledge of Allegiance came from a speech during their summer 1935 convention when their leader, Joseph Rutherford, called attention to the persecution that their fellow religionists were suffering in Germany because of their steadfast refusal to engage in the idolatrous "Hitler salute." In his speech, he also raised the question of whether the American practice, which at the time consisted of a military-style salute followed by extending the arm forward to eye level, wasn't similarly idolatrous. Many Jehovah's Witnesses concluded it was. Thus, out of allegiance to their beliefs and sympathy for their fellow believers in Germany, their children began refusing to participate in a pledge that they considered idolatrous.

However, school officials saw it differently. To them, refusing to recite the pledge was probably un-American. It was definitely a case of defiant insubordination. Beginning with the case of Carleton Nichols, a third-grader in Lynn, Massachusetts, and then spreading to Pennsylvania and throughout the nation, schools began expelling Jehovah's Witness children who refused to salute the flag.

In Minersville, Pennsylvania, where the Gobitas children went to school, their teachers and some classmates supported them in their decision to refrain from pledging allegiance. Other children taunted them and showered them with pebbles when they walked to and from school. School Superintendent Charles E. Roudabush was outraged.

Under Pennsylvania law, the children could be punished only if they had broken a formal rule. To get the authority he needed in order to take action against the Gobitas children, Roudabush called a meeting of the school board for November 6, 1935. At that meeting, Walter Gobitas explained the rationale for his children's decision. Lillian and Billy submitted their own statements.[19] But the school board gave Roudabush what he wanted—a formal ruling that all students and teachers be required to salute the flag as part of daily exercises—and Roudabush immediately announced the expulsion of the Gobitas children "effective immediately."[20] Walter Gobitas retorted, "I'm going to take you to court for this."[21]—and he did.

The case entered the federal court system in the spring of 1937 under the misspelled family surname as *Gobitis v. Minersville School District*. In district court, Judge Albert Maris, a Quaker, first turned aside the school district's motion to dismiss the case as without merit, and then, at trial, ruled for the Jehovah's Witnesses saying that their children were exercising their right of conscience guaranteed to them by the state and federal constitutions. According to Judge Maris, the school district was using the flag salute as a way of imposing an unconstitutional test as a condition for receiving the benefits of a public education.

The ruling gained favorable attention from Philadelphia newspapers, but it outraged Roudabush and his supporters.[22] With funds from patriotic organizations, the Minersville School District filed an appeal. When the Third Circuit Court upheld the ruling of the trial court, the school district again appealed.

Represented by attorneys Joseph F. Rutherford, George K. Garder, and Hayden Covington, and with *amicus curiae* briefs filed on their behalf by the American Civil Liberties Union and the Committee on the Bill of Rights of the American Bar Association, the Jehovah's Witnesses had reason to hope for another victory. Just two weeks earlier in the case of *Cantwell v. Connecticut*, the U.S. Supreme Court had affirmed their right to engage in door-to-door proselytizing. But according to the June 3, 1940, opinion written by Justice Felix Frankfurter, the pledge had nothing to do with religion. It had everything to do with patriotism and national unity, which the court saw as essential to national security. There was no reason to deny a duly elected legislative body such as a school board the "right to awaken in the child's mind considerations as to the significance of the flag contrary to those implanted by the parent" through whatever means it saw fit.[23] Only Justice Harlan Fiske Stone dissented.

Well over 200 secular and religious newspapers and magazines published editorials and articles criticizing the *Gobitis* opinion.[24] Many were especially critical of Justice Frankfurter, who wrote the opinion, for seeming to sacrifice his long-standing support of civil rights on the pyre of wartime hysteria. To the public and to many politicians, however, the decision seemed right. To them, it signaled court approval for taking any action that might be deemed necessary to counter the Jehovah's Witness menace.

This court decision sparked the worst outbreak of repression and violence directed at a religious minority that the United States has ever seen. Thirty-one states enacted laws or took other steps to expel Jehovah's Witness children for refusing to salute the flag. Towns that hadn't already taken such steps enacted new laws or dusted off old, seldom-used ones to harass and punish Jehovah's Witnesses as they attempted to proselytize. The Gobitas family received threats of arson and physical harm. For a time, Minersville residents boycotted their grocery store. But the family got off lightly compared to many other Jehovah's Witnesses. Anti-Witness rioting broke out in all but four states. Virtually everywhere, there were beatings, burnings, shootings, castrations, and cases of Jehovah's Witnesses being tarred and feathered or forced to drink castor oil.

Through it all, Jehovah's Witnesses continued going door-to-door and preaching on street corners. Their young men continued to claim conscientious objector status. Their children refused to pledge allegiance. When they were met with violence, harassment, or punishment at the hands of the law, they continued to file court cases.

When courts in Kansas, Minnesota, and Washington refused to follow the Supreme Court's reasoning in the *Gobitis* case and the Civil Rights Section of the Justice Department issued an opinion that United States attorneys and local officials should take steps to reduce repression and vigilantism aimed at Jehovah's Witnesses, the Witnesses' head attorney filed a new case in August 1942 challenging the expulsion of their children for refusing to recite the Pledge of Allegiance.

During its spring 1943 session, the U.S. Supreme Court heard the appeal of the case of *West Virginia State Board of Education v. Barnette*. On Flag Day, June 14, 1943, the Court announced its decision—*Gobitis* had been wrongly decided. Expelling children or otherwise punishing them for failing to adhere to a compulsory ritual violated their constitutional rights. In his opinion for the court, Justice Robert Jackson wrote:

> If there is any fixed star in our constitutional constellation, it is that no official, high or petty, can prescribe what shall be orthodox in politics, nationalism, religion, or other matters of opinion or force citizens to confess by word or act their faith therein. If there are any circumstances which permit an exception, they do not occur to us now.[25]

Through their relentless efforts to obtain their right to act in accordance with the tenets of their faith, the Jehovah's Witnesses ushered in an era of increasing civil rights for everyone. In the 1960s, Justice Jackson's words formed the backdrop for Supreme Court rulings on school prayer; in the 1970s, the Court revisited them in cases in which they found flag desecration and other offensive anti-government and anti-war sentiments constitutionally protected speech. But whether today's more conservative Supreme Court would be as likely to protect individual rights against the power of governments is an open question.

Although the Jehovah's Witnesses secured the right of children to refrain from saying a pledge, the Pledge of Allegiance itself has generated new controversies since Congress added the words "under God" to it in 1954, at the height of the Cold War, to underscore differences between the American democratic capitalist system and "godless communism."

On June 14, 2004, Flag Day and the 50th anniversary of its decision in the *Barnette* case, the U.S. Supreme Court overturned the verdict of the Ninth Circuit Court of Appeals in the case of *Newdow v. U.S. Congress*. Without addressing the substantive question of whether the words "under God" constitute an unconstitutional establishment or endorsement of religion on which the Ninth Circuit Court, as well as the Fourth Circuit Court in an earlier similar case, had based their conclusions, the high court simply ruled that Charles Newdow, an atheist, was not the custodial parent, and therefore did not have the necessary standing to bring a suit intended to shield his daughter from a sentiment he considered offensive.

In 2007, the Supreme Court further curtailed the First Amendment rights of students in public schools when, in the case of *Morse v. Frederick*, it overturned the Ninth Circuit Court of Appeals verdict that the Juneau-Douglas High School principal, Deborah Morse, could not punish student Joseph Frederick for unveiling a sign with the message "Bong Hits 4 Jesus" in front of television cameras while standing on a public sidewalk across from the school during the 2002 Winter Olympics Torch Relay in Juneau, Alaska. In the majority opinion, Chief Justice John Roberts argued simultaneously that Frederick's sign was not constitutionally protected political speech and that the school could punish him for displaying a message contrary to the school's anti-drug stance because the school had released students from classes in order to watch the parade. In a concurring opinion, Justice Clarence Thomas went even further, saying that students have no First Amendment rights.[26]

Even a very liberal court cannot protect against public outrage or from repercussions from employers acting under contract law when people fail to honor time-honored patriotic symbols and customs.

In 1995, Denver Nuggets basketball player Mahmoud Abdul-Rauf, a Muslim, created an uproar when he refused to stand for the singing of the national anthem before games. The NBA suspended him for that action. Some letter writers to Denver papers thought he should have been banned for life, but the suspension lasted only one game because Abdul-Rauf agreed to a compromise that allowed him to stand silently with eyes downcast or closed during the singing of the national anthem.

In 2007, an announcement by Keith Ellison, the first Muslim elected to Congress, about his plans for the swearing-in ceremony led radio talk show host Dennis Prager to tell his audience that the newly elected representative from Minnesota's Fifth Congressional District should not be allowed to take the oath of office on the Quran instead of the Bible. Such an act, he said, "undermines American civilization" and will do "more damage to the value system that has formed this country than the terrorists of 9-11."[27] Many religious and political conservatives, including Representative Virgil Goode, a Republican from Virginia, essentially agreed. Some people, however, found it even more scandalous that so many of their fellow citizens failed to recognize that the Constitution clearly states there can be no religious test for public office. Taking the oath of office by swearing on a Bible is custom, not law.

THE GREATEST

They called him "The Louisville Lip." He called himself "The Greatest." His parents named him Cassius Marcellus Clay Jr., after his father who was named for a nineteenth-century abolitionist and politician. As an amateur prize fighter, he won six Kentucky Golden Gloves titles, two national Golden Gloves titles, an Amateur Athletic Union National Title, and the gold medal in the Light Heavyweight division at the 1960 Olympics in Rome.

When Clay turned professional after the Olympics, boxing was a moribund sport. But with Clay on the scene, people who never cared much about boxing began to pay attention. His good looks were part of his appeal, but it was his brash pronouncements about his opponents and their ultimate fate that made for the kind of good theater that translated into public interest and box office receipts. That his comments sometimes rattled his opponents, causing them to lash out at him, made the theater even better, especially when he confounded his opponents and the experts by backing up his boasts with the promised victory.

Before his 1964 title fight against Sonny Liston, Clay taunted his opponent, telling anyone who would listen how he intended to win the fight. Although his prefight commentary infuriated Liston, most experts took it as nothing more than hype. His recent victories had been unimpressive; few thought his strategy would work. But against all odds—and the oddsmakers—Clay defeated Liston to become the world heavyweight champion. He had, indeed "float[ed] like a butterfly and st[u]ng like a bee."[28]

Then almost overnight, Clay went from media darling and fan favorite to a controversial, even despised, character. On March 25, 1964, Malcolm X (Chapter 4, "A Monster and/or a Martyr"), announced that Clay had renounced the Baptist faith in which he was raised to become a member of the Nation of Islam. In place of his "slave name," Cassius Clay was now Muhammad (one who is worthy of praise) Ali (fourth rightly guided caliph).

At a time when the United States was beginning to grapple seriously with its legacy of slavery, Nation of Islam doctrine was controversial. It was also scary. An offshoot of traditional Islam, "Black Muslims," as members were often called, promoted black empowerment. They also proclaimed a racist message of hatred toward whites and all things white. That Clay, who had gained so much from a society he now claimed was racist, should join a religion that preached segregation and even race warfare, seemed inexplicable.

When Ali failed the armed forces qualifying exam later in 1964 because of inadequate writing and spelling skills, rumors spread that the Black Muslims were behind it. Ali had purposefully failed the exam. Although Ali had barely managed to graduate from high school, suspicions mounted as Ali mouthed off about whites, the draft, and his boxing opponents. Rumor turned into "fact" in 1966 after the military revised its qualifying test and rescored previous results.

Now classified 1-A, Ali initially boasted that the government wouldn't draft him to serve in Vietnam because he was too popular and because the tax paid on his boxing income was worth more to the government than his body was worth in military uniform.[29] When Ali was drafted, he refused to respond when he was called forward by his birth name. As a member of the Nation of Islam, he also claimed conscientious objector status. If that weren't enough, he also said, "I ain't got no quarrel with those Vietcong" and "no Vietcong ever called me nigger."[30]

Even members of Ali's family were appalled. An April 11, 1966, *Sports Illustrated* article by Jack Olsen quoted Ali's aunt, Mary Turner, as saying, "He's gonna mess himself up so won't nobody go see him…. Most folks feel like I do: when their sons get ready to go to the Army, they'll just pack the suitcases and go."[31] The American Legion, other patriotic and civic organizations, and politicians condemned Ali as an unpatriotic "yellow nigger."[32] The media fed the frenzy, with the *Chicago Tribune* waging a venomous campaign against holding the next Ali fight in that city.[33]

In 1967, Ali was convicted for refusing induction into the military and sentenced to five years in prison. The boxing commission suspended his license to fight professionally in the United States and, although he had successfully defended his title nine times, stripped him of his heavyweight crown. For three years, while appealing his case, Ali supported himself with loans from friends and from occasional speaking engagements at anti-war rallies on college campuses.

But as opposition to the war in Vietnam increased, opinions about Ali's alleged treason changed. First Georgia, the only state without a boxing commission, granted him a license for a 1970 fight against Jerry Quarry. Then the New York State Supreme Court ruled Ali had been unjustly denied a boxing license and granted him a license. His December victory in Madison Square Garden over Oscar Bonavena paved the way for the fights that cemented Ali's place in boxing history and in popular culture.

In "The Fight of the Century" at Madison Square Garden on March 8, 1971, Joe Frazier handed Ali his first professional loss, but after a string of victories, Ali reclaimed his title on October 30, 1974, by defeating Frazier at a match held in Kinshasa, Zaire, that has become enshrined in popular culture. "The Rumble in the Jungle," as the fight was billed, is the subject of Norman Mailer's book *The Fight*, and of the Academy Award-winning 2006 documentary *When We Were Kings*. In 1975, Ali again defeated Frazier in a match fought in Quezon City in the Philippines. That "Thrilla in Manila," is generally considered one of the greatest fights of the twentieth century.

Ali retained his title until February 1978 when he lost to the 1976 Olympic champion, Leon Spinks. Although he defeated Spinks in a 1979 rematch, it quickly became apparent that Ali was no longer the fighter he once was. In 1980, he fought and lost to Larry Holmes on a technical knockout. He retired in 1981 as a three-time world heavyweight champion with a professional record of 56 wins, 36 by a knockout, and five losses.

Even before the 1980 loss to Holmes, the Mayo Clinic had diagnosed Ali as having a hole in the membrane of his brain. In 1983, he was diagnosed with Parkinsonism and ultimately with Pugilistic Parkinson's syndrome.

In retirement, Ali, whose racial and social views had softened since leaving the Nation of Islam for the Sunni branch of traditional Islam, devoted himself to philanthropic work on behalf of civil rights and social justice. He also reaped numerous honors and accolades. His hometown of Louisville, Kentucky, named a street in his honor. In 1999, the Kentucky Athletic Hall of Fame named him the "Kentucky Athlete of the Century" and *Sports Illustrated* named him the "Sportsman of the Century." He had the honor of lighting the torch to open the 1996 Summer Olympics in Atlanta.

But Ali's real legacy rests with the courageous stand he took in 1964. By proclaiming himself a member of the Nation of Islam and taking a new name, he made it easier for generations of Americans to adopt a religion outside the Judeo-Christian mainstream and to live and work openly under an Arab/

People called him a traitor when as a member of the
Nation of Islam he refused to serve in the military, but
three decades later they cheered as the former Olympic
and world boxing champion Muhammad Ali carried the
Olympic torch during opening ceremonies of the 1996
Summer Games in Atlanta. AP photo, Doug Mills.

Muslim name. By refusing to be drafted, he contributed to changes in law that
made it possible for those who are not long-time members of traditional peace
churches to claim and win conscientious objector status.

In 1971, the Supreme Court overturned Ali's conviction for refusing to be
drafted. In 1987, the California Bicentennial Foundation for the U.S. Constitution selected him as personifying the vitality of the U.S. Constitution and
Bill of Rights. In 2005, he received the Presidential Medal of Freedom and
the "Otto Hahn Peace Medal in Gold" from the United Nations Association
of Germany for his work with the U.S. civil rights movement and the United
Nations.

THE RADICAL PRIESTS

In an era marked by civil rights demonstrations and anti-Vietnam War protests, the Berrigan brothers were a part of it all. They were priests, poets, and
pacifists. In the late 1960s, they would also have ranked at or near the top of

almost anyone's list of most controversial activists. Even many of those who generally shared their opinions thought they sometimes went too far.

Daniel joined the Jesuits immediately after graduating from high school; he was ordained into the priesthood in 1952. Younger brother Philip attended college for one semester before being drafted and serving in the artillery during World War II. Deeply affected by his war experiences and by the racism he saw during his days in boot camp in the South, he entered a seminary run by the Josephites who specialized in serving African American parishes. He was ordained in 1955.

Almost immediately, Philip became active in the Civil Rights movement, marching for desegregation and participating in sit-ins and boycotts. The Josephites transferred him from the parish he served in New Orleans largely because of his militancy. In 1965, Daniel's role in organizing the antiwar Clergy Concerned About Viet Nam contributed to the decision by his religious superiors to banish him to Latin America. But if those transfers were intended to make the Berrigans think twice about being so involved in controversial issues, the strategy didn't work. While still involved in civil rights efforts, Philip became increasingly active in the peace movement. Daniel grafted economic and social justice elements onto his antiwar protests.

In 1967, Philip Berrigan joined with artist Tom Lewis, poet and teacher David Eberhardt, United Church of Christ pastor and missionary James L. Mengel, and noted theologian and Trappist monk Thomas Merton to stage one of the most dramatic antiwar protests of the era. On October 17, the men made their way to the Baltimore Customs House where they passed out copies of *Good News for Modern Man*, a popular version of the *New Testament* written in vernacular English. They also poured a mixture of their own blood and duck blood on Selective Service records.

Philip called the group's dramatic gesture a constructive one meant to protest American foreign policy. In his "Musings from Baltimore City Jail," he wrote that the protest was directed at a country "which cannot welcome its black people, cannot leave the Vietnamese people alone, cannot temper overseas economic greed, cannot but slide from the Bomb to the ABM systems."[34] But the authorities could not accept his reasoning. The "Baltimore Four," as the protesters became known, were convicted. Berrigan's sentence was six years in prison for destroying government property, but he served only a few months.

After his release on bail, Philip joined with his brother, Daniel, and seven other Catholics to stage an even more dramatic protest. In May 1968, the men entered the draft board in Catonsville, Maryland, where they removed 378 draft files and took them outside where they burned them with a homemade version of the napalm used by the American military because of its ability to inflict horrible burns on human targets. The "Catonsville Nine" issued a statement calling on their church and others to cease being silent accomplices to the government's race and war crimes.[35]

They were arrested. While awaiting trial, Daniel, along with Boston University professor emeritus Howard Zinn, undertook an unauthorized trip to Hanoi to negotiate the release of three pilots being held by the Viet Cong.[36] FBI director J. Edgar Hoover denounced Berrigan and Zinn as traitors for violating the government's policy against negotiating with North Vietnam. While they were in Vietnam, the U.S. military bombed locations where Berrigan and Zinn were known to be. But the pilots became the first American POWs to be released unharmed by North Vietnam.

Both Berrigans were convicted at their 1969 trial for burning draft records. Daniel went underground, causing him for a time to be on the FBI's "Ten Most Wanted" list, but he was eventually apprehended and served his prison sentence. After serving their sentences, both Daniel and Philip resumed their activist ways.

Philip helped found Jonah House to provide support to those in the antiwar movement. In 1973, he left the priesthood and later married Elizabeth McAlister, who worked at Jonah House. Daniel spent some time in France where he met with Thich Nhat Hanh, an exiled Vietnamese Buddhist monk and fellow peace activist.

On September 8, 1980, the Berrigans and six others trespassed at the General Electric Nuclear Missile plant in King of Prussia, Pennsylvania. They damaged nuclear warhead nose cones and poured blood over documents and files. They were arrested and charged with 10 felony and misdemeanor counts. Following 10 years of appeals, they were sentenced and then paroled in consideration of time already served. But since then, their Plowshares Movement, which takes its name from biblical verses in *Micah* and *Isaiah* that speak of turning swords into plowshares, has been involved in more than 70 similar protests in the United States and abroad.

In addition to being active in the pro-life movement, Daniel has staged or participated in protests of the 1991 Gulf War, the Kosovo War, and the U.S. invasions of Afghanistan and of Iraq. Philip's final act of protest was in December 1999 when he and others from the Plowshares Movement again engaged in an antiwar protest by banging on A-10 Warthog warplanes at an Air National Guard base. For that action, he was convicted and sentenced to 30 months in jail. He was released in December 2001 and died a year later, on December 6, 2002, at age 79.

Except for the liberal lay-edited *Commonweal*, which supported the Berrigans in frequent articles and regularly published their writings,[37] their Roman Catholic Church and most of its publications generally ignored them. Although they took care to distance themselves from the Berrigans' antiwar stance, the *Boston Globe* and the *New York Times* called their sentencing as members of the Catonsville Nine too harsh.[39] But like FBI Director Hoover, most veterans groups and many politicians, civic leaders, and average citizens thought they deserved more than the sentences they got.

Although few protests and demonstrations have ever matched those of the Berrigan brothers for drama and for divisiveness, religiously motivated demonstrations and protests are relatively common. Most of them are local, rating no more than a brief story or two in local media. Only a handful receive national attention. Instead of attracting new support for a cause or engendering outrage from opponents, protests and demonstrations tend to be met with a yawn.

Whether the Berrigans' protests contributed in any real way to the resolution of issues they cared so passionately about and for which they spent so many years in jail is open to debate. But in taking their stand, they did manage to call attention to their concerns. In doing so, they joined a long list of American religio-political activists who have had, and may be having, an impact.

Religion inspired many to join the abolition movement and support the Union during the Civil War; clergy and laypeople joined with the Rev. Martin Luther King in support of civil rights. A march in Washington in 1943 by 400 rabbis helped pave the way for more Jewish refugees from Nazi persecution to enter the United States. In the late 1970s and early 1980s, members of the Maryknoll order attracted attention for their opposition to American involvement in Nicaragua and El Salvador. Sister Gwen Hennessey and Sister Dorothy Hennessey, who live in the Dominican religious center in Dubuque, Iowa, have become well known for their protests of the Army's School of the Americas in Fort Benning, Georgia, which they and many others believe teaches torture and murder techniques to South Americans. The 2005 movie *Dead Man Walking* made Sister Helen Prejean a heroine to those who oppose the death penalty. In 2007, the United Church of Christ and the Presbyterian Church-USA announced plans to help undocumented immigrants by reviving the Sanctuary Movement that in the 1980s saw 500 Catholic, Jewish, and Protestant congregations from at least seven different denominations provide safety for political refugees from Central America who couldn't get, or couldn't wait for, legal clearance to enter the United States.

THE MONUMENT

It started with a plaque and a prayer. No sooner had Alabama Governor Guy Hunt appointed Roy Moore to replace Etowah County Circuit Judge Julius Swann, who had died in office, than Moore hung a wooden Ten Commandments plaque on the courtroom wall, just behind his bench. Almost immediately, he also began opening court sessions with a Christian prayer asking for divine guidance for jurors.

At first no one much noticed or cared, but that changed a year later with the case of two male strippers, known professionally as "Silk" and "Satin." When their case for murdering a drug addict went to trial in Judge Moore's courtroom in June 1993, their defense attorney protested the opening prayer.

The American Civil Liberties Union sent a letter to Judge Moore threatening a lawsuit if he continued to start court sessions with a prayer.

Although the ACLU took no further action at that time, Judge Moore used the incident to his advantage in his 1994 bid to win a full term as judge for the Etowah County Circuit Court. His claims that the ACLU's actions were blatant intimidation intended to undermine the moral underpinnings of the nation and the law resonated with Alabama voters. Judge Moore won in a landslide over attorney R. D. Pitts, who had unsuccessfully prosecuted the "Silk and Satin" case in Judge Moore's courtroom.

After the election, the ACLU made good on its threat by filing a lawsuit claiming that both the plaque and the prayer were unconstitutional. Although that suit was dismissed on technical grounds, newly elected Governor Fob James instructed the state's attorney general, Bill Pryor, to file suit in support of Moore. In 1996, state circuit court Judge Charles Price ruled that the plaque could remain in the courtroom, but the prayers were unconstitutional.

Immediately after the ruling, Judge Moore held a press conference to announce that he would defy the court's ruling that he must cease opening court sessions with prayer. He also told the assembled reporters that he displayed the Ten Commandments in his courtroom for a religious reason. His purpose, he said, was to affirm the Commandments' place as the moral underpinnings of American law.[39]

That assertion led Judge Price to issue a new ruling that gave Judge Moore 10 days to remove the Commandments plaque from his courtroom, but Moore again vowed to ignore the new order. He also appealed the court's decision. The Alabama Supreme Court then issued a temporary stay against the ruling, but never actually ruled on the merits of the case.

In 1999, at the urging of the Christian Family Association, Judge Moore announced from his Etowah County courtroom that he was entering the race for the position of chief justice of the Alabama Supreme Court. During his campaign, he promised to use his position as chief justice to ensure that God would not be banished from public life.

Again the message struck a responsive chord with voters. In spite of receiving little support from the business community or the Republican Party, both of whom generally favored the incumbent Harold See, Judge Moore easily won first the primary, and then the general election against Sharon Yates.

Chief Justice Moore was sworn in on January 15, 2001. He immediately began planning a display much grander than the plaque that adorned his courtroom. Late on the night of July 31, 2001, Chief Justice Moore oversaw the installation of his monument to the moral underpinnings of the law in the rotunda of the state judicial building. The 5,280-pound granite monument was three feet wide, three feet deep, and four feet tall. On its base were quotes from the Declaration of Independence, the national anthem, and several of the nation's founding fathers. On top, as its crowning element, were two tablets inscribed with the Ten Commandments.

The next morning, Chief Justice Moore called a press conference in the central rotunda to proclaim that the monument was his response to a cry from the people for an official acknowledgment of the God who is the foundation for the nation and its laws. At Chief Justice Moore's invitation, Coral Ridge Ministries, an evangelical Christian organization that had helped pay for Moore's appeal of Judge Price's ruling, was the only organization allowed to film the installation and unveiling. Coral Ridge Ministries used its proceeds from sale of its video to cover legal expenses that Moore incurred in the ensuing court case, titled *Glassroth v. Moore*.[40]

That case began on October 31, 2001, when the Alabama ACLU, Americans United for Separation of Church and State, the Southern Poverty Law Center, and assorted other organizations filed suit in the U.S. District Court for the Middle District of Alabama. The monument, they claimed, violated the First Amendment's Establishment Clause.[41]

Moore argued in court that he would not remove the monument because doing so would force him to violate the Alabama Constitution whose preamble prescribes a duty to invoke "the favor and guidance of almighty God" if justice is to prevail. That means, he continued, that one "must first recognize the source from which all morality springs." His intent, he said, was to mark "the beginning of the restoration of the moral foundation of law to our people" and a "return to the knowledge of God in our land."[42] But U.S. District Judge Myron Thompson disagreed. On November 18, 2002, he ruled that the monument must be removed because it violated the Establishment Clause of the First Amendment.

In another context, Moore's monument might have passed constitutional muster. A carving of Moses, flanked by Confucius and Solomon, adorns the exterior of the building in Washington, D.C., that houses the Supreme Court of the United States; the courtroom itself features friezes of 18 lawgivers including Solomon, Mohammed, and Augustus Caesar. In the 1984 case of *Lynch v. Donnelly*, the U.S. Supreme Court ruled that a Christmas display that included a manger scene was constitutional because the religious figures were surrounded by secular figures of snowmen and Santa Claus.

But, as Judge Thompson explained in his ruling in the case of *Glassroth v. Moore*,

If all Chief Justice Moore had done were to emphasize the Ten Commandments' historical and educational importance ... this court would have a different case before it.... But the Chief Justice ... went far, far beyond. He installed a two-and-a-half ton monument in the most prominent place in a government building, managed with dollars from all state taxpayers, with the specific purpose and effect of establishing a permanent recognition of the "sovereignty of god," the Judeo-Christian God, over all citizens in this country, regardless of each taxpaying citizen's individual personal beliefs or lack thereof.[43]

Judge Thompson's ruling required Moore to remove the monument by January 3, 2003, but stayed his order after Moore appealed. On June 4, 2003, the Eleventh Circuit Court of Appeals upheld the lower court's ruling. It also noted that different Christian traditions use different wordings and numberings for the Commandments. Therefore, "choosing which version … to display can [also] have religious endorsement implications."[44]

With that ruling in hand, Judge Thompson ordered Moore to remove the monument from public areas of the state judicial building by August 20, but Moore remained defiant. Moore's intransigence could have cost the state a $5,000 fine for each day after the deadline that the monument remained in place, but on August 21, the eight other justices on the Alabama Supreme Court unanimously overruled Moore and ordered the monument removed.

The next day, the Alabama Judicial Inquiry Commission filed a complaint against Moore with the Alabama Court of the Judiciary whose members included the governor, lieutenant governor, judges, lawyers, and other legal experts. That move had the effect of suspending Moore from his position as chief justice pending a full hearing by the Court of the Judiciary. The monument was moved to a nonpublic area of the judicial building on August 27. Then, on November 13, the Court of the Judiciary issued its decision. Judge Moore had violated the Alabama Canons of Judicial Ethics. Because he had refused to obey court decisions and indicated he would continue to do so, his contempt of court meant that the penalty should be his removal from office.

The monument was finally removed from state property on July 19, 2004, but Moore still refused to give up. He would, he said, continue his battle to give proper credit to the Ten Commandments by becoming a candidate in the 2006 gubernatorial race on the Republican ticket. But this time the voters were not with him. Moore lost in the primary by a 2-to-1 margin.

Although Moore lost his court case and ultimately failed to win an elected government position, he always had, and still has, many supporters. Surveys conducted during the first court case showed that 88 percent of Alabama citizens supported him; they elected him to judgeships twice; and when the Eleventh Circuit Court of Appeals announced its decision, thousands of supporters, including the Rev. Jerry Falwell, rallied in his support on the judicial building lawn. After his failed bid to become Alabama's governor, Moore began taking his monument and his message on the road. People still show up to see his monument and hear him speak at churches, veterans' organizations, and other venues around the country.

Moore's supporters generally believe that the rulings against his plaque, his courtroom prayers, and his monument both undermine what they see as the Christian underpinnings of public morality and good government and also violate the Free Exercise clause of the First Amendment. To them, the court decisions that went against him are just another example of what they call "activist judges" who ignore the clear will of the people.

But like the organizations that filed the original lawsuits against Moore, many other religious people see it differently. They point to testimony given in the original court case showing that both lawyers and citizens of different faiths changed their work habits or their path to avoid the monument. Both Moore's religious intent in displaying it and the people who gathered there to pray created the appearance of state endorsement of a particular faith—and that violates the Establishment Clause.

In the last 50 years, as the nation's religious diversity has increased because of the Free Exercise clause, cases like *Glassroth v. Moore* that arise under the Establishment Clause have become more common than they once were. The Mount Soledad cross in a San Diego city park has been in the news and in court for 20 years. The administration of President George W. Bush asked the United States Supreme Court to hear the appeal of a similar case in which the Ninth Circuit Court of Appeals ruled that a cross on federal land on the California-Nevada border is unconstitutional. In November 2008, the high court agreed to hear a case from Utah dealing with the request of Summum to have a monument to the tiny sect's "Seven Aphorisms" placed alongside one to the Ten Commandments in Pioneer Park in Pleasant Grove, Utah. Cases like these will most likely continue to pop up and cause controversy for years to come.

Like cases involving school prayer and the recitation of the Pledge of Allegiance (this chapter, "Soldiers of the Lord"), cases like those that revolve around religious symbols on public property underscore the inherent tension between the Free Exercise and Establishment Clauses. While the founding fathers were intent on guaranteeing the freedom to believe as one chooses, they also wanted to guard against the problems they saw as arising from official government involvement in religion. But they gave precious little guidance on how to adjudicate the boundaries between the Free Exercise Clause and the Establishment Clause. Therefore, regardless of how a court rules in an individual case, the losing side will very likely find the decision scandalous.

GOD DAMN AMERICA

The Rev. Jeremiah Wright earned his theological degrees from the University of Chicago Divinity School and the United Theological Seminary in Dayton, Ohio. He had taught classes at Chicago Theological Seminary and Garrett Evangelical Seminary, and served on the Board of Trustees for Chicago Theological Seminary and the Board of Directors of Evangelical Health

Systems and for the Black Theology Project. For his work, he had received seven honorary doctorates, including ones from his alma maters and from Lutheran-affiliated Valparaiso University. When he retired from the parish ministry in February 2008, Northwestern University announced plans to award him his eighth honorary degree.

But before that could happen, sermons he had delivered years earlier triggered a scandal with serious political implications. On March 13, 2008, ABC news reported that on September 16, 2001—the Sunday after 9/11—the Rev. Wright had said in his sermon that the United States had brought on Al Qaeda's attacks through its own terrorist activities. "We bombed Nagasaki, and we nuked far more than the thousands in New York and the Pentagon, and we never batted an eye," he told his congregation.[45]

To make matters worse, two years earlier he had said, "The government wants us to sing 'God Bless America,' … but I say God damn America … for killing innocent people.… God damn America for treating our citizens as less than human. God damn America for as long as she acts like she is God and she is supreme."[46] Both the Rev. Martin Luther King and Malcolm X (Chapter 4, "A Monster and/or a Martyr") had said much the same thing about American foreign and domestic policies, but that was a long time ago. Even those who remembered were willing to pass their comments off as outbursts of righteous indignation coming, as they did, in the midst of a struggle for equal rights for black Americans.

Televangelist Pat Robertson said the events of 9/11 were a sign of God's righteous anger at a society so morally lax as to condone abortion and homosexuality.[48] Most Americans responded with little more than a yawn.

The Rev. Wright's words might also have been excused or ignored except for the fact that for 36 years he had been the pastor of Chicago's Trinity United Church of Christ, whose best known parishioner was Democratic presidential hopeful Barack Obama. Obama had credited Wright with bringing him into the faith; Wright had officiated at his marriage and had baptized his children. The title for Obama's memoir *The Audacity of Hope* came from a sermon by Wright.

In the context of a presidential race being fought against the backdrop of President George W. Bush's War on Terrorism and U.S. policy in Iraq and the Middle East, the Rev. Wright's words seemed to many to be unpatriotic—maybe even un-American. To many, they also seemed downright un-Christian.

During his time as pastor of Trinity, Wright had become well known for delivering sermons in which he parsed biblical passages line by line. His preaching was as firmly rooted in the Bible as that of other prominent clergy who, from time to time, said outrageous things.[49] But unlike them, his interpretation was rooted in black liberation theology.

Like Wright himself, black liberation theology was a product of the 1960s. During the struggle for civil rights, its twin messages that blacks can be proud of their race because people of all races are equally lovely in God's eye and that God, through Jesus, stands with and for the poor and oppressed found a receptive audience. Black liberation theology helped many inner-city congregations like Trinity grow by keeping within the Christian fold young blacks who otherwise might have joined the much more Afro-centric and separatist Nation of Islam (Chapter 4, "A Monster and/or a Martyr") or simply have dropped out of what they had come to believe was a "white" and a "slave" religion.[50]

In the 1960s, most Christians were willing to tolerate black liberation theology as, at worst, a reasonable if somewhat misguided way to offer hope to African Americans in their struggle to gain full political and social rights. But 40 years later, the theology espoused by the Rev. Wright, and apparently embraced by his parishioners, seemed less benign.

Although the United Church of Christ, Trinity's parent denomination, was overwhelmingly a white, middle-class denomination, Trinity, though a multiracial congregation, was comprised mainly of blacks, many of whom came from lower socioeconomic groups. The church operated a variety of social service programs catering to Chicago's poor and disadvantaged. In his sermons, however, Wright was as likely to rail against blacks who failed to take responsibility for problems of their own making as he was to condemn exploitation of them by wealthier citizens of any race or by the government. But in the context of the 2008 election campaign, both the congregation's motto, "Unashamedly black and unapologetically Christian," and the fact that the congregation counted among its membership many influential black politicians and business leaders, sparked fears of the black power, black nationalist, and black separatist movements that had seemed so dangerous in the 1960s and 1970s (Chapter 4, "A Monster and/or a Martyr"; this chapter, "The Greatest").

But at its core, the flap over the Rev. Wright's sermons was not about Wright and his theology. It was about Barack Obama. For him, his 20 years as a member of Trinity and his close association with the Rev. Wright, whom he had appointed to his African American Religious Leadership Committee, raised questions about his policies, his judgment, and his religion.

Both his Democratic primary opponent Hillary Clinton and Republicans had long contended that Obama was too inexperienced and naïve to be president. But to those criticisms religious and political conservatives now began to insinuate that Obama was really a closet racist whose interests and policies would hurt true, *that is* white, Americans, their values, and their country. After all, his pastor had said, "God damn America." With a funny name, a Kenyan father, and a bit of early education in an Islamic school, Obama might not really be a Christian. He certainly couldn't possibly have America's interests at heart. He didn't even wear a flag pin in his lapel.

While conservative political voices were generally more strident, Democrats, too, found the episode troubling. In a tight race between Obama and Hillary

Clinton to become the presidential candidate on the Democratic ticket, Democrats worried about the effect of Wright's scandalous words on their chances in November.

Bloggers of all stripes joined in. As facts, lies, half-truths, rumors, speculations, and allegations swirled around him, Obama and his campaign staff went into damage control mode. On March 18, Obama gave a major speech at Philadelphia's Convention Center in which he tried to put Wright's words in the context of the black experience while simultaneously distancing himself from his pastor's more radical comments and laying claim to his basic message that he was the candidate best suited to bridge racial, cultural, and religious divides that had for too long bedeviled the country.

The speech might have laid the scandal to rest had it not been for the Rev. Wright.

The next day, Wright went out of his way to call Obama's speech unfair to him, politically motivated, and insincere. He appeared on television talk shows and gave speeches, many of them containing new, and to many, equally outrageous, comments.[51]

On March 28, Obama removed the Rev. Wright's name from the list of members of his African American Religious Leadership Committee, a move that apparently fueled Wright's anger. On April 28, Wright told the National Press Club in Washington, D.C., that the attacks on him were also attacks on black people and their religion. In a speech the next day, Obama called Wright's performance at the Press Club a self-aggrandizing spectacle. Wright's comments, he said, were nothing more than angry rants with no basis in reality.[51]

On May 1, Northwestern University dropped its plans to give Wright his eighth honorary degree. At the end of the month, Obama announced that he was no longer a member of Trinity United Church of Christ.

Even as Obama was dealing with fallout caused by words his pastor had spoken years earlier, the Republican presidential candidate, John McCain, found himself answering questions about his relationship with televangelists Rod Parsley and Ted Hagee, whose support for him raised questions about McCain's judgment and his international policy similar to those that Wright's comments raised about Obama.[52] But distancing himself from a couple of clergymen who supported him and whose rhetoric was common in conservative Protestant circles was much easier for McCain to do than it was for Obama to lay to rest questions raised by his long-standing association with a pastor whose kind of political rhetoric had not been heard from Christian clergy since the 1960s and 1970s (this chapter, "The Radical Priests").

Although the scandal had the potential to wreck Obama's political aspirations, that didn't happen. He wrested his party's nomination from Hillary Clinton, who at the outset of the campaign was expected to win easily. During the presidential campaign he agreed to let Rick Warren, pastor of the

Saddleback mega-church in California and popular *Purpose Driven Life* author, interview him about his religion in a joint televised appearance with his Republican opponent John McCain. He sent letters and emissaries to conservative pastors.[53] He trimmed the Republican margins in suburbs, among so-called blue-collar "Reagan Republicans" and even among evangelical Christians by recruiting workers, opening campaign offices, and making campaign appearances in Republican strongholds. McCain's selection of Sarah Palin as his vice presidential running mate energized the Republican conservative religious core, but did not play well with independent voters. When the stock market crashed in October, McCain was doomed. In the end, even Karl Rove, who masterminded the elections of George W. Bush and other Republicans for over a decade, had to concede that Obama ran a masterful campaign, out organizing and out maneuvering McCain and the Republicans during the election as he had done with Clinton and her supporters in the primaries.[54]

In the end, the Rev. Wright, for all his real accomplishments as pastor of Trinity United Church of Christ, became little more than a footnote in an historic election. Barack Hussein Obama made history. The man with a white mother, a black Kenyan father, a funny Afro–Middle Eastern name, some education in an Islamic school in Indonesia, and a seemingly radical and unpatriotic pastor in Chicago won the 2008 U.S. presidential election.

FOR FURTHER READING

Aman, John. 2004, July. It's about God. *Christianity Today*, p. 58.

Berrigan, Dan. 1968, April 26. My brother, the witness. *Commonweal*, p. 646.

Berrigan, Dan. 1968, September 27. From the Catonsville Nine: Greetings. *Commonweal*, pp. 195–196.

Berrigan, Philip. 1967, November 17. Musings from Baltimore City Jail. *Commonweal*, pp. 180–182.

Berrigan, Philip. 1968, December 6. Berrigan from jail: "Truth creates its own room." *Commonweal*, pp. 333–334.

The Berrigan Brothers: They rob draft boards. 1968, June 7. *Time*, p. 62.

Cronin, Mary M. 2006, Autumn. The liberty to argue freely: Nineteenth-century obscenity prosecutions and the emergence of modern libertarian free speech discourse. *Journalism Monographs* 8(3): 190–195.

Dart, John. 2003, September 6. Court orders judge's monument moved. *Christian Century*, pp. 12–13.

Eastland, Terry, ed. 1995. *Religious liberty in the Supreme Court: The cases that define the debate over church and state.* Grand Rapids, MI: Wm. B. Eerdmans Publishing Company, pp. 25–58.

Franklin, Robert M. 2007, May 31. Obama's faith: A civil and social gospel. *Sightings*. Chicago: Martin Marty Center at the University of Chicago Divinity School.

Gorski, Eric. 2008, March 18. Message of Obama pastor forged in civil rights movement. *Atlanta Journal and Constitution*. Retrieved May 23, 2008, from http://www.ajc.com/news/content/news/stopries/2008/03/18/wright_0319.html.

Green, Joshua. 2005, October. Roy and his rock. *The Atlantic*, pp. 70–71, 74–76, 78–82.

Haggard, Ted. 2004, April. Decalogue debacle. *Christianity Today*, p. 98.

High, Stanley. 1940, September 14. Armageddon, Inc. *Saturday Evening Post*, pp. 18–19, 50, 52–54, 58.

Levy, Leonard W. 1993. *Blasphemy: Verbal offense against the sacred, from Moses to Salman Rushdie.* Chapel Hill: University of North Carolina Press, pp. 413–423.

McCarten, John. 1939, June. Father Coughlin: Holy medicine man. *American Mercury*, pp. 129–141.

Noonan, John T., Jr., and Edward McGlynn Gaffney, Jr. 2001. *Religious freedom: History, cases, and other materials on the interaction of religion and government*, 2nd ed. New York: Foundation Press, pp. 212, 378–391.

Olsen, Jack. 1961, April 11. Cassius Clay: The man, the Muslim, the mystery: Part I, A case of conscience. *Sports Illustrated*, pp. 88–90, 92, 95–96, 101–102, 104.

Packer, George. 2008, March 31. Comment: Native son. *New Yorker*, p. 39.

Plimpton, George. 1964, June. Miami notebook: Cassius Clay and Malcolm X. *Harper's Magazine*, pp. 54–61.

Ryan, John A. 1938, December 30. Anti-Semitism in the air. *Commonweal*, pp. 260–262.

Sanneh, Kelefa. 2008, April 7. Project Trinity. *New Yorker*, pp. 30–36.

Chapter 7

RITUALS THAT RANKLE

James Madison and Thomas Jefferson were the architects of American religious freedom. But of the two, it is Jefferson's commentary that has shaped both public opinion and the law. About the freedom to believe whatever one will and to worship however one sees fit, he wrote that the free exercise of religion was "meant to comprehend, within the mantle of its protection, the Jew and the Gentile, the Christian and Mahometan, the Hindoo, and Infidel of every denomination."[1]

In arguing against an establishment of religion, Jefferson wrote:

[T]o suffer the civil magistrate to intrude his powers into the field of opinion, and to restrain the profession or propagation of principles on supposition of their ill tendency, is a dangerous fallacy.... [I]t is time enough for the rightful purposes of civil government for its officers to interfere when principles break out into overt acts against peace and good order.[2]

Hidden within those words lies a problem at least as severe as any that arise from the inherent tension between the Free Exercise Clause and the Establishment Clause. In giving government tacit permission to regulate—to interfere with—behavior, Jefferson provided a way to interfere with the free exercise of religion by regulating—even outlawing—behaviors that are an integral part of public worship.

In Jefferson's time, there were a handful of Jews, somewhat more Roman Catholics, and Protestant majority of Christians divided among a dozen or so denominations in the United States. Today there are members of at least 1,000 world and alternative religions who worship in this country alongside Christians from over 200 denominations and sects. Just as beliefs differ greatly both among and within religions, so, in some cases, do their manners of worship. The scandals that arise from religious rituals—manners of worship—that differ markedly from the mainstream are the subject of this chapter.

When Jefferson wrote that "Hindoos" and "Mahometans" should have religious freedom, the idea of extending protection to them was a radical notion.

Jefferson most likely picked those religions simply because they were as exotic, as foreign to Americans' religious practices, as any he could have imagined. But in promising them religious freedom while simultaneously inviting government interference with religious behavior, he could not have known that 200 years later American Christians in Michigan and New Jersey would find it scandalous that their Muslim neighbors were building mosques from which the call to worship would emanate five times a day.[3]

Whatever Jefferson may have known about the Hindu and Muslim religions most likely came from books. In his time there were no Hindus or Muslims in the country. But there were Indians with their own religions. There were also blacks who had practiced their own religions in Africa before they were brought to this country as slaves. Yet Jefferson didn't see fit to include their faiths in his list of protected religions; they still tend to be overlooked or dismissed as somehow not "real religions." The "scandalous" practices of Native Americans seeking to freely exercise their freedom of religion are the subject of "The Paiute Messiah" and "A Casualty in the War on Drugs" in this chapter. "The Chicken Wars" is about a Cuban immigrant's quest to set up a church where people could practice a religion brought to the Caribbean by slaves the way they once had practiced the religion in Africa.

It isn't just minority faiths of ethnic and racial minorities that cause scandals. "Snakes and Strychnine" tells of a Christian sect whose religious practices most Christians find both bizarre and dangerous. The chapter's final section, "Dancing by Moonlight," tells of a tiny minority of people within the military whose manner of public worship many Christians considered almost as scandalous and dangerous as the name of the religion they practiced.

THE PAIUTE MESSIAH

The Buffalo were gone. Their children had been packed up and sent off to Indian schools where they were forbidden to speak their language, or learn about or even speak of their own culture. They had been herded into reservations where they were expected to farm, sometimes by raising crops for which the land was ill suited. When the rains didn't come and the crops failed, the government blamed their predicament on their own stupidity and laziness and cut their supplementary rations in half.

But their plight might be temporary. Wovoka said so.[4] When word of his vision spread through the West, tribes from Texas to the Dakotas sent emissaries to Nevada to learn more from the Paiute Chief himself. Among them was Kicking Bear, a Minneconjous, who, on October 9, 1890, in the Moon of the Drying Grass, brought the news to Sitting Bull, the great chief of the Lakota Sioux.

Wovoka, Kicking Bear said, had a vision in which the Great Spirit had told him that he was the Messiah, come back to earth as an Indian. Because white men had killed the first Messiah, he would help them set things right. A flood of lava would destroy white people and their civilization, but it would spare the Indians. The Indians who had died would arise and return to their land. They need fear the white man no longer. If they wore special shirts, the white man's bullets would not hurt them. The buffalo would also come back. All they had to do was dance the sacred dance.[5]

Sitting Bull doubted that the dead could come back to life, and, in spite of Kicking Bear's assurances, he worried about what government agents might do if his people embraced the new religion. But he also knew that his people wanted to join in the sacred Ghost Dance lest they be left out when the wondrous things Wovoka prophesied came to pass. In spite of his concerns, he had no real objection to the Ghost Dance.[6]

Thus, during the Moon of Falling Leaves, Kicking Bear taught the simple, shuffling round dance to Sitting Bull's people at Standing Rock. By mid-November, normal daily activities on the Sioux Reservation came to a halt. Children stayed home from school; no one worked in the fields. Everyone was dancing the Ghost Dance.

The religion of the Ghost Dance was, at its core, a peaceful one that differed from conventional Christianity only in the nature of its ritual and the events surrounding the Second Coming. Like the Christian Messiah, Wovoka

The Sioux danced the Ghost Dance in anticipation of the Second Coming of the Messiah, but the public and the military found the dance scandalous and dangerous. Library of Congress, *Illustrated London News*.

had told his followers that they must always do what is right; they should not lie, or steal, or fight. Like prophets from other millennial sects that sprang up during the Second Great Awakening earlier in the century, Wovoka foretold of a time when God's enemies would meet their doom and his faithful followers would inherit their just reward.[7]

At the time, however, nothing about the Ghost Dance seemed peaceful or Christian. To the press and the public, it fed into the widespread belief that efforts to civilize and Christianize the Indians had been in vain. As more and more Indians left the Pine Ridge agency to join with other dancers throughout the Badlands of Dakota Territory, agents of the Bureau of Indian Affairs became increasingly fearful of what they saw only as dangerous savages. To them, the Ghost Dance looked like a pernicious, fanatical war dance.[8]

First, Maj. James McLaughlin ordered Indian police to forcibly remove Kicking Bear from the reservation. Then, in response to a November 20 order from the Bureau of Indian Affairs, he compiled a list of Indian "fomenters of disturbance."[9] No sooner had the list been telegraphed to Bureau headquarters in Washington, D.C., than the Bureau sent word to General Nelson Miles at military headquarters in Chicago that he should take action against those on the list.

One of those "fomenters of disturbance" on the list was Sitting Bull. But Miles knew that using troops to arrest the chief would cause trouble. To avoid a confrontation, he called upon William "Buffalo Bill" Cody who had known Sitting Bull for years and was generally on friendly terms with him. Buffalo Bill was willing to help by persuading Sitting Bull to travel to Chicago for a conference with Miles. McLaughlin, however, vetoed the plan, so Miles ordered McLaughlin to capture and hold Sitting Bull. McLaughlin complied by sending a contingent of Indian police to find and arrest the chief.[10]

Early on the morning of December 15, Bullhead, an Indian lieutenant loyal to the government agents, led the native police to Sitting Bull's cabin near Standing Rock. But when Catch-the-Bear, who was both loyal to Sitting Bull and an old enemy of Bullhead, realized what was happening, he pulled out his gun and shot Bullhead. As he fell, Bullhead tried to shoot Catch-the-Bear, but the bullet hit Sitting Bull. Red Tomahawk, a sergeant in the native police, also fired, killing Sitting Bull with a single shot to his head.

Within minutes a fight broke out between Indians loyal to Sitting Bull and Indians in the native police. By the time it was over, 12 men were dead and three more lay wounded. Only the arrival of troops prevented further blood-shed, but their arrival did little to defuse the situation. As word of Sitting Bull's death spread across the Plains, panic ensued.

Fearing what might happen, the military sent out a detachment under Major S. M. Whitside with orders to round up the Indians and bring them back to the agency. Of special concern was Big Foot, a Minneconjous chief who was also on the troublemaker list.

By that time Big Foot and many of the other Indians were already heading back to the agency where they hoped they would be safe. Therefore, they readily complied with Whitside's orders to surrender their weapons and head back to the agency. But taking no chances, Whitside called for reenforcements from another contingent of the Seventh Cavalry.[11]

On the night of December 28, Big Foot and his band of 356 men, women, and children who had camped on the bank of Wounded Knee Creek were surrounded by 470 men from a party of scouts and Whitside's men from the Seventh Cavalry. During the night, a second contingent under Colonel James W. Forsyth arrived and took charge. With Forsyth's Hotchkiss guns trained on them, the Indians, who had already surrendered their weapons, were again ordered to give up their guns. But the order produced only a few more weapons, so the troops began a pat down for concealed weapons.

Indians say that Black Coyote, who was deaf, raised his rifle to give it to Forsyth's men.[12] The troops saw it differently; however it happened, there was a crash. Guns started firing. By some counts, at least 300 Sioux, many of them women and children, were killed on the morning of December 29, 1890. At least 60 others were wounded; many of those died later from their wounds. At least 25 soldiers also died, most likely the victims of friendly fire.

When the Indians defeated the Seventh Cavalry and General William Custer at the Battle of Big Horn, the press and the public called it a massacre. When the Seventh Cavalry under Forsyth defeated the Indians, they called it the Battle of Wounded Knee.

After Wounded Knee, a disheartened Wovoka counseled his followers to accept the white man's ways.[13] He again began using his Christian name of Jack Wilson. For America's native people, Wounded Knee marked the end of their 200-year quest to hold on to whatever remained of their land and their culture.

At the time, most white Americans saw their government's actions as both necessary and justifiable. There were, however, a few who raised concerns about the wisdom and the need to deal forcibly with Indian practitioners of what even they conceded was a strange, new religion.

In the 1891 report of the U.S. Commissioner of Indian Affairs, Dr. Valentine McGillicuddy, a former Bureau of Indian Affairs agent, was quoted as having offered this advice to military officials intent on taking action against the dancing Sioux:

> I should let the dance continue. The coming of the troops has frightened the Indians. If the Seventh-Day Adventists prepare their ascension robes for the second coming of the Savior, the United States Army is not put in motion to prevent them: Why should not the Indians have the same privilege?[14]

With Wounded Knee the Ghost Dance religion faded away. But as Dr. McGillicuddy realized, it would have died out of its own accord as so many other millennial religions have done after their prophesies have failed. While his words went unheeded at the time, both the Ghost Dance and his counsel concerning it stand as a cautionary tale.

Then as now, Americans and their government find it hard to exercise patience and a modicum of cultural sensitivity when confronted with a religion that they find scandalous and just possibly dangerous. A hundred years after Wounded Knee, Native Americans still find it hard to practice their religion free from government interference (this chapter, "A Casualty in the War on Drugs"). At the time the government ignored Adventists who gathered to await the Second Coming, but a hundred years later a standoff between an Adventist sect and the National Guard ended in a fiery inferno in Waco, Texas (Chapter 8, "Virgins and Guns").

SNAKES AND STRYCHNINE

There are reports of the practice of snake handling from 1903 in North Carolina and 1906 in California. At about the same time, James Miller brought it to Sand Mountain in northeastern Alabama. But many historians of American religion say the real beginning was in 1909 when George Went Hensley introduced snake handling to members of his small church in Grasshopper Valley, Tennessee. From Tennessee and Alabama the practice spread throughout the Southeast, and then into the Midwest and Canada.

At first many of the churches where snake handling was practiced were Pentecostal ones affiliated either with the Church of God or the Church of God of Prophecy, both of which frequently carried articles about the practice and its practitioners in their publications.[15] By the 1920s, however, both denominations had foresworn the practice. Therefore, strictly speaking, today there is no snake-handling denomination. The churches that practice snake handling are fiercely independent ones, linked together primarily by kinship, proximity, and shared belief.

That belief stems from a literal interpretation of Mark 16:17-18 where, in the King James version that the churches use, Jesus tells his followers:

> And these signs shall follow them that believe; In my name shall they cast out devils; they shall speak with new tongues; They shall take up serpents; and if they drink any deadly thing, it shall not hurt them; they shall lay hands on the sick, and they shall recover.

Because the churches take their mandate from the same Bible verse, the practice is similar in all churches. Worship begins with the singing of traditional gospel songs, followed by a sermon that is part explication of a Bible passage and part personal testimonial. More singing and testimonials follow. As their intensity increases, congregation members begin dancing ecstatically or speaking in tongues. When the spirit seems right, the minister or an elder of the congregation takes a rattlesnake or other poisonous snake indigenous to the region from its cage and holds it aloft so that the snake's tongue can just reach his face. After that, other men and women from the congregation may handle the snake. Sometimes instead of, or in addition to, handling the snake, they may pass their hands through the flames of a blowtorch or drink from a small vial of poison, usually strychnine.

For those who belong to snake-handling congregations, the snake handling, the fire, and the poison are both a demonstration to God of their faith in Him and a test of that faith. Most of the time no one is hurt. But the practices are inherently dangerous, so mishaps and fear of mishaps can cause problems.

That happened in Grasshopper Valley in 1919. When a large rattlesnake bit Garland Defriese, the congregation foreswore snake handling even though Defriese did not die from the bite. Some church members, however, concluded that Defriese had been bitten because he was a "backslider," or one who had lost faith in God or somehow become enmeshed in sin.[17] They and their pastor moved on, establishing a new congregation some miles away.

Splits of that kind occur from time to time. Each of them may be a scandal within a local congregation. But snake-handling congregations are tiny ones, located in remote rural areas. Their members are fundamentalist Christians who generally try to limit their contacts with what they consider the sinful, secular world. Most also rely on faith healing instead of traditional medical care. Therefore, both their practices and deaths from them, when they occur, generally escape notice.

However, on occasion outsiders find out. When that happens, a sheriff's department or the local police often find themselves compelled to react to a practice that their neighbors find both scandalous and dangerous. One of the first scandals of that kind happened less than a year after Lewis Ford managed to convince *Life* magazine to do a story that for the first time brought the "serpent handlers" of Appalachia to national attention.[18]

That scandal happened in 1945, just a few years after Tom Harden, the son of one of Hensley's first converts to snake handling, reintroduced snake handling into Grasshopper Valley at his Dolley Pond Church of God with Signs Following. Ironically, it came as the result of the death from a snakebite of Lewis Ford. The media took notice of his death and of the hundreds of people who attended his funeral.[19] When members of the congregation tried to hold a revival service in Chattanooga, the police arrested Harden and Hensley, his mentor, and took them to jail. After a hearing before Judge Martin A. Fleming, both men refused to pay their fine on religious grounds and were assigned to a work gang to pay off the fine at the rate of a dollar a day. On appeal, Judge Frank Darwin dismissed the charges. However, the next year

Judge Hamilton S. Burnett of the Tennessee Court of Appeals ruled that Ford had not died accidentally, but had purposefully handled the snake—so his widow was not entitled to collect on his insurance policy.

Between Lewis's death in 1945 and the Tennessee court ruling, there were at least six more deaths from snake handling: a pregnant woman and her unborn child in West Virginia; a man in Daisy, Tennessee; and three men in Cleveland, Tennessee, home of the Church of God, to which Hensley had belonged and which once had embraced snake handling. Both local and national media reported the deaths.[20]

On February 28, 1947, by a vote of 70 to 0 the Tennessee legislature passed a law prohibiting the handling of snakes. Other states followed suit. So did the city of Durham, North Carolina. The Durham law was a response to an interstate convention of snake handlers that was planned for the city even as court cases against Benjamin Massey and Hartman Bunn for engaging in the practice were pending in the North Carolina Supreme Court.

During the winter of 1947–1948, the convention got heavy coverage in the *Durham Morning Herald* and *Durham Evening Sun*.[21] Although many of the more than 1,000 people who attended the convention were local, most area residents found snake handling scandalous. At a time when mixing of the races in any setting was both rare and generally frowned upon, they also found it scandalous to see white people and black people worshipping together. But at first Police Chief H. E. King did nothing other than to point out to local residents that there were no laws against using blowtorches or drinking poison, and to remind worshippers of the local ordinance against snake handling. However, when the worshippers ignored his warning that snake handling was illegal, King ordered his troops to move in and make arrests.

Bunn was fined $50, which he refused to pay. On appeal, he told the court that he and his followers were willing to follow reasonable ordinances such as ones that required snakes to be kept a certain distance from a crowd, but they could not comply with an ordinance that sought to overrule a command from God.[22] The court, however, ruled that religiously inspired behaviors, unlike religious beliefs, are not protected by the First Amendment. Thus, Bunn's conviction and fine were upheld.

Over the next few years, other cases popped up in Alabama, Georgia, Kentucky, North Carolina, and Tennessee. In all of them, the snake-handling defendant was convicted and ordered to pay a small fine or serve a short jail sentence. Although Bunn threatened to take his case to the United States Supreme Court, that didn't happen. The closest the Supreme Court ever came to hearing one happened almost 30 years later when Liston Pack and other leaders of the Dolley Pond Church were arrested after two congregation members died from drinking strychnine.

In 1975, after a trial court in Tennessee ruled that Liston Pack and other leaders of the Dolley Pond Church must abide by an order enjoining them from handling snakes as part of their worship service, Pack appealed the decision. In a 5-0 decision for the court, Justice Joe Henry ruled against Pack saying, "the state has the right to guard against the unnecessary creation of widows and orphans."[23] Pack again appealed, this time to the state Supreme Court, where he lost again. Although that court acknowledged that "to forbid snake handling is to remove the theological heart" of the church, the court affirmed its finding in the 1948 case of *Harden v. State* that the state and the nation have an overriding "interest in having a strong, healthy, robust, taxpaying citizenry capable of self-support and of bearing arms and adding to the resources and reserves of manpower." Because of the state's interest in protecting public health and safety, the court concluded that snake handling was "too fraught with danger to permit its pursuit in the frenzied atmosphere of an emotional church service."[24]

With the help of the American Civil Liberties Union, Pack appealed that ruling to the United States Supreme Court. The court, however, declined to hear the case. Without a ruling from the nation's highest court, the rulings from state courts still stand.

If the United States Supreme Court were to hear a case, it might or might not agree with the conclusion of state courts that handling snakes as part of a worship service is unprotected by the First Amendment to the United States Constitution. The verdict would most likely depend on the wording of the law the defendant was said to have broken.

If snake handlers were accused of breaking a general law like the ones some states and many municipalities have that simply prohibit the keeping of poisonous snakes and other exotic animals, and if the Court were to follow the precedent it set in the 1991 case of *Employment Division v. Smith* (this chapter, "A Casualty of the War on Drugs"), the Court would undoubtedly uphold the conviction. If, however, the law specifically targeted snake handling in worship services as the laws in some states do,[25] the Supreme Court would more likely follow the precedent of *Church of Lukumi Babalu Aye, Inc. v. City of Hialeah, Florida* (this chapter, "Chicken Wars") in ruling that the law was an unconstitutional interference with the snake handlers' religious freedom.

But even if the Supreme Court were to give First Amendment protection to the handling of snakes during worship services, the ruling would be unlikely to help widows like Mrs. Ford collect insurance benefits if the policy were carefully crafted to exclude the paying of benefits in cases where the decedent knowingly participated in practices a reasonable person would consider inherently dangerous. Neither would a ruling protecting snake handling necessarily have any effect on cases like the 1991 one that saw Glen Summerford convicted of attempted murder of his wife, who claimed in court that she had been bitten when her husband forced her, against her will, to reach into the cage of poisonous snakes he kept for use during services at their Sand Mountain, Alabama, church.[26]

Whatever the outcome of court cases may be, the decision is unlikely to have much effect on true believers. In spite of convictions in courts of law and in the court of public opinion, the practice has continued unabated for over a century. So the scandalous practice of snake handling invites consideration of whether the government has a duty to protect believers in snake handling from a religious practice that is inherently dangerous and sometimes fatal to them, or whether it would be enough to protect nonbelievers through laws of the kind Bunn suggested during his trial in North Carolina in 1948.

A CASUALTY IN THE WAR ON DRUGS

On October 3, 1983, John Gardin, the director of the Douglas County Council on Alcohol and Drug Prevention and Treatment (ADAPT) in Roseburg, Oregon, fired Galen Black. Five months later, he fired Al Smith. Both men were recovered alcoholics who worked at the agency as counselors. Both men's offense was that they had taken peyote as part of a religious ceremony of the Native American Church.

Like virtually all drug and alcohol rehabilitation centers in the United States, ADAPT counseled those who came to it for treatment that any use of alcohol or drugs, no matter how minor and no matter the circumstances, would inevitably cause them to fall back into the grips of their addiction. If Black and Smith had been conventional Christians, taking a sip of wine during communion service might have been acceptable even though both men were recovered alcoholics. But from Gardin's perspective, sacramental wine wasn't like sacramental peyote. Peyote contains mescaline, a powerful hallucinogen. The federal government considers it a Class 1 narcotic. Oregon, unlike 23 other states with large Native American populations, makes no exemption for the religious use of peyote.

From the agency's perspective, firing Black and Smith was a simple personnel matter. Not only did their action undermine ADAPT's treatment philosophy, but it was also a criminal offense. Even though neither man had a history of drug abuse and both of them had used the drug in question as part of a religious ritual, keeping them on its staff would send the wrong message to the addicts they counseled. It would also be hard to explain to the government agencies and the private entities that funded ADAPT. But in making the decision to fire Black and Smith, Gardin and the ADAPT board of directors misjudged both men's motives and their reactions. It also misjudged public opinion.

When Black went to work at ADAPT, he knew little about Native Americans or their religion. But he took seriously ADAPT's mission statement promising culturally sensitive treatment for Native Americans and other racial and ethnic minorities, so he set out to learn about Native American religion.[27] For him, becoming knowledgeable on the subject seemed a good way to enhance his professional credentials. As part of his months-long quest to learn more about Native American religion, he attended his first peyote ritual on September 10, 1983. The ceremony spoke to him in ways that led him to believe he had found a spiritual home, so he eagerly told another counselor about his experience.[28] Word that he had taken peyote got back to Gardin, who immediately ordered Black to undergo a psychological examination to determine if he had relapsed. When Gardin got the report saying that Black was indeed in relapse and was exhibiting the kind of distorted and delusional thinking addicts use to justify their behavior, he offered Black three options. Black could agree to be admitted for in-patient rehabilitation, he could resign, or he could be fired. Declining all three options, Black offered a fourth one: the option of going to court.[29]

News that Black had threatened to go to court over his firing for the ritual use of peyote spread quickly throughout the Native American community. As they talked about Black and the issues his case raised, they found themselves increasingly fearful that if a white man who had attended just one peyote session went to court, the peyote ritual could easily be misunderstood in ways that would adversely affect their religious freedom. They took their concerns to Al Smith, a member of the Klamath tribe and the only Native American on the ADAPT staff.[30]

Unlike Black, who had relatively little professional experience and virtually none with the Native American Church, Smith's record on both counts was exemplary. After hitting bottom, Smith had turned to Alcoholics Anonymous in 1957, where he was counseled to turn his life over to a higher spirit. Unable to turn to the Christian God who had been forced upon him at the Indian boarding schools he had been shipped to as a youth and where he had been stripped of his Klamath Indian name, language, and customs, he turned to the half-remembered prayers of his grandmother's religion. Those Klamath prayers worked. Smith became a much sought after motivational speaker for Alcoholics Anonymous before turning his efforts to work on behalf of and with his fellow Native Americans in national agencies and as a rehabilitation counselor. Through that work, he learned more about Native American spirituality and the Native American Church. For more than a decade, he had been a part of the Church. Once or twice a year he took the sacred peyote.

From his own experience and his experience as a counselor, he knew that Native American religion, including the sacramental use of peyote, could help Native Americans overcome their addictions. After some soul searching, Smith asked his supervisor for permission to take a day off to attend a ceremony. The permission was not granted. Smith went anyway. He took the peyote and was fired for insubordination.[31]

To Black and to Smith, it was a matter of respect for Native Americans, their heritage, their culture, and most of all, their religion. But to ADAPT, neither that claim, nor the laws concerning religious freedom mattered much.

The men had been fired for job-related misconduct and insubordination. Therefore, the agency could not support their claim that they were entitled to unemployment compensation.

In hearings held in Roseburg in 1983 and 1984, both Black and Smith raised the religious freedom claim. Both the Oregon Employment Division and ADAPT pointed out that Oregon's drug law made no exemption for the religious use of peyote. Unlike the First Amendment to the U.S. Constitution and the constitutions of many other states that protect the "free exercise of religion," Oregon's constitution protects only "the right of conscience" and of "religeous (sic) opinion."[32] But for the Employment Division, the more important point was the need to protect the integrity of the state's unemployment insurance fund by denying claims for benefits to plaintiffs such as Black and Smith. For ADAPT the principle at stake was its right to fire employees for misconduct.

The referee who heard the case for the Oregon Employment Division ruled that Black's use of peyote was an isolated instance, but one that gave cause for concern. Therefore, ADAPT could adopt regulations labeling any use of peyote as misuse. Although Smith had willfully violated his employer's rules, he had been fired for following the dictates of his conscience. The state's only reason for denying unemployment benefits in this case would be to protect the integrity of the state's unemployment insurance fund. That was not the kind of "compelling interest" required by a string of cases stemming from the 1963 case of *Sherbert v. Verner* in which the U.S. Supreme Court ruled that a Seventh-day Adventist who had been fired for refusing to work on her Sabbath could collect unemployment benefits. Using that case as precedent, the referee ruled that both Black and Smith were entitled to receive unemployment compensation.[33]

Although Black got the compensation he wanted, the referee gave little support to his contention that his right to religious freedom had been violated; he was a white man with a short and rather tenuous connection to the Native American Church. But for Smith it was different. Not only had the referee seemed to accept his claim that his religious freedom was at stake, but the federal Equal Employment Opportunity Commission had filed suit accusing ADAPT of racism in its treatment of its only Native American employee. That fact troubled ADAPT. It raised some concern within the Employment Division, but both ADAPT and the Employment Division were even more upset by the fact that the referee's decision meant both men were to receive compensation in spite of what they considered obvious job-related misconduct. Therefore, ADAPT and the Employment Division decided to go to court.

That move sparked a flurry of editorials and letters to the editor, much of it critical. But instead of facing criticism for allowing employees to take peyote as ADAPT had feared would happen if the agency didn't fire Black and Smith, the criticism was over wasting taxpayer money with appeals to avoid paying a rather trivial amount of benefits to two employees who had taken part in an admittedly somewhat unusual ritual.

In the Appellate Court, the ruling was the same in both the case of *Black v. Employment Division* and *Smith v. Employment Division*. Oregon law provided no protection for Black or for Smith, but the Free Exercise clause of the First Amendment to the United States Constitution did. The state's interest in denying the men unemployment benefits was not the kind of "compelling interest" required in cases like this one by the U.S. Supreme Court's decision in *Sherbert v. Verner.*

Nevertheless, the Unemployment Division and ADAPT were determined to fight on. Before the case could reach the Oregon Supreme Court, however, ADAPT's insurance company refused to pay for any further legal proceedings. ADAPT found itself signing a consent decree under which it agreed to never again punish an employee for "non-drug sacramental use of peyote during a bona fide ceremony of the Native American Church," but took no further part in the case.[34]

In the Oregon Supreme Court, the Employment Division fared no better than it had at the appellate level. Still, it pressed on, amid mounting public opinion against further appeals.

In 1988, the U.S. Supreme Court heard the consolidated case of *Employment Division, Oregon Department of Human Resources v. Smith and Black*, but instead of issuing an opinion, the Court remanded the case to the Oregon Supreme Court with a request for clarification of Oregon law. In response, the Oregon Supreme Court simply reiterated its earlier opinion. Neither the Oregon Constitution nor state laws concerning drug use provided any protection for Smith and Black; however, under the "compelling interest" test of *Sherbert v. Verner*, the First Amendment to the United States Constitution did.

Finally, in 1991, the United States Supreme Court was ready to rule on the merits of the case. When it did, its 6 to 3 ruling shocked almost everyone. The U.S. Supreme Court not only overturned the verdict of the Oregon Supreme Court, it radically altered the law by limiting the "compelling interest" test only to those cases where the law was aimed at a particular religion or religious practice. Applying Oregon's drug law to members of the Native American Church struck at the heart of their religion, but that didn't matter because the law applied to everyone, not just to a religious practice.

In language reminiscent of that which the Court had used a century earlier in cases involving the Mormon practice of polygamy (Chapter 8, "The Revoked Revelation"), Justice Antonin Scalia wrote for the majority, "We cannot afford the luxury of deeming presumptively invalid, as applied to a religious objection, every regulation of conduct that does not protect an interest of the highest order." Because states could grant exemptions to generally applicable law, the proper remedy was with legislatures, not by an appeal to the court. That this would undoubtedly work to the disadvantage of minority religions was true, he concluded, but the "unavoidable consequence of democratic government must be preferred to a system in which each conscience is a law unto itself."[35]

As word of Scalia's opinion spread, religious organizations throughout the country quickly realized that the American Jewish Congress and the Council on Religious Freedom, who had joined the Association on American Indian Affairs in filing amicus curiae briefs on behalf of Black and Smith, were right. The case raised religious freedom issues that went far beyond the right of Native Americans to use peyote in their religious ceremonies. Scalia's opinion placed in jeopardy religious exemptions such as the ones that allowed for the sacramental use of wine even during Prohibition and that now protect those who allow children to partake of the sacrament.

Within a matter of weeks, a coalition of religious bodies banded together to take Scalia up on the part of his opinion that said relief should come from legislative bodies, not from the courts. In the end, they were successful.

After more than two years of intense lobbying by nearly 50 religious organizations ranging from the conservative Southern Baptists to the very liberal Unitarians, Congress undid much of what the Supreme Court had done by passing the Religious Freedom Restoration Act in November of 1993. A year later, Congress made it perfectly clear that it expected the "compelling interest" test to apply even to peyotists by passing The American Indian Religious Freedom Act.

Although Black and Smith lost their court case at the highest level, ultimately they won in Congress and, most importantly, in the court of public opinion. Although in the 1997 case of *City of Boerne v. Flores* the Supreme Court ruled that the Religious Freedom Restoration Act provided protection only against acts by the federal government, not by state and local governments, by then the high court had already begun to rethink its abandonment of the "compelling interest" test (this chapter, "The Chicken Wars").

THE CHICKEN WARS

Ernesto Pichardo was among the first wave of immigrants who came to the United States from Cuba in the aftermath of the 1961 Bay of Pigs invasion. In Cuba, like others of his generation, he was nominally Catholic. But by his teens, he had drifted away from Catholicism and into the Santeria religion that he had learned about from his mother. In Cuba she had practiced spiritualism and the Afro-Cuban Palo Monte religion. She had also become a Yoruba-Lukumi priestess.

In Cuba during the late eighteenth and early nineteenth centuries, slaves were forcibly baptized Catholic upon their arrival. By law, their masters were to make sure they practiced the Catholic faith. Although most slaves and many of their descendents became at least nominally Catholic, many others continued to practice their traditional religion under the cover of Catholicism.

Thus, in Cuba the traditional Yoruba-Lukumi religion from Yorubaland, in what is now Nigeria, became Santeria, or "the way of the saints," which became both a form of folk Catholicism and also a distinct religion.

In Cuba, each orisha, or divine spirit of the Yoruba-Lukumi religion, became associated with a Catholic saint. On a saint's day, people venerated the saint at a Catholic mass and then honored the orisha in a home ceremony; the same kind of dual ceremony took place in connection with major life events, in times of trouble, and when seeking spiritual guidance. But unlike Christians, who believe their God is everlasting and their saints were martyred for their faith, Santerians believe the orishas are alive, but are not immortal; they live in stones, believed to have come from Africa. To keep the orishas alive, they must be fed with prayers and supplications—and also with blood. Therefore, on their special day and on other festival occasions, Santerians sacrifice small animals, pour their blood over the stones where the orishas live, and then cook the meat and share it in a ceremonial meal.

That was the way Santeria was practiced in Cuba, and also the way Cuban Americans practiced it in the United States. But it wasn't the way Pichardo thought it should be. Although he was a white man with no real ties to Africa, he dreamed of a more institutionalized Santeria where orishas, divorced from their Catholic overlay, could be worshipped and fed publicly in temples as they had been in Yorubaland before slaves in the New World were forced to transmit their faith orally and practice it surreptitiously.

In 1974, Pichardo incorporated the Church of Lukumi Babalu Aye. ("Lukumi" is another name for Santeria, but it is also a Yoruban greeting used in Cuba to recognize others who share the same Afro-Cuban ethnic and religious heritage. In Cuba the Catholic patron saint Lazarus became equated with the orisha known as Babalu Aye.)

In 1987, after working for more than a decade to make his vision a reality, Pichardo announced plans to open the first public Santeria church at the site of an abandoned used-car dealership located just a few blocks from the main street and city hall in Hialeah, Florida.[36] When news of the new church broke, however, the public outcry was immediate.[37] Although Pichardo tried to placate the public by inviting politicians, academics, and members of the Santeria community to meet with him and showing them pictures of what the renovated building would ultimately look like, the meeting's only effect was to solidify opposition to his plans.

In response to that opposition, but perhaps also for his own political reasons, Hialeah mayor Raul Martinez, who at the time was under investigation for accepting kickbacks in zoning cases even as he was running for reelection against the man who had leased the dealership property to Pichardo, called a city council meeting on the matter for the night of June 9.[38] At that meeting it was Pichardo versus everyone else. Pichardo's efforts to explain that the First Amendment gave his Church the right to exist were shouted down.

Traditional Santerians said Pichardo's attempt to institutionalize their religion was a power grab; publicly practicing it was sacrilege. Catholic leaders groused about the rapid growth of Santeria among those who otherwise would remain Catholic. Other Christian leaders denounced Santeria as a dangerous, pagan cult. They decried animal sacrifice as sinful, barbarous, and a threat to public morals. Leaders in the Cuban establishment fretted about the damage it might do to the image of peaceful, law-abiding Cuban Americans, since the religion had become associated with murder and drug use through sensational news coverage of Santeria in other states and through the popular television show *Miami Vice* for which ironically Pichardo had served as a consultant. Concerns were raised about the harmful effects that witnessing an animal sacrifice would have on children. Everyone deemed the practice unsanitary and a danger to public health.[39]

Then there were the animal rights activists. Representatives from the Humane Society of the United States (HSUS), the Society for the Prevention of Cruelty to Animals (SPCA), and People for the Ethical Treatment of Animals (PETA) turned out in full force. Animal sacrifice, they said, was cruel. Animals would be made to suffer for no good reason.[40]

So a controversy rooted in the right of a small religious group to sacrifice chickens, rabbits, other small animals, and goats to feed their gods became known in the nation's press as "The Chicken War."[41] At the end of the June 9 meeting, the city council passed an emergency ordinance incorporating the state's animal cruelty law into its own statutes. At the same time, it passed Resolution 87-66 expressing its "commitment to a prohibition against any and all acts of any and all religious groups which are inconsistent with public morals, peace or safety."[42]

The Church of the Lukumi Babalu Aye held its first open house on August 7. Four days later, the city of Hialeah adopted another resolution affirming its "opposition to the ritual sacrifice of animals within the City of Hialeah, Florida."[43] A month later, the city council went even further. On September 8, it passed Ordinance 87-52, which prohibited the possession of animals meant for sacrifice or slaughter. On September 22, it passed Ordinance 87-71, which struck at the heart of the Santeria faith by prohibiting "the ritual sacrifice of animals," which it defined as meaning "to unnecessarily kill, torment, torture, or mutilate an animal in a ... ritual or ceremony not for the primary purpose of food consumption." For good measure, it also passed Ordinance 87-72 banning the slaughter of animals on property that had not been zoned for that purpose.[44]

Three days later, Pichardo filed a lawsuit in the U.S. District Court for the Southern District of Florida in which he claimed the actions by the city council were discriminatory and a direct violation of the Free Exercise clause of the First Amendment of the U.S. Constitution. But in spite of legal assistance from the American Civil Liberties Union, the case did not go well for Pichardo.

In his 50-page ruling delivered on October 5, 1989, Judge Eugene P. Spellman agreed with Pichardo that the Hialeah ordinances were "not religiously neutral but were to stop the practice of animal sacrifice in the City of Hialeah." However, he also concluded that did not really matter. The ordinances, he said, "were not passed to interfere with religious beliefs, but rather to regulate conduct." For doing that, the city had "three compelling secular purposes: 1) to prevent the cruelty to animals; 2) to safeguard the health, welfare and safety of the community; and 3) to prevent the adverse psychological effect on children exposed to such sacrifices."[45] This decision was affirmed in a one-paragraph, unsigned opinion handed down by the Eleventh Circuit Court of Appeals.

By the time the appellate court issued its decision in May 1991, the United States Supreme Court had scrapped the "compelling interest" test in ruling that Oregon could refuse to pay unemployment compensation to two drug counselors who had been fired for using peyote as part of a religious ceremony (this chapter, "A Casualty in the War on Drugs"). Even worse for Pichardo, two of the three justices who had dissented in that case were no longer on the Court. Justice William Brennan had been replaced by David H. Souter, about whom little was known; Clarence Thomas, who replaced the reliably liberal Justice Thurgood Marshall, was known to be unsympathetic to minorities' claims of violations of their civil rights.

Although his case appeared hopeless, Pichardo was convinced that the orishas had spoken and victory would be his.[46] So the case of *Church of the Lukumi Babalu Aye v. City of Hialeah, Florida* went to the United States Supreme Court.

Amicus curiae briefs filed by HSUS, PETA, the Washington Humane Society, and the Institute for Animal Rights Law supported the city of Hialeah. A brief filed by the U.S. Catholic Conference argued that the Court should readopt the "compelling interest" test, but supported neither side. Churches and religious interest groups were still smarting from the Court's decision in the peyote case, so the major brief supporting Pichardo and the Church of Lukumi Babalu Aye had 16 signatories: Americans United for Separation of Church and State, the American Jewish Committee, the American Jewish Congress, the Anti-Defamation League of B'nai Brith, the Baptist Joint Committee on Public Affairs, the Catholic League for Religious and Civil Rights, the Christian Legal Society, the Church of Jesus Christ of Latter-day Saints, the Evangelical Lutheran Church in America, the First Liberty Institute at George Mason University, the General Conference of Seventh-day Adventists, the Home School Legal Defense Association, the Mennonite Central Committee of the United States, the National Association of Evangelicals, People United for the American Way, and the General Assembly of the Presbyterian Church. Three other briefs were also filed by the National Jewish Commission on Law and Public Affairs, the Council on Religious Freedom, and the Rutherford Institute in support of Pichardo and his Church of the Lukumi Babalu Aye.

Whether it was the public outcry over its decision in the peyote case or the overwhelming support for the Church of the Lukumi Babalu Aye from mainstream religions and interested parties who often find themselves on opposite sides in church-state confrontations, will never be known. Supreme Court justices simply do not comment on such things.

However, whatever was the case, the orishas were right. All of the other justices agreed with Justice Anthony Kennedy when he wrote in the court's June 11, 1993, decision that

> Our review confirms that the laws in question were enacted by officials who did not understand, failed to perceive, or chose to ignore the fact that their official actions violated the Nation's essential commitment to religious freedom. The challenged laws had an impermissible object; and in all events the principle of general applicability was violated because the secular ends asserted in defense of the laws were pursued only with respect to conduct motivated by religious beliefs. We invalidate the challenged enactments and reverse the judgment of the Court of Appeals.[47]

The Court did not rule that behaviors, like beliefs, are absolutely protected by the First Amendment. Nor did it reinstate the "compelling interest" test. Indeed, the welter of concurring opinions make it impossible to tell when the Court might find a regulation permissible and when it might find one to be an unconstitutional infringement on the free exercise of religion. But in spite of the welter of sometimes conflicting concurring opinions, the case clearly indicates that neither conservative justices like Antonin Scalia nor more liberal ones like Ruth Bader Ginsburg will countenance laws that clearly target a religion and its practices, even if that religion is a minority one and an overwhelming majority find its religious practices abhorrent.

DANCING BY MOONLIGHT

As often happens, a story in a local newspaper created an uproar. But this time it wasn't a hard news story. It was a feature story about a religious ceremony. In that May 11, 1999, story, religion reporter Kim Sue Lia Perke told *Austin-American Statesman* readers about Wiccans, most of them soldiers, who had gathered by moonlight at a Boy Scout camp on the grounds of the Fort Hood military base near Killeen, Texas, to celebrate the vernal equinox.[48] The ceremony was neither secret nor anything new. Wiccans had met on the base for years to learn about their religion. For three years they had used the scout camp for their major ceremonies. Although few outsiders ever attended, the ceremonies were open to the public.

Perke's reporting, with its sidebars tracing the religion's history and describing its beliefs and its ceremonial practices, was sensitive and informative.[49] The most sensational element in the entire spread was a photo showing the

Wiccan high priestess and several others leaping over a campfire. Also, in accord with Wiccan terminology, Perke referred to some of the 40 Wiccans who participated in the Open Circle ceremony as "witches."

For people unfamiliar with Wicca, the term "witch" triggers two conflicting images. For some, "witch" is a construct cobbled together from Halloween costumes and familiar television shows: *Bewitched; Charmed; Buffy the Vampire Slayer;* and *Sabrina, the Teenage Witch.* For others, "witch" may include black-clad women on broomsticks, but it also triggers sinister images of evil spells, animal sacrifice, the occult, and even Satanism.

Perke's story made it clear that none of those images has much to do with Wicca, which she described as "a reconstruction of nature worship from tribal Europe and other parts of the world."[50] Wiccans generally hold ceremonies to mark each full moon, but their major holy days coincide with the summer and winter solstices and with the vernal and autumnal equinoxes. Although they also have a male deity, Wicca is essentially a goddess-oriented religion that calls for living in harmony with people and with nature. Core beliefs include the Wiccan Rede "'an it harm no one, do what you will" and the corollary that whatever one does, for good or for bad, will return to the doer threefold.

But in spite of Perke's efforts to convey the essence of Wicca to her readers, the story's immediate effect was to trigger outrage among those who insisted that Wiccans dancing by moonlight on a military base were really subversives engaged in satanic practices. Almost immediately, a local fundamentalist Baptist church launched a letter-writing campaign in protest of Fort Hood's practice of allowing Wiccans to use base facilities.[51] The *Times* of London and the London-based *Daily Telegraph* carried stories.[52] In his *O'Reilly Report* for Fox News, Bill O'Reilly labeled the Army's recognition of "white witchcraft" the "most outrageous news of the day."[53]

But most other American media picked up the story only after May 18 when Bob Barr, a Republican Congressman from Georgia, announced that he had sent letters to the Secretary of the Army and to the commanding officer at Fort Hood demanding that the military stop sanctioning the practice of Wicca on military bases. In his press release, Barr opined:

> If military personnel who consider themselves witches want to practice such nonsense outside of their military service, the Constitution may be construed to allow them to do so. The military, however, does not operate under the same restrictions as society in general and it is difficult if not impossible, to make the case that encouraging the practice of bizarre rituals makes a positive contribution to combat readiness.[54]

In subsequent press releases, speeches, and opinion columns, Barr pointed to the Wiccan belief that one should "do no harm" as evidence that Wiccans are pacifists who cannot possibly be good soldiers.[55]

In response to Barr's comments, Fort Hood spokesman Lt. Col. Benjamin Santos patiently explained to the media that contrary to Barr's assertion, the military must treat Wiccans the same as it treats members of Christian and other faiths. In the 1986 case of *Dettmer v. Landon*, the Fourth Circuit Court of Appeals ruled that Wicca is a religion and, therefore, entitled to protection under the First Amendment to the United States Constitution. Because other religions meet on military property, Wiccans must also be allowed to use military facilities for their meetings and ceremonies.[56]

Marcy Palmer, Wiccan high priestess of the Open Circle at Fort Hood, and David Oringsderff, president of the Open Circle's sponsoring congregation and himself a veteran with 30 years of military service, repeatedly explained that Wiccans don't worship Satan or engage in satanic practices; they don't even believe in a devil. The "spells" they cast have more in common with Christian prayers for divine assistance for themselves and others than with the "spells" cast on fairy-tale heroines like Sleeping Beauty. Just as the biblical commandment against killing does not mean that Christians are necessarily pacifists, neither do most Wiccans interpret the "do no harm" Rede as a prohibition on killing in the context of a legitimate war.[57]

But, in spite of the proffered lessons in constitutional and military law and in the theology of Wicca, Barr and other religio-political conservatives remained convinced that tolerating the religion would undermine both the moral fabric of the nation and its military readiness.

Claiming that only the legislature should decide this kind of matter, Barr attached an amendment to a military appropriation bill that effectively would have revived earlier efforts by Congressman Robert Walker, a Democrat from Pennsylvania, and Senator Jesse Helms, a Republican from South Carolina, to ban Wicca from military bases. On June 9, conservative activist Paul Weyrich announced that his Free Congress Foundation and 12 other conservative political and religious groups called on all good Christians to refuse to enlist or reenlist so long as the Army allowed what he variously called "witchcraft" and "satanic practices" on its military bases.[58]

On June 24, 1999, Texas Governor George W. Bush, who at the time was the Republican presidential candidate, told ABC's *Good Morning America* that he didn't consider Wicca a real religion. While he had no objection to the display of the Ten Commandments on government property or in government buildings (Chapter 6, "The Monument"), the Army, he said, should abandon its practice of allowing the practice of "witchcraft" on military bases.[59]

Even as Barr and other conservatives continued to rail against witches in the military, however, more tolerant voices began to make themselves heard. Letters and e-mails to the *Atlanta Journal and Constitution* made it very clear that even in Barr's conservative home state there were many people who found his interpretation of the First Amendment much more scandalous than a handful of witches dancing by moonlight on military bases.[60] So did organizations like the American Civil Liberties Union and People United for the American Way, both of which have a long history of supporting those who practice unconventional religions and those with no religious affiliation. Some prominent religious leaders joined in, most notably televangelist Pat Robertson.

Although Weyrich had assumed Robertson would support his call for Christians to boycott the military, at the conclusion of a June 30 segment on a Wiccan Summer Solstice gathering in Washington, D.C., Robertson told his viewers that instead of worrying "about a little coven of witches running around," they should be more concerned that a successful effort to prevent them from practicing their religion could lead to efforts to curtail their own religious freedom.[61]

In the end, that sentiment prevailed. Barr's legislation to prevent Wiccans from practicing their religion on military bases went nowhere. Although Wiccans kept their right to conduct their rituals on military bases, Wicca remains among the most misunderstood and most discriminated against alternative religions.

Even before Wiccans began holding their rituals at Fort Hood and on other military bases, military personnel could list Wicca as their religious affiliation on their dog tags. Army and Air Force regulations instructed military chaplains to offer appropriate support and comfort to Wiccans, regardless of their own religious preference. But the Department of Veterans Affairs refused to allow use of the pentagram symbol of their faith on headstones in military cemeteries until 2007, when a series of lawsuits and a well-publicized campaign by the widow of Sgt. Patrick D. Stewart, a highly decorated soldier who was killed while serving in Afghanistan, forced a change in policy.

If the military found the pentagram problematic, both the symbol and the practice of their faith cause more problems for the approximately 150,000 Wiccans who are not part of the military than they do for the 1,500 or so who serve in the nation's armed forces. Like the witches of the Open Circle coven at Fort Hood who found themselves individual targets of hate mail from members of local conservative churches, witches who openly practice their religion in nonmilitary venues find themselves the target of rumors, allegations, harassment, and sometimes vandalism and violence. Almost every year the media report lawsuits triggered by claims of religious discrimination against Wiccans in housing, in the public schools, and in the workplace.[62]

FOR FURTHER READING

Brown, Dee. 1972. *Bury my heart at Wounded Knee.* New York: Bantam Books, pp. 389–420.
Covington, Dennis. 1995. *Salvation on Sand Mountain.* New York: Penguin Books.
Dew, Spencer. 2006, July 20. New World blood libel. *Sightings.* Chicago: Martin Marty Center at the University of Chicago Divinity School.

Drinan, Robert. 1990, December 29. Religious freedom and the incoming Congress. *America*, pp. 512–514.

Epps, Garrett. 2001. *To an unknown god: Religious freedom on trial.* New York: St. Martin's Press.

Greenhouse, Linda. 1990, April 18. Use of drugs in religious rituals can be prosecuted, justices rule. *New York Times*, p. A22.

Greenhouse, Linda. 1993, June 12. Court, citing religious freedom, voids a ban on animal sacrifice. *New York Times*, pp. 1, 9.

Gwynne, S. C. 1999, July 5. I saluted a witch. *Time*, p. 59.

Haynes, Charles. 1999, June 27. Witches test our religious tolerance. *Freedom Forum.* Retrieved March 14, 2008, from http://www.freedomforum.org/templates/document.asp?documentID=9013.

Hood, Ralph W., Jr., and W. Paul Williamson. 2008. *Them that believe: The power and meaning of the Christian serpent-handling tradition.* Berkeley: University of California Press.

Kerstetter, Todd. 2003. "Mobocratic feeling": Religious outsiders, the popular press, and the American West. *American Journalism* 20(1): 57–72.

Neff, David. 1990, June 18. When religion makes us nervous. *Christianity Today*, p. 17.

Noonan, John T., Jr., and Edward McGlynn Gaffney, Jr. 2001. *Religious freedom: History, cases, and other materials on the interaction of religion and government*, 2nd ed. New York: Foundation Press, pp. 479–500, 547–551, 553–554.

O'Brien, David M. 2004. *Animal sacrifice and religious freedom: Church of the Lukumi Babalu Aye v. City of Hialeah.* Lawrence: University of Kansas Press.

Silk, Mark. 1999, Summer. Something Wiccan this way comes. *Religion in the News* 2(2): 9–10.

Vestal, Stanley. 1932/1989. *Sitting Bull: Champion of the Sioux.* Norman: University of Oklahoma Press, pp. 271–315.

Chapter 8

Problematic Practices

At their core, every religion is about the proper relationship between a people and their god or gods. But as a corollary, religions are also about how believers should order their everyday lives—about what constitutes a god-pleasing life.

Some religious teachings about what a god commands or condones are so widely shared that they give little cause for offense. Proscriptions against murder fall into that category. Differences in details such as those surrounding military service, abortion, and euthanasia lead to political controversies and sometimes to culture wars, but they rarely create a scandal.

However, there are religious teachings that deviate so markedly from societal norms that they do cause scandal. In the United States, these scandals most often stem from teachings about sex, marriage, and family life, especially when those teachings violate conventional wisdom about child care or seem to threaten public safety.

"Bible Communism" and "The Revoked Revelation" deal with scandals resulting from unconventional teaching about marriage that first came to light in the early nineteenth century. Although both the group and the practice described in the first section died as a result of scandal, the practice described in the second section continues to scandalize. Where once the concern was for public morality and for the welfare of women, today it is about the children.

That concern for children is also at the heart of the scandals described in "Of Miracles and Medicine." It also played a role in "Virgins and Guns," the last section in this chapter, but the real scandal in that one was two-fold: first, it was about a communal group whose activities seemed a threat to its neighbors; and, second, it was about government response to the perceived threat. "Ballots and Bioterrorism," the fifth section in this chapter, is also about a perceived threat from a religious community, but a threat that turned out to be a real one.

"A Tax Cheat or a Trustee?" is somewhat different. At the center of it is one of the new religions whose beliefs, recruiting methods, and communal lifestyle caused consternation in the 1970s. But the practice that seemed scandalous when it came to light is a fairly mainstream one. This one, like many of the other scandals in both this chapter and in Chapter 7, underscores the way Thomas Jefferson's dichotomy between constitutionally protected religious beliefs and unprotected behaviors can so easily be used as a mechanism for social control against an unconventional and unpopular religion.

BIBLE COMMUNISM

Like other Perfectionists of the early nineteenth century, John Humphrey Noyes was determined to help people overcome their sins so they might lead a more God-pleasing life. But for Noyes, motives were more important than behaviors. Therefore, the sins that needed to be overcome if people, as well as society itself, were to be perfected were selfishness, egotism, and greed.

According to Noyes, working hard was fine. The pride and acquisitiveness that came from working for wages were not fine, especially when they fostered an unwillingness to share. To overcome those sinful tendencies, Noyes taught that true Christians should live communally. Instead of owning property, they should share in all of the work of the community and receive from it whatever they needed.

For 30 years, the "Bible Communism" Noyes taught first to a handful of followers in Putney, Vermont, and then put fully into practice in 1848 in Oneida, New York, worked well. Within a year of its founding, the Oneida Association had attracted 87 members; within a few years, it had 200. At its peak, there were about 300 men, women, and children living in the Mansion House in Oneida, and several hundred more in satellite communities throughout New York and New England.

To support the community, Oneidans farmed, grew fruit trees, and developed a string of lucrative commercial enterprises. They stitched and sold carpet bags. They made and sold spoons and hunting traps—more than 100,000 a year by the 1850s to individual hunters as well as to the Hudson Bay Company.

People from surrounding communities flocked to Oneida to marvel at the technological devices they developed, used, and sometimes manufactured—the first lazy Susan, a washing machine, mop wringer, and mechanical potato peeler. Businessmen, community leaders, and even school children came to learn firsthand the management techniques that made the community such a financial success that it could give its members time to spend on the arts, let them take college-level courses at the Mansion House, and even send some of its young people to college.

If those who visited Oneida knew, most of them chose to ignore the fact that the work arrangements and management style that made Oneida such a business success were in large measure due to Noyes's unconventional views on marriage, which were at the heart of both his version of Bible Communism and also of the events that led to the move from Putney to Oneida.

As early as 1837, Noyes had confided his thoughts on marriage and the proper relationship between the sexes in a letter to David Harrison, a close friend. In that letter he wrote:

When the will of God is done on earth, as it is in heaven, *there will be no marriage*. The marriage supper of the Lamb, is a feast at which *every dish is free to every guest*. [Ital. in original] Exclusiveness, jealousy, quarrelling, have no place there, for the same reason as that which forbids the guests at a thanksgiving dinner to claim each his separate dish, and quarrel with the rest for his rights. In a holy community, there is no more reason why sexual intercourse should be restricted by law, than why eating and drinking should be—and there is as little occasion for shame in the one case as in the other.... The guests of the marriage supper may have each his favourite dish, each a dish of his own procuring, and that without the jealousy of exclusiveness. I call a certain woman my wife—she is yours, she is Christ's, and in him she is the bride of all saints.[1]

Although Noyes warned Harrison to be careful about showing the letter to others, others learned of it. When Theophilus Gates published a copy of it in his *Battle-Axe and Weapons of War*, Noyes valiantly tried to explain that he didn't advocate promiscuous free love of the kind that later became associated with the women's right movement[2] (Chapter 1, "The Voice of an Age").

According to Noyes, all men and all women within a perfect, holy community were married to each other. Intercourse within this kind of complex marriage was meant to be a mutually satisfying expression of love between a man and a woman, and between each man and woman and the entire community. Because sex wasn't meant just for procreation, practicing birth control was important. The method Noyes taught was male continence, technically coitus reservatus or intercourse to the point of pleasurable fulfillment just short of ejaculation.[3]

Although Noyes insisted his views on marriage were biblically based, putting the kind of "complex marriage" he advocated into practice most likely had more to do with lust than with a desire to establish the perfect, holy community.

After his first love, Abigail Merwin, married another man, he persuaded Harriet Holton to marry him even though he had warned her theirs would be no conventional marriage. It would be the foundation for a new religious community based on equality and sharing of all things. With the respectability that came with being married—and with the money Harriet brought to the union—Noyes set out to establish a community of like-minded Perfectionists in Putney. By 1840, through word of mouth and through his *Perfectionist* newspaper that he was able to continue publishing by using Harriet's money, he had attracted a small group of followers. By 1844, the Putneyites were practicing Bible Communism.

Within this little community and in the pages of his newspaper, Noyes expounded on complex marriage. Although he steadfastly maintained that the time had not come to establish the new marital order, by 1846 he had become impatient. He also had fallen in love with one of his married followers, Mary Cragin. Two months after telling his followers that the time to fully implement Bible Communism was at hand, he made love to Mrs. Cragin, after which he convinced his wife and Mary's husband, George, that they were to be the vanguard of the new order. After they agreed, a few others were admitted to the complex marriage circle. Although those within the circle were, for the time being, sworn to secrecy, complex marriage didn't remain a secret for long.

In the summer of 1847, Noyes, together with Mary Cragin, effected the faith healing of Harriet Hall, an invalid who had long belonged to a different Perfectionist community. Hoping to bring her and her husband, Daniel, into his group, Noyes gave him a detailed account of the sexual freedom members of his circle had under his Bible communism system. But instead of joining the group, Hall took the information to the state attorney's office in nearby Brattleboro.

The sheriff arrested Noyes. Noyes posted bail, but the arrest wasn't his only problem. Although he and Mary Cragin had apparently cured Harriet Hall, he failed to cure Mary Knight, who died from consumption. Physicians proclaimed him a quack. Pastors labeled the Putney community a den of iniquity. The Rev. Hubbard Eastman called Noyes "a hydra-headed monster of iniquity."[4] There was talk in the town of mob action to break up the pernicious ring of adulterers.

When jail seemed imminent, Noyes left town for his mother's home in Hamden, Connecticut. That ended talk of mob action, but it did nothing to shield Noyes's followers from the threat of further legal action. Therefore, Noyes and those of his followers who remained loyal moved to Oneida.

There, in 1848 on the fringes of civilization, Noyes and his little band of Perfectionists built their holy community on the twin pillars of Bible Communism and complex marriage. As information about the community spread through its newspaper and magazine and word of mouth, a steady stream of newcomers, most of them middle- and upper-class men and women, made their way to Oneida. For them, the attractions were the communal lifestyle, the community's entrepreneurial spirit, and, of course, the complex marriage.

As practiced at Oneida, complex marriage was not a licentious arrangement. Nor was it an exploitive one. As soon as they reached puberty, both girls and boys were expected to have their first sexual experience, usually with an older person who acted as their physical and spiritual guide. All men and women were expected to have multiple partners of varying ages, but men were to initiate sex only with women who were willing. While men undoubtedly enjoyed the arrangement, so did the women who had both greater protection and greater freedom than they would have had in a conventional marriage. The freedom to refuse sex and the practice of male continence offered women some protection from unwanted pregnancies and the inherent risks of bearing children; the communal lifestyle freed them from much of the drudgery of child rearing. Although more women than men engaged in child care and household tasks, and more men than women worked in the fields, all jobs, including supervisory ones, were open to both men and women.

At Oneida, women and men were considered equal partners, but they shared equally in all things under the watchful eye of Noyes, who with the assistance of a few close advisers, exercised tight control over everything from Bible interpretation to work arrangements and sexual liaisons. The method of control they used was mutual criticism.

As with those who expressed deviant beliefs and with those who did not do their share of the work, behaved in an unseemly manner on the job, became too attached to a particular job or too inclined to seek advancement, those who seemed disinclined to engage in sex, who failed to take a partner's wishes into account, or who developed a too close attachment to one partner were subjected to public criticism. In extreme cases of deviant beliefs and behaviors, members might be expelled from the community. More often, those who failed to conform to societal norms in the workplace found their job assignments changed; those whose transgressions were sexual found their choice of mates either proscribed or severely restricted.

For 30 years the system worked well. By 1870, however, Noyes found himself facing pressures that were both internal and external. Internally, the pressure came from young people, second generation Oneidans, who felt they should be able to have their first sexual encounter with a person of their own choosing, but it also came from some older, long-time community members who questioned Noyes's right to tell them with whom they should or should not have sex. Wanting a stronger voice in the governance of the community and in the details of their own work and sex life than the practice of mutual criticism allowed, they now presented a challenge to Noyes's role as the undisputed head of the community.

Externally, the challenge came from Anthony Comstock's crusade to rid the nation of anything he considered obscene. When Comstock persuaded Congress to pass legislation prohibiting the dissemination of information about sexual matters and birth control through the mail, Noyes responded by expunging all information about complex marriage and male continence from Oneida publications. But it was too late. Prudery was on the ascendant.

In 1873, the Rev. John W. Mears, a Presbyterian from nearby Clinton, New York, launched a campaign to rid the nation of the "corrupt concubinage" practiced at Oneida.[5] By 1879, Mears had assembled a coalition of Episcopalian, Presbyterian, and Methodist clergy to his cause. Area newspapers came to the defense of the Oneida community because it contributed so greatly to the area's economy,[6] but in late June, under a headline proclaiming the Oneida Community far worse than the polygamous Mormons (this chapter, "The Revoked Revelation"), the Syracuse *Standard* published news that arrests and prosecutions of Noyes and other Oneidan leaders were imminent.[7]

The next night, June 23, 1879, Noyes quietly slipped downstairs from his quarters in the Mansion House at Oneida. After first putting on his boots, he made his way to Canada, traveling through the night, first by foot and then by carriage, train, and finally by ferryboat.

The story in the *Standard* turned out to be false. There was no threat of an imminent arrest, but Noyes never again set foot in the United States. With Noyes gone, whatever was left of the communal unity that had sustained Oneida for so long disappeared. By August, Oneidans voted to give up complex marriage. The next year, they gave up on Bible communism. Ownership of their communal property and their business enterprises, including the spoon factory, were transferred into a corporation, Oneida Community, Ltd. Shares in its stock were parceled out to community members. Noyes himself received a generous allowance from the new company that allowed him to live out the remaining six years of his life in comfort in a house overlooking the American Falls on the Canadian side of the Niagara River.

Although Noyes's experiment in Bible communism ultimately failed, the name "Oneida" lives on as a respected brand of flatware manufactured by the corporation that grew out of Noyes's vision of perfecting society through the practice of Bible communism and complex marriage. And, as was true over a century ago, the Oneida Manor House and factories still play host to a steady stream of visitors who are curious about what was and what remains of the most successful American experiment in religiously inspired communal living. For those who want to learn even more, important documents from Noyes and the Oneida Community are housed in the Syracuse University library.

THE REVOKED REVELATION

Wherever the Mormons went, trouble followed. After they left Kirtland, Ohio, for a new home in Missouri, a war against them forced them to move again, this time to Nauvoo, Illinois. But in 1844, after a few years of relative peace, an angry mob succeeded in burning their buildings and killing Joseph Smith, the founder, president, and prophet of their religion. Under his successor, Brigham Young, they made the long trek to the Utah Territory where they hoped they could practice their religion in peace. Again, however, trouble followed.

Part of their problem stemmed from suspicion born of simple jealousy. Because they lived in relatively homogeneous, closely knit communities, their organizational skills and industriousness made the Mormons seem both an economic and a political threat to their neighbors. Mostly, though, the problem stemmed from their religion. To the nation's Christian majority, it was bad enough that the Mormons believed Jesus had visited the Native Americans or that they believed the angel Moroni had given Joseph Smith *The Book of Mormon*, which to Mormons is Holy Scripture on a par with the Bible itself. Even worse were their practices—especially polygamy, or plural marriage, as they called it.

According to the Church of Jesus Christ of Latter-day Saints, God revealed the doctrine of plural marriage to Joseph Smith in 1831 and commanded him to live by it. While the Mormons were still living in Nauvoo, Smith cautiously told a few other leaders about the revelation, but few outside of his inner circle knew of it until after the Mormons had been driven out of Nauvoo and had begun to make a home for themselves in the Utah Territory. There, under their new leader, Brigham Young, they learned about this new and "highest form" of marriage. With Young's encouragement, and with his example, those men who were financially secure enough to do so began taking more than one wife.[8]

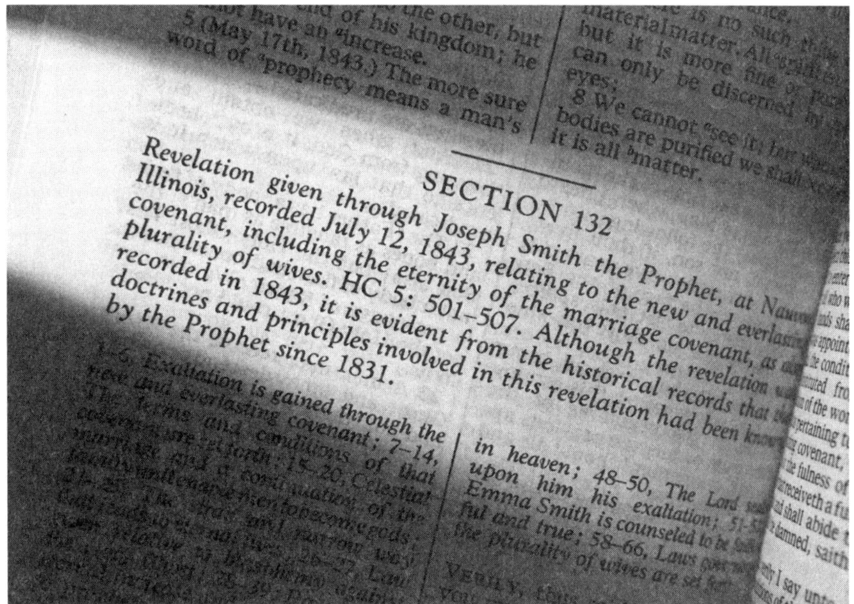

Although the Church of Jesus Christ of Latter-day Saints ended the practice in 1890, Joseph Smith's revelation that Mormons should practice plural marriage is recorded in Section 132 of the Church's Doctrine and Covenants. AP photo, Douglas C. Pizac.

As news that the Mormons had begun practicing polygamy spread throughout the country, the public outcry against the scandalous Mormons made it expedient for public officials to take action—so polygamy joined slavery as a burning issue. In the months leading up to the 1856 presidential election, the Republican Party platform called for Congress to exercise its "sovereign power over the Territories of the United States ... to prohibit in the Territories those twin relics of barbarism, polygamy and slavery."[9] For states-right Democrats of the era, joining a crusade against polygamy seemed a good way to siphon off support for abolition, so they rallied behind President James Buchanan's decision to send troops into the Utah Territory in an effort to root out that "barbarous practice."[10]

Although the federal government effectively made its presence felt in Utah, the "Mormon War" of 1857–1858 launched by President Buchanan failed to accomplish its goal of stamping out polygamy. In the face of continuing Mormon resistance, Congress embarked on a 30-year quest to legislate polygamy out of existence.

In 1862, Congress passed and President Abraham Lincoln signed into law "An Act to punish and prevent the Practice of Polygamy in the Territories of the United States." The law nullified acts of the territorial legislature that incorporated the Church of Jesus Christ of Latter-day Saints and that legalized plural marriages. It also imposed a $500 fine and five-year jail term as punishment for men who were found to have more than one wife, but not for men who merely engaged in cohabitation.

The Mormons, who considered the Declaration of Independence and the Constitution to be divinely inspired, could not believe a mere law could trump their First Amendment right to practice a tenet of their faith. Therefore, they rallied behind Brigham Young's secretary, George Reynolds, when he was indicted in 1874 for marrying Amelia Jane Schofield after he was already married to Mary Ann Tuddenham. To their dismay, the 1879 case of *Reynolds v. United States* went against them.

After accepting Thomas Jefferson's distinction between protected beliefs and behaviors that sometimes may be punished, the Supreme Court then drew on English common law and the writings of Judge James Kent (Chapter 6, "Satan's Hoary-headed Apostle") to label polygamy a serious offense against "peace and good order ... [that] has always been odious among the northern and western nations of Europe, and, until the establishment of the Mormon Church, was almost exclusively a feature of the life of Asiatic and of African people."[11]

That Reynolds acted in accord with his religious beliefs made no difference. To grant a religious exemption from the law of the land for polygamy would invite "anarchy." "To permit this," Chief Justice Morrison R. Waite wrote in his opinion for a unanimous court, "Would be to make the professed doctrines of religious belief superior to the law of the land, and in effect to permit every citizen to become a law unto himself. Government could exist only in name under such circumstances."[12] The law was deemed constitutional, Reynolds's conviction was upheld. But the conviction did nothing to persuade the Mormons that they should renounce the practice of plural marriage.

Faced with Mormon intransigence, the Republicans in 1880 again made the crusade against that "odious" practice a plank in their party platform.[13] Congress passed more laws, each more draconian than the last. On four occasions the Mormons challenged the laws in court; on four occasions the Supreme Court upheld the federal government's right to pass laws aimed at preventing the religiously inspired practice of polygamy. The last of those challenges was to the Edmunds-Tucker Act of 1887, which allowed for the forfeit and seizure of the Temple and other Church assets so long as the Church countenanced defiance of federal law concerning polygamy.

In the 1890 case of *The Late Corporation of the Church of Jesus Christ of Latter-Day Saints v. United States/Romney v. United States*, two justices would not have allowed the government to confiscate Church property, but all agreed that "the State has a perfect right to prohibit polygamy, and all other open offenses against the enlightened sentiment of mankind, notwithstanding the pretense of religious conviction."[14]

As the name of the case suggests, Congress thought it had finally solved the Mormon Question by authorizing the confiscation of Church property. With the Court's decision upholding that part of the law, the Church of Jesus Christ of Latter-day Saints might have faded away. But that didn't happen.

In September 1890, Church president Wilford Woodruff told the faithful that he had prayed for guidance and God had inspired him to call upon Mormons to forgo the practice of polygamy.[15] Because their religion teaches that whoever is the President and Prophet of their Church may receive new and authoritative revelations, Mormons accepted the document explaining this new message that President Woodruff presented to them as "authoritative and binding." That document, called the "Manifesto," became a part of the Church's Doctrines and Covenants.[16] In return for that decision, the Church kept its property. On January 4, 1896, Congress admitted Utah to the Union as the 45th state.

While most Mormons had no problem believing that the same loving God who in 1831 had authorized polygamy now counseled them to abandon the practice for the good of His own true Church, there were those for whom Woodruff's "Manifesto" and the nation's response to it made the command to forgo polygamy seem more a matter of political expedience than a binding statement of God's will. Now, more than a hundred years later, there are still those who, for religious reasons, practice polygamy. Although they either left the Church of Jesus Christ of Latter-day Saints or were expelled from it, they still call themselves Mormons.

As many as 10,000 of these Mormons belong to the Fundamentalist Church of Jesus Christ of Latter-day Saints (FLDS), but there are many others who have gathered around a leader who is unaffiliated with any organized religion but whom his followers accept as the true Prophet and Teacher of their Mormon faith. Most fundamentalist Mormons live in southern Utah, southern Nevada, and northern Arizona, but there are also enclaves in Idaho, Oregon, South Dakota, Texas, and the western provinces of Canada, and perhaps in other regions.

Because polygamy is illegal in the United States, most fundamentalist Mormons live in remote, rural areas where, for the most part, they manage to practice their faith unmolested. Occasionally, however, their activities intrude into public consciousness in ways that make them impossible for state and federal authorities to ignore. In some cases a polygamist claims that God has commanded him to take action against someone who does not share his beliefs. More often, information about polygamy, as practiced within a community, leads to government intervention as it did in 1953 in a raid on the FLDS community at Short Creek on the Utah-Arizona border.

Scandals of the first type may occur in any religion (Chapter 4, "Domestic Terrorists," "Another Domestic Terrorist"). Religiously inspired crimes against others differ only in their targets and in the doctrines the perpetrators claim as justification. In the few instances where fundamentalist Mormons have targeted those who do not share their faith, it has been because they believed God had commanded them to act in order to perpetuate or protect His sacred command to practice plural marriage. The most recent, notorious scandals of this type are the 1984 murder of Brenda Wright Lafferty and her 15-month-old daughter, Erica, and the 2002 kidnapping of Elizabeth Smart.

When Allen Lafferty came home from work on July 24, 1984, he found his wife and baby were dead. At first, the police suspected that Allen was the murderer, but that was not the case. The killers were Allen's older brothers, Dan and Ron. Ron had served a term on the Highland, Utah, city council; Dan had run for sheriff of Utah County. Both had been devout members of the Church of Jesus Christ of Latter-day Saints, but over the years they had become convinced that the Church had erred when it accepted the Manifesto. Dan and Ron converted all of their brothers to their fundamentalist understanding, but some of the wives resisted. Foremost among those wives was Brenda Lafferty. Not only had she tried to convince her husband that the fundamentalist Mormonism of her brothers-in-law was a heretical religion, but she had also counseled Ron's wife to leave her husband, who had become increasingly abusive as he became more convinced of the rightness of authoritative patriarchy and polygamy. The brothers killed Brenda because God told them that only a "blood atonement" would do; for the Kingdom of God to go forward, Brenda had to die for her sins of resisting appropriate male authority and refusing to accept polygamy. Her daughter also had to die because she would have grown up to be just like her mother. Although the brothers insisted they had acted as God told them to, the court had no trouble finding both men guilty of murder. Ron received the death penalty; Dan was sentenced to life in prison at the Point of the Mountain state prison. There he shares a cell with Mark Hofmann who is serving time for forgery[16] (Chapter 3, "The Salamander Letter").

Unlike Brenda and Erica Lafferty, 14-year-old Elizabeth Smart was not murdered. During the night of June 5, 2002, she was abducted from the bedroom she shared with her 9-year-old sister, Mary Katherine, in the family home in an upscale Salt Lake City suburb. By the time Mary Katherine felt safe enough to tell her parents that Elizabeth had been taken, Elizabeth and her kidnapper had been gone for hours.[17] At the time Mary Katherine had told her parents that the kidnapper's voice sounded familiar, but it took her four months to figure out whose voice she had heard. The man was Immanuel, a street preacher who had done a bit of work on the family's home. Using information the family provided, the police made a composite drawing of the man. But when they refused to release it to the public, the Smarts released the drawing at a press conference.[18] Almost immediately a woman called and identified Immanuel as her brother, Brian David Mitchell, a fundamentalist Mormon unaffiliated with any organized group. A few weeks later, after seeing the drawing on a February 15 episode of *America's Most Wanted*, an elderly couple spotted Immanuel walking down a busy street in the Salt Lake City suburb of Sandy in the company of two women, one older and one quite young. The man was indeed Immanuel/Mitchell. The older woman was his lawful wife, Wanda Barzee. The younger one was Elizabeth Smart. Immanuel had stalked her, kidnapped her, "married" her in a ceremony he performed himself, and then consummated the marriage by raping her. He had done so, he said, in response to a command from God to take for himself seven young wives.[19] Although on three occasions courts have found Immanuel/Mitchell incompetent to stand trial, he remains incarcerated on charges that include kidnapping, sexual assault, and burglary.

Fundamentalist Mormons, like members of other religions, do, on occasion, believe their God has told them to commit acts that target those who do not share their beliefs, but that kind of crime is relatively rare. More common are the scandals that arise from the practice of polygamy itself because it is a routine part of their everyday life. Because polygamy is so abhorrent to outsiders, both social service agencies and the government have tried for years to root out the practice. But the practice is so ingrained in polygamous communities that they have, for the most part, adopted a sort of "live and let live" approach, taking action only when activities within isolated polygamous communities come to public notice in a way that makes them impossible to ignore. Among the most notorious recent scandals of this type are the arrest and convictions of Warren Jeffs and the government raid on the Yearning for Zion ranch in Texas.

Jeffs was the leader of the Fundamentalist Church of Jesus Christ of Latter-day Saints centered in the Colorado City-Bountiful, Utah, area. But unlike his father, Rulon Jeffs, whom people described as warm and loving, Warren was autocratic. As Prophet of the FLDS Church, Warren Jeffs claimed the authority to give male members women, many of them young teenagers, as their wives and also to take the women away and reassign them to other men. That practice of assigning and reassigning wives led to some dissent within the community and also brought him to the attention of Utah authorities in 2003. Upon learning that the state was planning to arrest him, Jeffs went into hiding.[20] In May 2006, the FBI put him on its Ten Most Wanted List as a fugitive from the law. Three months later, Nevada state police found and arrested him when they stopped the car in which he was traveling for failing to have a visible license plate. In a Nevada court on August 28, Jeffs agreed to return to Utah to stand trial. At his September 2007 trial in St. George, Utah, Jeffs was convicted and sentenced to two consecutive prison terms of five years to life for forcing a 14-year-old girl to marry her 19-year-old cousin. In February 2008, he pled guilty to additional sex charges stemming from the arranged marriages of three young girls to older men.

In 2004, while Jeffs was on the lam, the FLDS Church bought 1,700 acres of land in west Texas where members began building a new community. Although people in the area were suspicious when hundreds of men, women, and children dressed in pioneer garb seemed to be living at what the purchaser of the land had said was to be a hunting lodge, few really knew what was going on at the ranch the settlers called Yearning for Zion for several years. That changed quickly when, on March 29, 2008, a woman who said she was 16 called a women's shelter. Yearning for Zion was a FLDS settlement, she said; she had been forced to marry at 15, she had a baby and an abusive polygamous husband, and she wanted out. In response to her call, Texas authorities did as they had done at Short Creek half a century earlier. Supplemented by agents from the Federal Bureau of Investigation, they swarmed to the ranch looking for the young woman who had called for help. Although they never found her and later concluded the call was a hoax,[21] they found evidence of underage women with children. In accord with a court order, mothers and children were rounded up and removed from the compound. Although those with children under four were allowed to stay with their children, many very young children were taken from their mothers and placed in protective custody. Separated from their children and forced to submit to DNA testing, which, along with seized documents, authorities expected would provide evidence of both underage marriage and incest, some of the women fought back in court. Two months after the raid, the Texas Supreme Court ruled the state had overstepped its authority by taking all of the children from their mothers because very clearly most of the children were not in imminent danger. On June 2, the mothers and their children were allowed to go back to their Yearning for Zion homes.

While newspaper headlines proclaimed their return a victory for the fundamentalist Mormons,[22] spokespersons from both child-protective agencies and the anticult network fretted about the safety of the children.[23] At the time, however, both ignored the fact that in ruling the women and children could return to their homes, the Texas Supreme Court gave the trial court great latitude to impose conditions on the women and their children. In her order allowing the return, Texas District Judge Barbara Walters, who initially had ruled for the state, gave the state almost everything it wanted:[24] Among the more draconian of the conditions she imposed on the community were ones requiring parents to stay in Texas, take parenting classes, open their homes to inspection by child-welfare agents whenever they wished, and allow the children to be examined in connection with any subsequent investigation of child abuse.

In spite of those conditions, life will almost certainly go on at Yearning for Zion much as it was before the raid. But as with the raid at Short Creek, the raid on Yearning for Zion will most likely do more to bond fundamentalist Mormons to their faith and to each other than it will do to stamp out polygamy.[25]

The scandalous crimes fundamentalist Mormons have sometimes committed against outsiders, as well as incontrovertible evidence that some men within polygamous communities are abusive, suggest that sometimes government action is warranted against those who engage in practices that they claim to be religiously inspired. But neither an official change in Church doctrine nor prosecutions under laws that make polygamy illegal have been able to stamp out the practice. Therefore, the long history of failed attempts to deal with what outsiders to the faith see as the problem of polygamy raises questions about whether a change in law might be warranted. In the nineteenth century, the Supreme Court warned that granting a religious exemption for polygamy would invite anarchy; but since then, legislatures and courts have found ways to protect religious practices that a majority find strange (Chapter 7, "The Chicken Wars," "A Casualty of the War on Drugs," "Dancing by Moonlight") while still making it possible to prosecute those whose actions clearly harm or endanger others, in spite of their protests that they are doing God's will (Chapter 1, "Hudson River Mystery"; Chapter 4, "Domestic Terrorists," "The Good Mother"; Chapter 7, "Snakes and Strychnine"; this chapter, "Of Miracles and Medicine").

OF MIRACLES AND MEDICINE

In 1890, John Alexander Dowie came to Chicago from his native Australia where he had gained a reputation as a gifted healer. For Dowie and his followers, relying on healing through prayer, anointing with oil, and the laying on of hands by a pastor or church elders instead of on modern medicine was purely scriptural. To make that point, Dowie most often quoted Isaiah 53:5 from the Old Testament, but sometimes he also cited Mark 16:18 or James

5:13-15 from the New Testament. Illnesses, he taught, are the devil's work; only God could overcome the power of the Devil.

In sermons and in his publication *Leaves of Healing*, Dowie touted the number of people who flocked to his Christian Catholic Church or checked themselves into one of the "divine healing homes" he set up as places where they could live at nominal cost while praying and studying the Bible in anticipation their illnesses would soon be cured.[26] Dowie branded medical science as "bosh."[27] In return, Chicago newspapers called him a quack, a charlatan, and a con artist as they trumpeted his failures[28]—and they were many.

On April 27, 1894, for example, the headline over a *Chicago Daily Tribune* story about the death of eight-year-old Homer Harrison was "Dies in Dowie's Den."[29] In 1899, the city was up in arms because outbreaks of scarlet fever and diphtheria within the city seemed traceable to a refusal by Dowie's followers to quarantine their afflicted children or even to report their illnesses to authorities. The most notorious case, however, was the 1901 death in childbirth of Emma Judd and her infant son.

When H. W. Judd, Emma's husband, told the coroner that he had not called for a physician to help with what was obviously a difficult birth but had instead relied on Dowie for prayers and anointing, state officials set out to prosecute Judd, Dowie, and two elders for neglect. Newspaper headlines screamed for conviction; demonstrators burned Dowie in effigy as they protested outside his church.[30] A grand jury, however, refused to return an indictment. There simply were no laws requiring medical care for children.

Although Dowie escaped conviction in that case, as he had done on numerous other occasions, his follower, J. Luther Pierson, was not so lucky. In May 1901, even as the Judd case was in the news in Chicago, Pierson found himself in court in White Plains, New York, on charges of criminal neglect stemming from the death of his daughter from catarrhal pneumonia. Although he told the court he knew his daughter was probably dying, he said he relied on prayer as Dowie taught because he believed illnesses were the work of the Devil. He did not regret that decision, he told the court. He regretted only that his faith was not strong enough to save her.[31]

The judge, however, found Pierson guilty as charged. Instead of paying the fine, Pierson castigated the law. The judge then sentenced him to jail, saying from the bench, "The trouble with him is that he will do the same thing over again."[32]—and the judge was right. The day after Pierson was sentenced to jail, his two-month-old son, whom he had treated with prayer before his exasperated wife took the boy to a doctor, died of catarrhal bronchitis. Still adamant that relying on prayer had been the right thing to do, Pierson appealed his conviction.

Although a panel of the New York Supreme Court in Brooklyn overturned Pierson's conviction, in 1905 in the case of *People v. Pierson*, the Court of Appeals of New York found against him. The court acknowledged that "there are people who believe that Divine power may be invoked to heal the sick and that faith is all that is required," but it also cited the United States Supreme Court's decision in the case of *Reynolds v. United States*, which drew a sharp distinction between beliefs that are protected by the First Amendment and behaviors such as polygamy that are not protected[33] (this chapter, "The Revoked Revelation"). By 1905, medical science had advanced to the point where people of faith regularly called in doctors, the court pointed out. Therefore,

> the law of nature, as well as the common law, devolves upon the parents the duty of caring for their young in sickness and in health, and of doing whatever may be necessary for their care maintenance and preservation, including medical assistance if necessary, and an omission to do this is a public wrong which the state, under its police powers may prevent.[34]

At the time, newspapers and law journals hailed the verdict in the Pierson case as signaling the end of the scandalous practice of denying children medical care that could have saved their lives. Westchester County, New York, prosecutors stepped up their efforts against members of the Church of Christ, Scientist whose children were also dying. The case chosen was that of Esther Quimby.

Where Dowie's followers based their belief in faith healing solely on the Bible, members of the Christian Science religion grounded theirs both in the Bible and in the teachings of their spiritual leader and Church founder, Mary Baker Eddy, whose recovery from an early life marked by illness and then a subsequent injury sustained in a fall led her to publish the first edition of *Science and Health with Key to the Scriptures* in 1849. In it, she explained that illnesses are imaginary. They should be treated by helping people overcome the kind of erroneous thinking that created the illusion of illness. To aid in that process, the Christian Science Church trained and credentialed practitioners to minister to the sick through prayer and, more importantly, through an explication of Eddy's teachings.

At the time, newspapers and much of the public found the Church of Christ, Scientist and its healing practices every bit as scandalous as those of Dowie and his Christian Catholic Church. But in spite of frequent, sensational media accounts of children who died while being treated by practitioners instead of by physicians,[35] the Church grew. By 1890, less than 20 years after its official founding, the Church had 9,000 members. Among those members were John and Georgianna Quimby.

When the Quimbys' daughters, Esther and Bessie, became ill in October 1892 with what appeared to be tonsillitis, the family called in John C. Lathrop, a prominent Christian Science practitioner, instead of a medical doctor. Under Lathrop's care, Bessie recovered, but Esther died. The coroner determined the cause of death was diphtheria and vowed to make a test case of her death by filing manslaughter charges against both her parents and her practitioner. In response, the Church and its members rallied in support of Lathrop and the Quimbys.[36]

At the grand jury hearing, Christian Science proponents forcibly argued that there was "no generally accepted standard of care," that medical practice was a hodge-podge of different and conflicting schools, each of which sometimes lost patients.[37] Christian Science was just another variant that also sometimes failed to cure, but that should not mean parents and practitioners who lost a child were guilty of manslaughter or even neglect. The state, however, brought in medical experts whose testimony proved more persuasive. The grand jury ruled not only that the girl's life could have been saved had she received medical care, but that her illness and death were a threat to others because she had not been properly diagnosed and then quarantined as the law required. The jury determined that both the Quimbys and Lathrop should be prosecuted under the state's manslaughter law.

In response to that decision, Mary Baker Eddy issued a statement instructing members that "until public thought becomes better acquainted with Christian Science," practitioners would refrain from treating infectious or contagious diseases. Members were to be "prompt and unfailing in their obedience" to health regulations.[38]

Whether Eddy's order had any real effect on the outcome of the case would be pure speculation, but the trial court found the Christian Science argument about conflicting standards of care more persuasive than the grand jury did. In spite of the New York court's decision in the Pierson case, there simply were no laws at the time mandating medical care for sick children. As in the Dowieite cases from Chicago and in previous ones involving Christian Scientists in Massachusetts and New York, the state failed to obtain a conviction.

Those failures emboldened the American Medical Association and others to press for legislation requiring parents to provide their children with basic necessities, including medical care. They also encouraged prosecutors to try harder to gain convictions against those whose willingness to allow children to die without benefit of medical care the public found scandalous.

During the first half of the twentieth century, the number of times Christian Science parents were brought to trial was matched only by the number of times Jehovah's Witnesses found themselves fighting for their religious freedom[39] (Chapter 6, "Soldiers of the Lord"). In legislatures, the Church of Christ, Scientist mounted a vigorous campaign to ward off laws mandating conventional medical care for their children; in courtrooms from Massachusetts to the Dakotas, the Church helped parents accused of neglect or manslaughter mount a vigorous defense.

In court, the Church won some cases while losing others. As with the Jehovah's Witnesses, the points they raised in court helped establish their religion as just another legitimate option within the panoply of American Christian religions.

Initially Christian Science efforts also helped defeat laws requiring traditional medical care for children. But as the rights of children, independent of those of their parents and guardians, became more firmly established, state laws defining a failure to provide medical care as child neglect or child abuse became more common, and religious exemptions to those laws became less common. The Church turned its lobbying efforts toward the federal government, and its efforts paid off.

In 1972, at a time when President Richard Nixon was in office and two of his top aides were Christian Scientists, the Department of Health, Education, and Welfare (HEW) adopted new regulations stating that "A parent or guardian legitimately practicing his religious beliefs" could not be judged neglectful simply for a failure to provide a child with medical treatment."[40] Today many of the religious exemptions written into law by states that did not wish to lose federal funding for child protection programs under the HEW directive remain on the books even though HEW rescinded its requirement for religious exemptions in 1983.

In spite of efforts to use the law to punish parents whose children's deaths are deemed preventable, child deaths in faith-healing communities remain common. In an article published in the April 1998 issue of the medical journal *Pediatrics*, coauthors Seth Asner and Rita Swan, a former Christian Science adherent whose child died as a result of her reliance on Mary Baker Eddy's teachings, documented 172 deaths during the preceding 20 years.[41] Of those, 64 came from the Faith Assembly; the second largest number, 24, were Christian Science cases. There were also multiple child deaths within the Church of the First Born in Colorado, Indiana, Oklahoma, and Oregon, and more scattered ones in smaller sects throughout the nation.

Almost all of those cases were conventional ones involving the death of a child whose life could have been saved with standard medical treatment. In prosecutions stemming from those deaths, courts have routinely cited the opinion from the Pierson case to buttress their claim that parents who let their children die without seeking medical care must be punished for their neglect.

Although courts still sometimes refuse to convict parents whose children die, the same reasoning they use in their efforts to prosecute parents who rely on faith healing carries over into cases involving religiously inspired methods of child discipline that are at odds with current public opinion about appropriate techniques. Potentially, they also may impact other parental decisions on such seemingly mundane matters as what and how much to feed a child or the age at which a child may be left home alone.

Each court case of this kind necessarily pits the rights of the child against those of the parent. Each conventional faith-healing scandal also raises questions about how much authority the government should have to force parents to conform to societal standards, especially when those standards conflict with parents' deeply and sincerely held religious beliefs.

That latter question took center stage when Rebecca Corneau gave birth to her fifth child, a daughter, on October 16, 2000, at the Neil J. Houston House, a state-run birthing facility for prison inmates in West Roxbury, Massachusetts. Corneau was a member of The Body, a tiny religious community in Massachusetts, whose belief in faith healing stems from teachings culled from Herbert J. Armstrong's Worldwide Church of God and Carol Balizet's Home in Zion Ministries mixed together with members' revelations, or "first leadings," which the group understand as commands from God.

Corneau followed the teachings of her religion when she gave birth to her fourth child without the help even of a midwife. Her son died; Corneau said he had been stillborn. The state found the case difficult to investigate because of the religious group's penchant for burying their dead children deep in the wilds of Maine's Baxter State Park and then refusing to reveal the location of the graves to authorities. Even before authorities managed to find the child's body and examine it to determine that, as they had suspected, the child's life could easily have been saved, an investigation into the case turned up enough evidence of religiously inspired physical abuse and medical neglect to declare the couple unfit parents and place their surviving children in protective custody. Therefore, when Corneau showed up visibly pregnant at a court hearing, Bristow County District Attorney Paul Walsh decided to do something to make sure her fifth child didn't die needlessly as he was convinced had happened to her son.

Walsh sought and got the court order that required Corneau to spend the last months of her pregnancy under medical supervision and then deliver the child with physicians present at the birth. In granting the order that sent Rebecca Corneau to the Houston House, the court relied on decisions stemming from the refusal on religious grounds of Jehovah's Witnesses to allow blood transfusions. In those cases dating from the 1960s, courts had ruled that adults have the right to direct their own medical care even if the decisions prove fatal. They do not, however, have the right to endanger a child or even a fetus by refusing to allow lifesaving treatment.[42]

The Corneau case, however, was different from the Jehovah's Witness cases. It also differed from a 1991 case in which a judge granted Philadelphia health officials the power to hospitalize gravely ill children and vaccinate unaffected ones as a measles epidemic swept through a religious school operated by Faith Tabernacle, a fairly traditional Christian faith-healing sect. In those cases, the government stepped in to save children whose lives were clearly in danger. Here, the government stepped in to ward off a potential danger to an unborn child. In doing so, the court order undermined both statutory law and constitutional principles.

In acting to protect the life of the child Corneau was carrying, the court seemingly granted personhood to a fetus—a status rarely granted to an unborn child who is killed as the result of a physical assault on a pregnant woman. While anti-abortion/pro-life activists applauded the action because it buttressed their position that a fetus is a child entitled to life, pro-choice advocates and women's rights organizations such as the National Organization for Women used the "slippery slope" argument to point out that if Corneau could be locked up because of some harm that might befall her unborn child, other women could be locked up if some zealous district attorney decided that women's decisions about diet, smoking, drinking, or even an exercise regimen might possibly have an adverse effect on their unborn child.[43]

Like Corneau, those women, and maybe even some men under some unforeseen circumstance, might, in effect, be jailed for something that had not yet happened. Therefore, the decision to hold Corneau at the Houston House until she gave birth seemingly ignored the principles of due process and "innocent until proven guilty" that are both enshrined in the Bill of Rights and are also the bedrocks of the American criminal justice system.

The urge to protect innocent life, especially when it is the life of a child, is strong. Every death that results from a failed faith healing is a tragedy for the parents whose child died in spite of their best efforts to do what they thought was best for their child. To outsiders to the faith, each preventable child death is a scandal. But each of these scandals requires careful consideration about how much weight should be given to the First Amendment guarantee of religious freedom, how much weight should go to majority opinion regarding a minority religion and its practices, and how much authorization and/or discretion the government should have to step in and enforce contemporary societal standards.

A TAX CHEAT OR A TRUSTEE?

The Internal Revenue Service (IRS) said the Rev. Sun Myung Moon cheated on his income taxes. In 1973, he had opened an interest-bearing account at Chase Manhattan Bank. Into that account he made deposits, many of them consisting of so much money in currency and small bills that on occasion it took tellers an hour to count it all.[44] From time to time he also made withdrawals for his own personal use. Each year he reported those withdrawals as personal income when he filed his income taxes. He did not report the more than $100,000 in interest the account earned over a period of three years.

The Rev. Sun Myung Moon was the founder and spiritual leader of the Holy Spirit Association for the Unification of World Christianity, more commonly called simply the Unification Church. As a teen in his native Korea, Moon had a vision in which he said Jesus told him to complete the mission of reconciling humanity to God that he had been unable to finish because he had been killed before he could marry and raise a holy family. After World

War II, Moon founded the Unification Church and set out to gain converts. In North Korea, his evangelism landed him in jail. After American forces freed him in 1950, Moon took his message to South Korea and to Japan, where his fiery preaching and fervent anticommunism gained him a loyal following. Then, in 1971, Moon set out to convert America.

In the United States, however, Moon found it much easier to generate controversy than to attract adherents to his Church. Like the 3 million Unification Church members in Asia, his 30,000 to 40,000 Americans followers called him "Father." To them, he was a prophet, a spiritual leader, and the embodiment of their faith. Most Americans, however, saw nothing religious about him. Over the course of a decade, the media were full of tales told by former "Moonies" whose families and friends had stepped in with rescues and de-programmings. The religion, they said, preyed on unsuspecting young people. They had been seduced or kidnapped, held captive, and brainwashed. Moon was a dangerous cult leader who needed to be stopped.[45]

In spite of public opinion that was overwhelmingly negative, the Holy Spirit Association for the Unification of World Christianity was a real religion. Moon was a religious leader. The first money he deposited in that bank account came from his devotees in Japan who gave it to him to use in his missionary work in the United States. Subsequent deposits of currency and small bills came from his American followers who got the money selling flowers for the Church or sometimes by begging.

If the amount of money Moon had at his disposal and the amount he took for himself and claimed as income was unusually large, neither the fact that the account was in his name alone nor the fact that he failed to report as income the interest on the account was terribly unusual. Catholic bishops and archbishops, televangelists, and parish ministers often have bank accounts in their name from which they can withdraw funds at their discretion. If those accounts are interest-bearing ones, they do not report the interest as personally taxable income; neither must their churches, as nonprofit entities, report the income to the IRS and pay taxes on it.

The only difference between those accounts and the one Moon held in his name is that on those accounts the person whose name is on the account is formally designated a trustee for a church or other religious organization. Moon was not officially designated as a trustee, but many tax experts say that may not matter.[46] Although the law on the subject can be somewhat Byzantine, if the donors of the money Moon deposited into the account intended the money to go to the Unification Church, they may have created an implicit trust with Moon, as head of the Church, as the trustee.

But to the IRS, what Moon had done looked like tax evasion. None of the complexities of church organization or the finer points of tax law seemed to matter at his October 1981 trial in federal district court. The prosecution maintained that Moon was simply a greedy, tax-cheating businessman. To buttress that case, they had only to point to the size of the bank account, the $636,000 Westchester County, New York, estate the Church bought for Moon using money from the bank account that Moon recorded as a loan to the Church, and the number of ostensibly church-owned businesses Moon controlled: companies dealing in pharmaceuticals, titanium, and ginseng tea that had made him wealthy before he came to the United States; New York real estate; fishing fleets; and then the *Washington Times*, which the Church bought to the consternation of almost everyone even as Moon was standing trial.

To Moon's attempts to raise a religious defense built around the theology and workings of the Church and his role in it, the prosecution responded with threats to raise in court all the negative publicity about the Church, whether or not any of it was germane to the case at hand. The judge raised no objection to the prosecution's strategy. His charge to the jury left the impression that religion was irrelevant. If Moon had used money from the account for his own purposes, then the interest should have been reported as income by him.

In October 1981, the jury responded with a guilty verdict. Moon was fined $25,000 and sentenced to 18 months in jail. Forty organizations came to Moon's aid as he mounted his appeal. Among them were the National Council of Churches, the United Presbyterian Church, the American Baptist Church, the Unitarian Universalist Association, the African Methodist Episcopal Church, the National Association of Evangelicals, and the Catholic League for Religious and Civil Rights. In their amicus curiae brief, they warned:

> when someone's religious beliefs and practices become relevant to refuting the charges against him, treating him as though religion had nothing to do with the matter is the very essence of unfairness and discrimination.... Upholding the conviction in this case would establish the dangerous principle that courts may simply disregard the religious reasons for, and the religious meanings of, someone's conduct.
>
> The principle that religious notions and explanations must at least be fully taken into account ... is critical to all faiths.[47]

Although judges from the Court of Appeals for the Second Circuit found the religious persecution aspects of the case troubling, the panel of judges upheld the lower court's verdict by a 2 to 1 vote. An appeal for an en banc hearing failed, as did one to the United States Supreme Court. Moon served 13 months of his 18-month sentence.

Since his release from jail, Moon has spent much of his time in Asia. The *Washington Times*, whose purchase by the Unification Church was greeted with a mixture of fear and derision, has settled in as a staunchly conservative, pro-capitalist, anti-communist alternative to the *Washington Post*. Other Church businesses seem to be thriving. If the Church isn't growing, neither has it disappeared. No longer as controversial as it was in the 1970s, it rarely makes

Rev. Moon waves to his followers and to reporters following his July 4, 1985, release from the Federal Correctional Institution in Danbury, Connecticut, where he served his sentence for tax evasion. AP photo, Bob Child.

the news except on those occasions when members whose marriages have been arranged by their spiritual leader are united in a mass wedding ceremony that provides a photo opportunity journalists find hard to resist.

The warning issued by those 40 religious organizations who signed the amicus curiae brief on behalf of the Rev. Moon, however, seems prescient. The 1990 majority opinion penned by Supreme Court Justice Antonin Scalia in the case of two alcohol and drug counselors who were denied unemployment compensation after being fired for ingesting peyote during a religious ritual seemed to allow, if not compel, courts to ignore religious motivations in cases where the defendant claims a religious reason for breaking a generally applicable secular law (Chapter 7, "A Casualty in the War on Drugs").

BALLOTS AND BIOTERRORISM

It started at an ashram in Poona, India. There, Bhagwan Shree Rajneesh taught all beliefs are false. "Do what you will" is the only law. Any other rule is a kind of social control that stifles people's true selves.[48] Spiritual seekers from the United States and Western Europe made their way to Poona to learn first-hand from the guru who called himself "The Awakened One"—and to enjoy the freedom promised by his law that there is no law. The money they paid to hear his lectures and to participate in his encounter groups made

Bhagwan and his ashram wealthy. During the 1970s, he was one of the most popular and sought-after Indian mystics of that era. However, for all his popularity among his Western devotees, he was not very popular with his Hindu neighbors.

They found it offensive that he called his devotees "sanyassins," a term Hindus apply only to a holy person who has attained a status akin to godhood. They found appalling the sexual orgies that sometimes degenerated into rape, the drugs, and the assorted acts of violence and general mayhem that broke out among those living in his lawless society. When he called their religion and their country "old, ancient and rotten," it was too much.[49]

Local authorities blocked Bhagwan's plans to expand his ashram. India began denying entry visas to Westerners headed for Poona. The guru then obtained a visa on the grounds he sought medical care in the United States. In May 1981, he showed up in Montclair, New Jersey, at a mansion his devotees had bought for him. But he didn't intend to stay there. He planned to build a new community like the one he had in India. Toward that end, he dispatched his top aide, who went by the name Ma Anand Sheela, to find a place where he and his followers could live as they pleased without interference from societal rules.

In June 1981, Sheela paid $5.75 million for the Big Muddy Ranch, a 64,000 acre worn-out cattle ranch, in the high desert country of eastern Oregon. In July, Bhagwan and some of his followers moved there, only to find they weren't quite as far from society's rules as they had hoped.

The Big Muddy Ranch, now renamed Rancho Rajneesh, was zoned as agricultural land. When she bought the land, Sheela had promised that no more than 40 people would live there. But many more sanyassins moved in. Almost immediately they began improvements that smacked of commercial development. Under Oregon's strict land use and zoning laws, the Land Conservation and Development Commission (LCDC) had the power to block the group's planned improvements. So the newcomers began to covet the nearby tiny town of Antelope and its urban development district where they could legally establish commercial enterprises.

Thus the battle for Antelope began. It was a culture war from the beginning,[50] but it was also a political one. By and large Oregonians are a tolerant people with a "live and let live" philosophy. But Oregon is also home to many Christian fundamentalists. Its high desert country is politically and socially quite conservative, so the people of Antelope were not happy to have so many sanyassins wearing bright "sunrise colors" and beaded necklaces with photographs of their guru in their midst.

When the Bhagwan's followers applied for a business permit to open a printing plant and an office complex, Antelope city officials refused to grant it. The Rajneeshees went to court and won. In response, the residents of Antelope scheduled an election to disincorporate the town. If there were no town, there would be no urban development district. The Rajneeshees would have to deal with the powerful LCDC if they wanted to build in the area.

To block that possibility, Bhagwan's followers made use of Oregon's generous voter registration law. Under that law, people who had spent a night in a district and said they planned to remain in it could register even on election day and vote in the election. Sanyassins moved into Antelope. They won the election. By a 55–42 vote, disincorporation failed.

The Rajneeshees also filed papers to incorporate their Rancho Rajneesh. To assure a favorable vote, they bought cattle at a high price from a county commissioner whose approval they needed. They got his vote, and they got their city. They called it Rajneeshpuram, and quickly deeded it to their newly created Rajneesh Neo-Sannyassin International Foundation.

With the creation of that Foundation, followers of the guru who taught that there is no religion now had created a religion. The town, now owned by the Foundation, had its own pink-clad security force. It also had control of development within the city limits as well as control over access to the city and movement within it.

But their right to incorporate their town was being challenged in court. To make sure they could continue with their development plans even if they lost their town in court, the Rajneeshees put up three candidates for election to Antelope's seven-member city council. On election day, they wrote in names for all other candidates on the ballot. When the results of the November 1982 election were in, the Rajneeshees held 9 out of 10 city positions, including that of the mayor, treasurer, and town marshal.

Once in office, the Rajneesh officials renamed all the streets after Hindu gods. They raised taxes, apparently hoping to drive out long-term Antelope residents, and contracted out the police service to the Rajneesh Peace Force from Rajneeshpuram. Their actions upset almost everyone who was not one of the guru's devotees.

The Immigration and Naturalization Service began looking into Bhagwan's immigration status—he had come to the United States on a medical visa, but had not sought any medical care. Bhagwan sought permanent residence as a "religious worker," but preached a religion he said was not a religion.[51] Moreover, he had entered one of his periodic periods of silent withdrawal, so he couldn't really be doing any religious work even if his beliefs really did constitute a religion.

But if the guru had withdrawn from public life, Sheela had not. Claiming religious persecution from intolerant, close-minded Oregonians, as she had done since the group's arrival in the state, Sheela angered Governor Vic Atiyeh by sending him an open letter stating that "Oregon can hardly prosper if it is filled with stagnant, dilapidated little towns like Antelope—places where indolent old people go to mark time until they die."[52]

Sheela demanded the right to give the invocation when the state legislature opened its biennial session, got what she wanted, and then showed up with armed guards. Her invocation, "I go to the feet of the Awakened One; I go to the feet of the commune of the Awakened One; I go the feet of the Absolute Truth of the Awakened one,"[53] violated the requirement that the invocation be nonsectarian. It also set up a wave of negative publicity and protests as even the more liberal and tolerant people from Oregon's populous Willamette Valley concluded they had a dangerous cult in their midst.[54] In April 1983, after the Rajneeshees took control of Antelope and set up their Foundation-owned town, she published a letter warning, "[W]e are here in Oregon to stay at whatever the cost.[55]

Sheela meant business. Not content to control Antelope and Rajneeshpuram, she hatched a plan to take over Wasco County, where Antelope and Rajneeshpuram were located. In the summer of 1984, she announced a Share-a-Home program under which any urban homeless person over the age of 18 could come to the ashram. Transportation would be provided; in Rajneeshpuram, the homeless would get shelter, food, and a job. Coincidentally, the offer was good just until October 17, the last day to register to vote in the fall elections.

The media reacted to the program with both bemusement and bewilderment, but many homeless people responded to the offer[56]—many, but not enough to enable the Rajneeshees to use them to take over the county government, especially because the state had made it harder for them to register. To prevent vote fraud, the state now required new voters in Wasco County to register in The Dalles, the county seat, located on the Columbia River some hundred miles away.

Threatening letters arrived at the homes of state officials and newspaper reporters looking into the goings on at Rajneeshpuram. The Rajneesh community filed a lawsuit against their enemies—everyone from President Ronald Reagan down to their Wasco County neighbors. They called the lawsuit *God v. the Universe*.[57]

In 1983, after the Antelope election, Mike Sullivan, the district attorney in neighboring Jefferson County, inexplicably fell ill from what appeared to be arsenic poisoning. During 1984, two county commissioners contracted salmonella poisoning after visiting Rajneeshpuram. Bhagwan's doctor also became ill. Then between September 6 and 26, while the voter registration campaign was going on, more than 700 people contracted salmonella poisoning after eating at salad bars in at least 10 different restaurants in The Dalles area.

That, however, was the beginning of the end. On September 16, Bhagwan Shree Rajneesh reasserted himself. On that date, he called a press conference to announce that Sheela and 14 associates had fled. They were on their way to Europe. Over the next week, he called more conferences at which he revealed Sheela's treachery. He invited government authorities to visit his town.[58]

Law enforcement agents who swarmed the ranch in response to Bhagwan's invitation turned up evidence implicating the guru in immigration fraud that included mass weddings designed to gain green cards for foreign-born sannyas-sin. They also found evidence of massive bugging and wiretapping. Under-neath Sheela's cabin they found a fully equipped biological-warfare laboratory.

As investigators had suspected, the strange illnesses were the work of the Rajneeshees. The salmonella poisonings in The Dalles were the largest bioter-rorist attack within the United States. They were also a dry run for an even bigger attack just before the November election. Sheela had planned an attack that would sicken Wasco voters. If they couldn't make it to the polls, she and her cabal within Rajneeshpuram would take over the county.

Federal and state grand juries looked into the evidence. When it became clear he was about to be indicted, Bhagwan's lawyers began negotiating terms for a voluntarily surrender. But on October 27, Bhagwan Shree Rajneesh, along with some others, took off in two rented Lear jets.

Alerted to the hasty departure by an informant, Oregon officials contacted their counterparts in North Carolina. When the planes touched down in Charlotte, Bhagwan and his entourage were arrested. A few hours later, Sheela and two of her associates were captured and arrested in Germany. Both Bhag-wan and Sheela were extradited to Oregon.

Bhagwan pleaded guilty to immigration charges; under a plea bargain he paid a large fine and agreed to leave the country. He returned to India, where he then ran an ashram and spiritual retreat center until he died on January 19, 1990, at age 58.

Sheela and her codefendants pleaded guilty to federal immigration charges and state charges of attempted murder, assault, and arson. She was sentenced to two 20-year sentences and ordered to pay $500,000 in fines and restitution. The sannyassins scattered. The Big Muddy Ranch that had become Rajneesh-puram lay empty and then was sold.

Although the Rajneeshees are no longer a threat, they came as close to using American law to take over secular government and in its place establish a theocracy as any religious group has ever done—or even tried to do.

VIRGINS AND GUNS

The Millerites, followers of William Miller whose belief that Jesus, the Messiah, would return to earth in all His glory failed to materialize, gave rise to the Seventh-day Adventist Church. In 1934, after the Seventh-day Adven-tists disfellowshipped Victor Houtoff for the heretical beliefs he published in his "Shepherd's Rod" manifesto, some Adventists followed him to Texas. There, at their Mt. Carmel on the Brazos River near Waco, Houtoff's Shepherd's Rod community first became known as the Davidian Seventh-day Adventists and then as the General Association of Davidian Seventh-day Adventists. When Houtoff died, his death touched off a series of power struggles within the community that ended in 1987 with Houtoff's successor, Benjamin Roden, in jail and Vernon Howell, a relatively new convert to the faith, in control at Mount Carmel.

Under Howell, the world came to know the General Association of Davidian Seventh-day Adventists simply as Branch Davidians. Both the group's official name and its more common one stem from members' belief that they are the last in an unbroken lineage of true believers whose heritage can be traced back to the biblical House of David into whom Jesus, the Messiah and Savior, was born. Under Howell, Branch Davidians also came to believe that their leader is a messiah, or anointed one, in the biblical tradition of King David and of the Emperor Cyrus (Koresh, in Persian). In 1991, to make that belief perfectly clear, Howell legally changed his name to David Koresh.

Koresh's followers began calling themselves Students of the Seventh Seal. As an apocalyptic sect, they took their end-time beliefs and their preferred name from the Book of Revelations, and especially from the parts of that book that tell of a remnant of 144,000 true believers who will be spared from the tribulation and of the Seven Seals whose breaking marks the passage of end-time stages. Their leader, they believed, was the "cleansing angel" of Revelations who would prepare the world for the New Jerusalem. Toward that end all faithful female adherents were to be his perfect mate. Through them he would create a new lineage of "righteous seed," who would erect a restored House of David and ultimately rule the world. But before that day, there must be the final battle of Armageddon. That battle would begin in the United States with an attack by the government on Mt. Carmel, which Koresh had renamed "Ranch Apocalypse."

To his followers Koresh was the messiah whom God had called upon to unlock the messages behind the Seven Seals. Some of those messages had already been unlocked, so they knew they were living in the time of the Fifth Seal. Armageddon would soon be upon them.

The Branch Davidians who lived at Mt. Carmel spent much of their time studying the Bible and listening to sermons from their leader. They also worked diligently to fortify their compound and lay in supplies for the forthcoming battle.

But they were not a particularly reclusive group. Koresh, who fancied himself something of a musician, occasionally jammed with groups that were part of the Waco music scene. Children sometimes were home-schooled; other times they attended public school. Their mothers generally spent their days at Mt. Carmel, but most men worked in town, some in businesses unconnected to the religion and others in ones that, though owned by Davidians, counted outsiders among their customers and clients.

Neither were they a closed society. Over the years, a few people came to Mt. Carmel to live, while others left the compound and the faith. Fellow believers from Australia, California, and other states sometimes visited Mt. Carmel. Those who lived at Mt. Carmel sometimes visited Branch Davidians who did not live with them. On occasion members also visited apostate friends or relatives or ones who had never been a part of the faith.

That openness to visits with outsiders led to trouble when 14-year-old Kiri Jewell went to Michigan to spend Christmas with her father in 1991. Although Kiri had visited her father on other occasions since her parents' divorce, this time, with the help of a former member who had failed to wrest control of a Davidian community in Australia away from Koresh, he sent her for deprogramming. After four months of intensive efforts by former Davidians, Kiri gave her father what he wanted—she told a judge in a Michigan court that she wanted to live with her father instead of going back to Mt. Carmel to live with her mother.[59]

After the judge awarded custody of Kiri to her father, she took her story to the media. On television and in newspaper interviews, she repeated stories of polygamy, illicit sexual relations between adult males and very young girls, and other forms of child abuse she had heard about from former members of the Australian community who had been brought to Michigan to aid in her deprogramming. To those stories, she added ones of sexually abused young virgins and of harsh physical punishments meted out to children, including infants and toddlers—stories that were, she said, based on things she had seen or experienced while living at Mt. Carmel.[60]

When media around the country picked up Kiri's stories, Texas launched an investigation. Although the Texas Department of Children's Protective Services turned up no evidence of illicit sex between adult Davidians and minors at the compound, or of any other kind of physical or sexual abuse,[61] reporters managed to find a few former Davidians who told tales of child abuse similar to the ones Kiri had told.[62]

To outsiders those new media reports of abuse suggested that social service workers must not have conducted a very thorough investigation. David Koresh was clearly a dangerous cult leader who used religion to condone, promote, and practice all kinds of child abuse.

While the image of Koresh and his followers as dangerous to innocent children was still fresh in people's minds, a new image of him and his followers as a danger to their neighbors began to take shape. Unlike the image of Davidians as child molesters, this one grew out of a story told by an outsider with no real connection to or interest in the group.

This new image began to take shape in May 1992 when United Parcel Service in Waco informed the McLennan County Sheriff's Department that one of its drivers had reported that a box he was delivering to Mt. Carmel had broken open, and in it were guns, inert grenade casings, and black powder. At about the same time, a few Mt. Carmel neighbors reported what they thought was gunfire at Mt. Carmel.[63] To the government and to the public, weapons and reports of gunfire could mean only one thing—that Koresh had a band of brainwashed followers, trained in the use of lethal weapons, who were preparing to attack their peaceful neighbors.

By June the Federal Bureau of Alcohol, Tobacco, and Firearms (BATF) had launched an investigation into the Branch Davidians. The BATF also placed their compound at Mt. Carmel under round-the-clock surveillance and began training for what it felt sure would be a forthcoming attack by Koresh's fanatical followers. By the end of February 1993, the BATF became convinced it was time to take further action.

On Sunday morning, February 28, BATF agents, armed with a warrant to search for illegal weapons, moved toward Mt. Carmel in what they thought would be a surprise move. The Davidians, however, had received advance warning and taken up defensive positions. As the agents entered the compound, shots rang out. A Davidian called 911 for help. After more gunfire, the raid ended in a ceasefire.

Four children left the compound and were taken into protective custody. Five Davidians and four BATF agents were dead. Because federal agents had been killed in the line of duty, the FBI took command of what degenerated into a lengthy standoff between the Branch Davidians and government forces who had them surrounded. For the 51 days of the siege, communication with Koresh and his followers was either through or approved by FBI negotiators.

During the first few days, conversations between Koresh and FBI-approved negotiators led to an agreement that those who wanted to leave the compound could do so. Nineteen children and some adults left. But after word came back to the Davidians that the children had been taken into protective custody and the adults who had left with them had been arrested, no one else left the compound.

Koresh also apparently agreed to give up peacefully, first if the government would agree to the broadcast of a message from him, and then if he were given time to complete his exposition on the meaning of the Seven Seals. But instead of surrendering on the agreed upon date, Koresh informed government agents that the Lord had instructed him to wait a little longer.

That decision by Koresh convinced the authorities that waiting longer would be pointless. With negotiations suspended and conditions at Mt. Carmel apparently deteriorating, Janet Reno, the U.S. attorney general under President Bill Clinton who had first come to national attention by prosecuting child abuse cases in Florida, approved a final assault on Mt. Carmel for the sake of the children who, the FBI said, were being held hostage and in imminent danger.[64]

In preparation for that assault, the FBI cut off water and electricity to the compound. It also stepped up its psychological warfare that included shining bright lights into the compound all night and bombarding the Davidians with nonstop recordings of Nancy Sinatra tunes, Buddhist chants, and the sounds of rabbits being killed.

On April 19, 51 days after the siege began, the FBI pumped tear gas into the compound through holes it had first punctured in the walls of the buildings.

However, even as the levels of tear gas increased to dangerous levels, no Davidians emerged from the compound.

After six hours, a woman came out carrying a computer disk with Koresh's treatise on the Seven Seals. At the same time, three fires broke out simultaneously in different parts of the main building. Twenty minutes later there was an explosion. Seventy-four Davidians, including David Koresh, died in the fiery inferno that was Mt. Carmel.

In 1993, public opinion polls showed that the overwhelming majority of Americans thought the scandalous beliefs and behaviors of the Branch Davidians at Mt. Carmel fully justified the government's actions against them.[65] Although the BATF and the FBI believed their actions were necessary to protect the children from further abuse and the community from attack by the Davidians, the official report of an investigation by Congress made it clear that both agencies were guilty of misinterpreting and mishandling the situation.[66]

An examination of the children who left Mt. Carmel during the early days of the siege confirmed the Protective Service's earlier conclusion that the Davidians did not physically abuse their children—neither was there any evidence of pedophilia. Although the Davidians believed Koresh had the right to take for himself multiple wives of his own choosing, DNA testing showed that neither he nor any other adult male Davidian had produced any children through liaisons with underage girls.

Neither was the community in imminent danger. Although the Branch Davidians had accumulated a huge arsenal, their purpose was defensive. They had no plans for attack. Moreover, the Davidians had legally acquired all of their weapons, with the exception of a few automatics, and kept the records on them required by Texas law.

The FBI and the BATF chose to accept the opinions of experts from the anticult community whose reputation depends on their ability to convince people to leave alternative religions. This decision was made in spite of warnings from biblical scholars and other experts who study apocalyptic and alternative religions from a more neutral historical or social science perspective. They were concerned that a strategy developed for dealing with terrorists and hostage-takers would not work with members of an apocalyptic religion.[67]

No one can say for sure what would have happened if the BATF and the FBI had acted differently, but the decision to confront the Davidians with a show of force made the fiery finale inevitable. For the Davidians who died at Mt. Carmel, both the siege and the conflagration confirmed their belief that they were indeed living in the time of the Fifth Seal, when a battle between true believers and the forces of evil, personified by the government, would end in a purifying fire that would pave the way for the Second Coming.

Although 74 Branch Davidians died at Mt. Carmel, there are still Branch Davidians living in Waco and in small communities scattered throughout the nation and the world. Like those who died in the inferno, they still believe they are the remnant of true believers.

Thus, like the other scandals described in Chapters 7 and 8, the story of the Branch Davidians raises important questions about the meaning and scope of religious freedom as guaranteed by the First Amendment. As Michael Barkun notes in his "Reflections after Waco" in the June 2–9, 1993, *Christian Century*:

> If the state is not to consign all new and unusual religious groups to the realm of outcast "cults," how is it to differentiate among them? Should the state monitor doctrine to distinguish those religious organizations that require particularly close observation? News reports suggest that Islamic groups may already be the subjects of such surveillance—a chilling and disturbing prospect. Who decides that a group is dangerous? By what criteria? If beliefs can lead to actions, and if those actions violate the law, how should order and security be balanced against religious freedom?[68]

Although the Branch Davidians may not have been a threat to their neighbors, there are individuals and groups, some of them heavily armed, who may be or may become a true threat. Therefore, the story of the Branch Davidians, with their huge arsenal, also raises significant questions about protection for versus limitations on the Second Amendment right to "keep and bear arms."

FOR FURTHER READING

Barkun, Michael. 1993, June 2–9. Reflections after Waco: Millennialists and the state. *Christian Century*, pp. 596–600.

Epps, Garrett. 2001. *To an unknown god: Religious freedom on trial.* New York: St. Martin's Press, pp. 66–89.

Fogarty, Robert S. 1993, April 12. "Cults," guns and the Kingdom. *The Nation*, pp. 485–487.

Gaffney, Edward McGlynn, Jr. 1993, May 21. Reaction to Waco: Enforcing the law; Consider the Bill of Rights. *Commonweal*, pp. 5–6.

Gallagher, Eugene V. 2008, Fall. FLDS 1, Texas 0. *Religion in the News* 11(2): 6–8, 25.

Goodman, Ellen. 2000, September 10. Just how far can the state go in protecting an "unborn child"? *Boston Globe*, p. F7.

Isikoff, Michael. 1985, August 26. New Moon. *The New Republic*, pp. 14–16.

Kantrowicz, Barbara. 1993, May 3. Day of judgment: How the cult standoff with the FBI escalated into a fiery finale. *Newsweek*, pp. 22–27.

Klaw, Spencer. 1993. *Without sin: The life and death of the Oneida Community.* New York: Penguin Books.

Krakauer, Jon. 2004. *Under the banner of heaven.* New York: Anchor Books.

Lewis, James R., ed. 1994. *From the ashes: Making sense of Waco.* Lanham, MD: Rowman & Littlefield.

Mason, Debra L. 1986, January 21. Sect member goes on trial in baby's death. *Columbus Dispatch.* In Judith M. Buddenbaum and Debra L. Mason, eds., *Readings on Religion as News.* Ames: Iowa State University Press, pp. 371–375.

McClaughry, John. 1983, December 12. The uneasy case against Reverend Moon. *National Review*, pp. 1611–1612.

Miller-McLemore, Bonnie J. 2007, May 3. Christian discipline of children. *Sightings*. Chicago: Martin Marty Center at the University of Chicago Divinity School.

Morse, Jodie. 2003, March 24. The missing nine months. *Time*, pp. 44–48.

Murr, Andrew. 2006, March 22. Polygamist on the lam. *Newsweek*, p. 37.

Murr, Andrew. 2006, September 11. The polygamist's life. *Newsweek*, p. 25.

Noonan, John T., Jr., and Edward McGlynn Gaffney, Jr. 2001. *Religious freedom: History, cases, and other materials on the interaction of religion and government*, 2nd ed. New York: Foundation Press, pp. 288–307, 912–915.

Perry, Seth. 2008, April 17. Look at this tangle of thorns. *Sightings*. Chicago: Martin Marty Center at the University of Chicago Divinity School.

Peters, Shawn Francis. 2008. *When prayer fails: Faith healing, children, and the law*. New York: Oxford University Press.

Riley, Michael, Richard Woodbury, Julie Johnson, and Elaine Shannon. 1993, May 3. Tragedy in Waco. *Time*, pp. 27–45.

Von Drehle, David. 2008, May 5. The sins of the fathers. *Time*, pp. 32–35.

Notes

CHAPTER 1

1. Maria Monk 1836, January 19. Awful disclosures. *New York Herald.* In Judith M. Buddenbaum and Debra L. Mason, eds. *Readings on religion as news.* Ames, Iowa State University Press, 2000, p. 93.

2. Ibid., p. 89.

3. Judith M. Buddenbaum. 1987, Summer-Autumn. "Judge … what their acts will justify": The religion journalism of James Gordon Bennett. *Journalism History* 14(2–3), p. 66, n. 52.

4. Ibid., p. 54.

5. A revival in Sarasota Springs. 1840, May 15. In Buddenbaum and Mason, *Readings on religion as news,* p. 100.

6. Buddenbaum, "Judge … what their acts will justify," p. 62.

7. Alan Bjerga. 2001, Winter. The trials of faith: Discussion of religion and the Beecher adultery scandal, 1870–1880. *American Journalism* 18(1), p. 76; Amanda Frisken. 2004. *Victoria Woodhull's sexual revolution: Political theater and the popular press.* Philadelphia: University of Pennsylvania Press, p. 85.

8. Paul A. Carter. 1971. *The spiritual crisis of the Gilded Age.* DeKalb: Northern Illinois University Press, pp. 118–132.

9. Bjerga, The trials of faith.

10. George Hackett. 1988, February 29. A sex scandal breaks over Jimmy Swaggart. *Newsweek,* p. 30.

11. Richard N. Ostling. 1988, March 7. Now it's Jimmy's turn. *Time,* pp. 46–48.

12. James G. Houghland, Jr., Dwight Billings, and James R. Wood. 1990, September. The instability of support for television evangelists: Public reactions during a period of embarrassment. *Review of Religious Research* 32(1): 56–65; Ron Givens. 1988, June 6. Back in the limelight again. *Newsweek,* p. 7; John Schwartz. 1988, April 11. Jimmy Swaggart: breaking away. *Newsweek,* p. 6.

13. Sins of the fathers. 2002, March 4. *Newsweek,* pp. 48–53; Globe Spotlight Team. 2002, January 6. Church allowed abuse by priest for years. *Boston Globe.* Online version retrieved January 21, 2008, from http://www.boston.com/globe/spotlight/abuse/coverage/jan-02.htm.

14. Sacha Pfeiffer. 2002, January 31. Famed "street priest" preyed upon boys. *Boston Globe.* Online version retrieved January 21, 2008, from http://www.boston.com/globe/spotlight/abuse/stories/013102-shanley-spotlight.htm.

15. Globe Spotlight Team. 2002, January 31. Scores of priests involved in sex abuse cases. *Boston Globe*, p. A1.

16. Ibid.

17. Chester Gillis. 2002, July 29–August 5. Cultures, codes and publics. *America*, pp. 8-11.

18. Vatican shifts on expulsion of sex abusers. 2002, May 13. *America*, p. 5.

19. Timeline: U.S. Church sex scandal. 2008. *BBC News.* Retrieved January 21, 2008. http://www.newsvote.bbc.co.uk/1/hi/world/americas/3872499.st

20. Ibid.

21. Philip Jenkins. 2004. *The new anti-Catholicism.* New York: Oxford University Press.

22. Martin E. Marty. 2002, July 31. Facing the fallout. *Sightings.* Martin Marty Center at the University of Chicago.

23. Andrew Lee. 2006, January 5. Christian groups in Colorado Springs. *Sightings.* Martin Marty Center at the University of Chicago.

24. Jonathan Darman and Andrew Murr. 2006, November 13. A pastor's fall from grace. *Newsweek*, p. 34.

25. New Life Church. 2006, November 2. News release from New Life Church, Colorado Springs, Colorado.

26. James Dobson. 2006, November 2. News release from Focus on the Family, Colorado Springs, Colorado.

27. Eric Gorski and Mike McPhee. 2006, November 3. Haggard admits meth buy. *Denver Post.* Retrieved January 22, 2008, from http://www.denverpost.com/search/ci-4597552.

28. Katie Kerwin McCrimmon. 2006, November 4. Polygraph results indicate deception. *Rocky Mountain News.* Retrieved January 22, 2008, from http://www.rockymountainnews.com/news/2006/nov/04.

29. Overseers Board. 2006, November 4. News release from New Life Church, Colorado Springs.

30. Eric Gorski. 2006, November 5. Disgraced Haggard: I am a "deceiver and a liar." *Denver Post.* Retrieved January 22, 2008, from http://www.denverpost.com/search/ci-4607865.

31. Gayle Haggard. 2006, November 5. Gayle Haggard's letter to New Life Church. *The Gazette* (Colorado Springs). Retrieved January 22, 2008, from http://www2.gazette.com/display.php?id+1326185&secid=1.

32. Eric Gorski. 2007, February 6. Haggard says he is "completely heterosexual." *Denver Post.* Retrieved January 22, 2008, from http://www.denverpost.com/search/-ci5164921.

33. Kevin Simpson and Eric Gorski. 2006, November 12. Pastor's case stirs debate. *Denver Post.* Retrieved January 22, 2008, from http://www.denverpost.com/search/-ci4644918.

34. Entrepreneurs R us. 2006, December. *Christianity Today*, pp. 22–23.

CHAPTER 2

1. Paul E. Johnson and Sean Wilentz. 1994. *The kingdom of Matthias*, New York: Oxford University Press, p. 54.

2. Ibid., p. 59.

3. Ibid., p. 79.

4. Ibid., p. 81.

5. Ibid., p. 40.

6. Ibid., pp. 92–94.

7. Ibid., p. 101.

8. Ibid., p. 105.

9. Ibid., pp. 119–120.

10. Ibid., pp. 135–137

11. Ibid., pp. 145–147.

12. Douglas R. Brown, Wesley R. Iversen, H. Michael Rood, Douglas D. Smith, and Paul N. Williams. 1972, March 30. Boys Town: Lucrative income of a well-known child-care home. *West Omaha Sun.* In Heinz Dietrich Fischer, ed. *Local reporting, 1947–1987: From a county vote fraude [sic] to a corrupt city council.* New York: K. G. Saur, 1989, pp. 170, 174.

13. Ibid., p. 170.

14. Boys Town bonanza. 1972, April 10. *Time*, pp. 17–18; The money machine. 1972, April 10. *Newsweek*, p. 55.

15. Jean Seligman. 1987, June 8. The inimitable Tammy Faye. *Newsweek*, p. 69.

16. Ibid.; Russell Watson. 1987, June 8. Heaven can wait. *Newsweek*, pp. 62–63.

17. Andrew Kopkind. 1987, April 6. Jim Bakker's lost America. *Esquire*, p. 183.

18. Charles Shepard. 1987, March 7. Bakker treated for drug dependency. *Charlotte Observer*, p. 1A; Charles Shepard. 1987, March 20. Jim Bakker resigns from PTL. *Charlotte Observer*, p. 1A.

19. Kim A. Lawton. 1992, January 13. Broadcasters face ethics questions—again. *Christianity Today*, p. 43.

20. Robert Abelman. 1991, Spring/Summer. Influence of news coverage of the "Scandal" on PTL viewers. *Journalism Quarterly* 68(1/2):101–110.

21. Jim Bakker. 1996. *I was wrong.* Nashville: Thomas Nelson, p. 535.

22. Laurie Goodstein. 1995, June 4. Thou shalt not lie. *Washington Post.* In Buddenbaum and Mason, *Readings on religion as news*, p. 430.

23. Ibid., p. 437.

24. Larry Downing. 1996, October 28. The Asian connection. *Newsweek*, p. 27.

25. Jonathan Alter and Michael Isikoff. 1996, October 28. The real scandal is what's legal. *Newsweek*, pp. 30–31.

26. The clue in the letter. 1996, August 12. *Newsweek*, p. 49.

27. Ronald C. Kiener. 2008, Fall. The Postville raid. *Religion in the News* 11(2): 2.

28. Stephen G. Bloom. 2000. *Postville: A clash of cultures in heartland America.* New York: Harcourt; Kiener, The Postville raid; Pat Johnson. 2008, May 13. Biggest kosher meatpacker started by Jews in 1987. *Des Moines Register.* Retrieved November 6, 2008, from http://search.desmoinesregister.com.

29. Kiener, The Postville raid, p. 3.

30. Ibid.

31. Ibid., p. 24.

32. Ibid., p. 3; Alan Cooperman. 2004, December 31. USDA investigating kosher meat plant: Advocacy group's grisly video sparked outcry. *Washington Post*, p. A3.

33. Kiener, The Postville raid, pp. 3–5, 24. Alan Cooperman. 2007, July 7. Eco-kosher movement aims to heed tradition, conscience. *Washington Post*, p. A1.

34. Kiener, The Postville raid, pp. 3–5; Samantha M. Shapiro. 2008, October 12. Kosher wars. *New York Times.* Retrieved October 31, 2008, from http://www.nytimes.com/2008/10/12/magazine/12kosher-t.html.

35. Kiener, The Postville raid, p. 4; Orthodox Union. 2006, June 30. Prof. Grandin is satisfied with AgriProcessors slaughter practices. Retrieved November 6, 2008, from http://www.ou.org/news.

36. Kiener, The Postville raid.

37. Ibid.

38. Ibid., pp. 4–5, 24.

39. Ibid., p. 3; Julie Eilperin. 2004, May 3. Kosher meat plant sets off Iowa feud: Some fear release of salt water into river. *Washington Post*, p. A2.

40. Kiener, The Postville raid, p. 5.

41. Ibid., p. 24; Tony Ley. 2008, August 26. Packers taking advantage of workers nettles Obama. *Des Moines Register.* Retrieved November 6, 2008, from http://search.desmoinesregister.com.

42. Kiener, The Postville raid, p. 24; Tony Ley. 2008, September 10. Kosher group: Change plant's leadership. *Des Moines Register.* Retrieved November 6, 2008, from http://search.desmoinesregister.com.

CHAPTER 3

1. Arthur Conan Doyle. 1926. *The History of Spiritualism*, vol. 1. New York: G. H. Doran, pp. 88–89.

2. The Rochester rappers. 1853, April. *United States Democratic Review.* Retrieved February 11, 2008, from http://www.victorian-magic.blogspot.com/2006/05/rochester-rappers.html; See also, Doyle, *The history of spiritualism*, pp. 85, 247.

3. *Preliminary report of the Commission appointed by the University of Pennsylvania to investigate modern spiritualism in accordance with the request of the late Henry Seybert.* 1887. New York: J. B. Lippincott.

4. Daniel Stashower. 1999, August. The medium and the magician. *American History*, p. 41.

5. Ibid.

6. J. Malcolm Bird. 1924, July. Our next psychic: A preliminary account of the case that now comes before us, as it appears to the naked eye. *Scientific American*, pp. 28–29; J. Malcolm Bird. 1924, August. The "Margery" mediumship. *Scientific American*, pp. 88–89, 126.

7. Stashower, The medium and the magician, pp. 39, 42.

8. Ibid., p. 43.

9. Ibid.

10. Harry Houdini. 1925. "Margery" the Medium exposed. Retrieved May 2, 2007, from http://www.pbs.org/wgbh/amex/houdini/sfeature/margery1/html.

11. The psychic investigation: Claims of "Margery" to produce supernatural phenomena are rejected by the committee. 1925, April. *Scientific American*, p. 229.

12. Stashower, The medium and the magician, p. 46.

13. Ibid.

14. Bruce Bliven. 1926, November 3. Sister Aimee. *The New Republic*, p. 289.

15. Ibid., pp. 289–290. Sarah Comstock. 1927, December. Aimee Semple McPherson: Prima donna of revivalism. *Harper's Monthly Magazine*, p. 19; Aimee and the media (no date). Retrieved April 1, 2007, from http://.xroads.virginia.edu/~UG00/robertson/asm/media.html.

16. Comstock, Aimee Semple McPherson, pp. 11–15; Shelton Bissell. 1928, May 23. Vaudeville at Angelus Temple. *The Outlook*, pp. 126–127, 158.

17. Faithful cling to waning hope. 1926, May 20. *Los Angeles Times.* Retrieved April 10, 2007, from http://xroads.virginia.edu/UG00/robertson/asm/latimes.html.

18. David Warren Ryder. 1926, July 28. Aimee Semple McPherson. *The Nation*, p. 81; Bliven, Sister Aimee, pp. 292–293; John Updike. 2007, April 30. Famous Aimee. *New Yorker*, p. 76.

19. Updike, Famous Aimee, p. 76.

20. Ibid., p. 78.

21. Ibid., p. 79.

22. The search for the phantom will. 1976, April 20. *Time*, p. 21.

23. The Hughes will: Is it for real? 1976, May 10. *Time*, p. 30.

24. Ibid.; Susan Fraker. 1976, May 17. Howard Hughes: Heirs apparent? *Newsweek*, pp. 39–40.

25. Fraker, Howard Hughes: Heirs apparent? p. 39; Susan Fraker. 1976, May 24. Howard Hughes: A wealth of wills. *Newsweek*, p. 30.

26. The Hughes will: Is it for real?

27. John Hollenhorst. 2005, February 23. Dummar may have told truth after all. *Deseret News.* Retrieved May 2, 2007, from http://deseretnews.com/dn/view/0,1249,600114069,00.html.

28. Ibid.; Fraker, Howard Hughes: Heirs apparent? p. 40.

29. Hollenhorst, Dummar may have told truth.

30. Paul Foy. 2007, January 9. Judge tosses lawsuit over Hughes will. Associated Press. Retrieved May 2, 2007 from http://www.signonsandiego.com/news/nation/20070109-1151-wst-dummar-hughes.html.

31. Richard N. Ostling. 1985, May 20. Challenging Mormonism's roots. *Time*, p. 44; Jan Shipps. 1985, November 13. The salamander and the saints. *Christian Century*, p. 1021.

32. First "Hofmann" history-mystery. 1987, February 15. *Salt Lake Tribune*, Retrieved March 5, 2008, from http://www.utlm.org/onlinebooks/trackingreview.htm?FACT.

33. Dallin H. Oaks. 1987, October. Recent events involving church history and forged documents. *Ensign*, pp. 63–69. Retrieved March 5, 2008, from http://www.lds.org.

34. Gordon B. Hinckley. 1985, June 23. First Presidency message: Keep the faith. Published in September 1985 in *Ensign*, p. 3–6. Retrieved March 5, 2008, from http://www.lds.org.

35. Church releases statement on Mark Hofmann interviews. 1987, July 31. Published in October 1987, *Church News*, pp. 78–79.

36. Royal Ontario Museum. 2003, July 23. Royal Ontario Museum: Oded Golan's arrest/James Ossuary. Retrieved March 12, 2008, from http://www.rom.on.ca/news/releases/public.php?mediakey=vhggdo3048.

37. Burkhard Bilger. 2004, December 6. God doesn't need Ole Anthony. *New Yorker*, p. 76; Sean Rowe. 2006, June 11. Second coming: A jet settin', Scotch-sippin', Robert Tilton washes up in South Florida and he still wants your money. *Dallas Observer.* Retrieved March 3, 2008, from http://www.dallasobserver.com/1997-11-06/news/second-coming.

38. Bilger, God doesn't need Ole Anthony; David Pazstor. 1995, December 7. Goofin' on God. *Dallas Observer.* Retrieved March 3, 2008, from http://www.dallasobserver.com/1995-12-07/news/goofin-on-god.

39. Bilger, God doesn't need Ole Anthony, p. 78; Pazstor, Goofin' on God; John W. Kennedy, 1993, September 13. End of the line for Tilton? *Christianity Today*, pp. 78–82.

40. Bilger, God doesn't need Ole Anthony, pp. 76–78.

41. Ibid., p. 78.
42. Ibid.
43. Ibid.; Pazstor, Goofin' on God.
44. Rowe, Second coming.

CHAPTER 4

1. Mark Gado. 2006. *Killer Priest.* Westport, CT: Praeger, p. 58.
2. Ibid., pp. 58, 63–64.
3. Ibid., pp. 68–69.
4. Ibid., pp. 74–75.
5. Ibid., pp. 77, 79, 85–86, 89, 91–92.
6. Ibid., pp. 20–42.
7. Ibid., pp. 89.
8. Ibid., pp. 141–149.
9. Ibid., p. 144.
10. Ibid., p. 148.
11. Ibid., pp. 153–154.
12. Ibid., p. 157.
13. Ibid., pp. 177–180.
14. Ibid., p. 204.
15. Ibid., p. 143.
16. Malcolm's brand X. 1964, March 23. *Newsweek*, p. 32; Richard Lentz. 1993. The incorporation of Malcolm X. *American Journalism* 10(3–4):43–47.
17. C. Eric Lincoln. 1961. *The Black Muslims in America.* Boston: Beacon, pp. 76–77.
18. Walter Bell. 2007. Malcolm X: The legend emerges. *TruTV Crime Library.* Retrieved May 15, 2008, from http://www.crimelibrary.com/terrorists_spies/assassins/malcolm_x/index.html.
19. Walter Bell. 2007. Malcolm X: Plots, theories and facts. *TruTV Crime Library.* Retrieved May 15, 2008, from http://www.crimelibrary.com/terrorists_spies/assassins/malcolm_x/4.index.html.
20. Ibid.; Joe Purnick. 1995, May 8. An unlikely matchmaker for Shabazz and Farrakhan. *New York Times*, pp. B1, B6.
21. Death and transfiguration. 1965, March 5. *Time*, p. 23.
22. Black America. 1970, April 6. *Time*, p. 13; Lentz, The incorporation of Malcolm X, p. 63.
23. Kenneth L. Woodward. 1977, August 15. Temple trouble. *Newsweek*, p. 79; Marshall Kilduff and Phil Tracey. 1977, August 1. Inside Peoples Temple. *New West*, pp. 30–38. Retrieved February 20, 2008, from http://jonestown.sdsu.edu/AboutJonestown/PrimarySources/newWestart.html; Nightmare in Jonestown. 1978, December 4. *Time*, p. 18; Don Lattin. 2003, November 18. How spiritual journey ended in destruction. *San Francisco Examiner.* Retrieved February 20, 2008, from http://www.sfgate.com/cgi-bin/article.cgi?f=/c/a/2003/11/18/JONESTOWN.TMP.
24. Kilduff and Tracey, Inside Peoples Temple.
25. Jim Jones: Man who would be "God." 1978, December 15. *Christianity Today*, pp. 370–371; Messiah from the Midwest. 1978, December 4. *Time*, p. 23.
26. Nightmare in Jonestown, p. 18.

27. Ibid.

28. Ibid., p. 19.

29. Ibid., p. 20.

30. Jones and the disciples. 1978, December 13. *Christian Century*, p. 1176; Jim Jones: Man who would be "God," p. 371.

31. Abortion foes will borrow page from Nazi trials. 1996, December 31. *Oregonian*. Retrieved January 18, 2008, from http://nl.newsbank.com; Rene Sanchez. 1999, January 15. Abortion foes' Internet site on trial. *Washington Post*, p. A3.

32. Patrick Rogers. 1994, August 8. Is murder "justifiable" homicide? *Newsweek*, p. 22.

33. Michael D. Lemonick. 1995, January 9. An armed fanatic raises the stakes. *Time*, p. 35.

34. Clinic killings. 1995, January 27. *Commonweal*, p. 3.

35. John W. Kennedy. 1994, September 14. Killings distort pro-life message. *Christianity Today*, p. 56.

36. Ibid., p. 57.

37. Ibid.

38. Clinic shootings interpreted. 1995, January 18. *Christian Century*, p. 4; Jill Smolowe. 1995, January 16. Fear in the land. *Time*, p. 34; Clinic killings; Two families. 1996, February 23. *Commonweal*, p. 5.

39. Kennedy, Killings distort pro-life message.

40. Smolowe, Fear in the land, p. 36; Lemonick, An armed fanatic.

41. Alex Dominguez. 2008, November 1. Funeral protesters hit with verdict nearing $11M. *Indianapolis Star*, A5; Ben Nuckols. 2007, December 12. Gay-hating church scrutinized. *Indianapolis Star*, p. 12.

42. Iver Peterson. 1995, February 27. Resignation adds to mystery in bludgeoning of rabbi's wife. *New York Times*, p. D1.

43. Ibid.

44. Chronology: From a synagogue to a murder trial. 2001, October 16. *New York Times*, p. D1.

45. Ibid.; Peterson, Resignation adds to mystery, p. D7; Killer of rabbi's wife says he was told to fake a robbery. 2001, February 20. *New York Times*, p. D2.

46. Peterson, Resignation adds to mystery, p. D1.

47. Ibid.

48. Daren Fonda. 2003, June 9. How luck ran out for a most wanted fugitive. *Time*, p. 8; Michael Isikoff. 2003, June 9. Flushed from the woods. *Newsweek*, p. 35.

49. Isikoff, Flushed from the woods; Alan Cooperman. 2003, June 2. Is terrorism tied to Christian sect? *Washington Post*, p. A3.

50. Peter Wilkinson. 2003, July 10. The making of a maniac. *Rolling Stone*, p. 34.

51. Ibid., p. 32.

52. Ibid., p. 34.

53. Ibid.

54. Eric Rudolph. 2005, April 13. Statement. Retrieved February 12, 2007, from http://www.armyofgod.com/EricRudolphHomepage.html.

55. Timothy Roche. 2002, January 28. The Yates odyssey. *Time*, pp. 42–43.

56. Ibid., p. 46, 48; Deborah W. Denno. 2003. Who is Andrea Yates? A short story about insanity. *Duke Journal of Gender Law and Policy* 10(1): 61.

57. Roche, The Yates odyssey, p. 44; Suzanne O'Malley. 2004, March. Horror in Houston. *Readers Digest*, p. 132.

58. Roche, The Yates odyssey, p. 50.

59. Ibid., p. 59; Carol Christian and Lisa Teachey. 2002, March 6. Yates believed children doomed. *Houston Chronicle.* Retrieved February 20, 2008, from http://www.chron.com/disp/story.mpl/special/drownings/1268306.html.

60. Suzanne O'Malley. 2004. *Are you there alone? The unspeakable crime of Andrea Yates.* New York: Simon & Schuster, p. 29.

61. Roche, The Yates odyssey, p. 44, 46–48.

62. Ibid., p. 46; Denno, Who is Andrea Yates? p. 62.

63. Denno, Who is Andrea Yates? pp. 67–69.

64. Timothy Roche. 2002, March 18. Andrea Yates: More to the story. *Time.* Retrieved February 20, 2008, from http://www.time.com/nation/article/0,8599,218445,00.html; Terri Langford. 2002, March 8. Doctor: Yates knew killing was wrong. *Dallas Morning News,* p. 35A.

65. Bound, tortured, killed—and captured? 2005, March 7. *Newsweek,* p. 35.

66. A double life. 2005, December 2. BTK history. *Wichita Eagle.* Retrieved May 2, 2007, from http://www.kansas.com/216; BTK archive. 2007. *Wichita Eagle.* Retrieved May 2, 2007, from http://www.kansas.com/215.

67. Serial killer's big mistake. 2005, December 2. *Wichita Eagle.* Retrieved May 2, 2007, from http://www.kansas.com/215/story/19184.html.

68. Julie Sevig. 2005, August. After the Rader guilty plea: "Take note of what we do with evil," pastor urges. *The Lutheran.* Retrieved May 10, 2007, from http:www.thelutheran.org/article/article.cfm?article_id=5259&key=2765709.

69. Julie Sevig. 2005, May. Images of hope: Congregation echoes pastor, "Not the Dennis Rader I know." *The Lutheran.* Retrieved May 10, 2007, from http:www.thelutheran.org/article/article.cfm?article_id=5092&key=25928462.

CHAPTER 5

1. John Somerville and Ronald E. Santoni, eds. 1963. *Social and political philosophy.* Garden City, NJ: Anchor Books, p. 250.

2. David L. Holmes. 2006. *The faith of the founding fathers.* New York: Oxford University Press, p. 81.

3. John T. Noonan, Jr., and Edward McGlynn Gaffney, Jr. 2001. *Religious freedom: History, cases, and other materials on the interaction of religion and government,* 2nd ed. New York: Foundation Press, p. 210.

4. Leonard W. Levy. 1993. *Blasphemy: Verbal offense against the sacred, from Moses to Salman Rushdie.* Chapel Hill: University of North Carolina Press, p. 401.

5. Ibid., pp. 402–403.

6. Ibid., p. 403; Noonan and Gaffney, *Religious freedom,* p. 211.

7. Levy, *Blasphemy,* p. 404.

8. Ibid., pp. 404–405.

9. Ibid.

10. Ibid., p. 405.

11. *Joseph Burstyn v. Wilson.* 1952. (343 U.S. 495). Concurring opinion of Justice Felix Frankfurter. Online version retrieved April 16, 2007, from http://caselaw.lp.findlaw.com.

12. Ibid.

13. Ibid.

14. Ibid.

15. Ibid.

16. William J. Clancy. 1951, March 16. Freedom of the screen. *Commonweal*. Retrieved June 27, 2007, from http://www.commonwealmagazine.org.

17. "The Miracle" decision. 1952, June 13. *Commonweal*. pp. 235–236.

18. *Joseph Burstyn v. Wilson*, concurring opinion of Justice Felix Frankfurter.

19. Ibid.

20. *Joseph Burstyn v. Wilson*. 1952 (343 U.S. 495). Opinion of the court. Online version retrieved April 16, 2007, from http://caselaw.lp.findlaw.com.

21. Ibid.; Free cinema. 1952, June 2. *Time*, p. 22.

22. *Joseph Burstyn v. Wilson*. 1952 (343 U.S. 495). Appendix to opinion of Mr. Justice Frankfurter. Online version retrieved April 16, 2007, from http://caselaw.lp.findlaw.com.

23. According to John. 1966, August 12. *Time*, p. 38; Maureen Cleave. 1966, March 4. How does a Beatle live? John Lennon lives like this. *London Evening Standard*. Retrieved April 16, 2007, from http://www.standard.co.uk.

24. Blues for the Beatles. 1966, August 23. *Newsweek*, p. 94.

25. According to John.

26. Blues for the Beatles.

27. T.N.D. 1966, August 20. Of many things. *America*, p. 164.

28. Notes and comment. 1966, August 27. *New Yorker*, pp. 21–22.

29. Blues for the Beatles.

30. Maureen Cleave. 2005, October 5. The John Lennon I knew. *London Telegraph*. Retrieved April 16, 2007, from http://Telegraph.co.uk.

31. Robert Scheer. 1976, November. *Playboy* interview: Jimmy Carter. *Playboy*, pp. 63–86.

32. Ibid.; David Gelman. 1976, October 4. The great *Playboy* furor. *Newsweek*, p. 70.

33. Gelman, The great *Playboy* furor, p. 71.

34. Ibid.

35. Patrick Goldstein. 1989, March 12. Are Pepsi, Madonna on the rocks? *Los Angeles Times*, p. C76.

36. Pepsi cancels Madonna ad. 1989, April 5. *New York Times*, p. D2.

37. Lucy R. Lippard. 1990, April. The spirit and the letter. *Art in America*, p. 245, n. 1.

38. Ibid., p. 239; Cathleen McGuigan. 1989, July 3. When taxes pay for art. *Newsweek*, p. 68; Tom Matthews. 1990, July 2. Fine art or foul? *Newsweek*, pp. 46, 48–49.

39. McGuigan, When taxes pay for art; Comments on Andres Serrano. 1989, May 8. *Congressional Record*, p. 2, no. 15 in online version retrieved April 18, 2007, from http://www.csulb.edu/jvancamp/361_r7.html.

40. Mathews, Fine art or foul? pp. 48–49; Conservative groups raise uproar over art funding. 1990, April 23. *Christianity Today*, p. 53.

41. Lippard, The spirit and the letter, p. 239; William H. Honan. 1989, August 16. Artist who outraged Congress lives amid Christian symbols. *New York Times*. Retrieved August 18, 2008, from http://www.nytimes.com.

42. Kim A. Lawton. 1990, June 18. Taking aim at art. *Christianity Today*, p. 53.

43. An interview with Wendy Beckett. 1990. PBS. Retrieved April 18, 2007, from http://www.pbs.org/wgbh/sisterwendy.

44. Cathleen McGuigan. 1989, August 7. Arts grants under fire. *Newsweek*, p. 23.

45. Ibid.

CHAPTER 6

1. Unitarian Universalist Association. Undated. Abner Kneeland. Retrieved April 16, 2007, from http://www25.uua.org/uuhs/duub/articles/abnerkneeland.html; Noonan and

Gaffney Edward McGlynn, *Religious* Freedom: History, cases, and other materials on the interaction of religion and government, 2nd ed. New York: Foundation Press, p. 212.

2. Unitarian Universalist Association, Abner Kneeland; Leonard W. Levy. 1993. *Blasphemy: Verbal offenses against the sacred, from Moses to Salman Rushdie.* Chapel Hill: University of North Carolina Press, pp. 416–417.

3. Ibid.

4. Ibid., p. 418; Unitarian Universalist Association, Abner Kneeland.

5. Levy, *Blasphemy*, p. 414.

6. Ibid., p. 415.

7. Ibid., pp. 415–416.

8. Ibid., p. 418; Unitarian Universalist Association, Abner Kneeland.

9. Levy, *Blasphemy*, p. 419; Unitarian Universalist Association, Abner Kneeland.

11. John McCarten. 1939, June. Father Coughlin: Holy medicine man. *American Mercury*, p. 136; Ronald H. Carpenter. 1998. *Father Charles E. Coughlin: Surrogate spokesman for the disaffected.* Westport, CT: Greenwood Press, p. 31.

12. Carpenter, *Father Charles E. Coughlin*, p. 31; McCarten, Father Coughlin, p. 129.

13. John A. Ryan. 1938, December 30. Anti-Semitism in the air. *Commonweal*, pp. 260–262; Coughlin's "communists": Fellow churchmen embarrassed but radio priest talks on. 1938, December 26. *Newsweek*, pp. 26–27.

14. Donald Warren, 1996. *Radio priest Father Charles Coughlin: The father of hate radio.* New York: The Free Press.

15. Sam Zagoria. 1984, February 22. What Jesse Jackson said. *Washington Post*, p. A20.

16. James R. Dickinson and Kathy Sawyer. 1984, June 28. Mr. Farrakhan—and reaction. *Washington Post*, p. A23; Edward D. Sargent. 1984, June 30. Metropolitan A.M.E. pastor blasts Farrakhan statements. *Washington Post*, p. B1.

17. Martin E. Marty. 2006, August 7. Extra Ecclesiam. *Sightings*. Chicago: Martin Marty Center at the University of Chicago Divinity School.

18. Shawn Francis Peters. 2000. *Judging Jehovah's Witnesses.* Lawrence: University of Kansas Press, p. 26.

19. Ibid., pp. 36–37.

20. Ibid., p. 38.

21. Ibid.

22. Ibid., p. 41.

23. Ibid., p. 58; Noonan and Gaffney, *Religious freedom*, p. 383.

24. Peters, *Judging Jehovah's Witnesses*, pp. 66–67.

25. Noonan and Gaffney, *Religious freedom*, p. 389.

26. Judy Wang. 2007, Fall. Chipping away. *Student Press Law Center Report*, pp. 20–23.

27. Pierre M. Atlas. 2007, January 4. Religious tolerance means allowing oath on Quran. *Indianapolis Star.* A8; NCC's FaithfulAmerica delegation meets with Rep. Virgil Goode. 2007, January 30. *NCC News.* Received January 31, 2007, from nccnews@ncccusa.org.

28. Peter Finley, Laura Finley, and Jeffrey Fountain. 2008. *Sports Scandals.* Westport, CT: Greenwood Press, pp. 132–133.

29. Ali up. 1966, February 25. *Time*, p. 26.

30. Finley, Finley, and Fountain, *Sports scandals*, p. 132; Jack Olsen. 1966, April 11. Cassius Clay: The man, the Muslim, the mystery: A case of conscience. *Sports Illustrated*, p. 90.

31. Olsen, Cassius Clay, p. 90.

32. Ibid.

33. Ibid.; Finley, Finley, and Fountain, *Sports scandals*, p. 132.

34. Philip Berrigan. 1967, November 17. Musings from Baltimore City Jail. *Commonweal*, p. 180–182.

35. John Deedy. 1968, June 7. News and views. *Commonweal*, p. 346.

36. The Berrigan Brothers: They rob draft boards. 1968, June 7. *Time*, p. 62.

37. Dan Berrigan. 1966, April 9. *Commonweal*, pp. 34–35; Philip Berrigan. Musings from Baltimore City Jail, pp. 180–182; John Deedy. 1968, January 12. News and views. *Commonweal*, p. 426; Dan Berrigan. 1968, April 26. My brother, the witness. *Commonweal*, p. 646; John Deedy. 1968, May 10. News and views. *Commonweal*, p. 220; John Deedy, News and views (1968, June 7); Cleaver and Berrigan. 1968, June 14. *Commonweal*, pp. 372–373; The Berrigan case. 1968, June 14. *Commonweal*, p. 373; John Deedy. 1968, June 21. News and views. *Commonweal*, p. 394; Dan Berrigan. 1968, September 27. From the Catonsville Nine: Greetings. *Commonweal*, p. 195–196; Philip Berrigan. 1968, December 6. Berrigan from jail: "Truth creates its own room." *Commonweal*, pp. 333–334; Dan Berrigan. 1969, October 10. The bishop and the ghosts of Filetto. *Commonweal*, pp. 39–42.

38. John Deedy. News and views (1968, June 21).

39. John Dart. 2003, September 6. Court orders judge's monument moved. *Christian Century*, p. 12.

40. John Aman. 2004, July. It's about God. *Christianity Today*, p. 58.

41. *Glassroth v. Moore*. 2002. 229F Supp 2d (M.D. Ala. 2002). Retrieved April 15, 2008, from http://www.findlaw.com.

42. Ibid.

43. Ibid.

44. Ibid. See also, Lawrence Webb. 2003, August 29. Seven suggestions and three commandments. *Sightings*. Chicago: Martin Marty Center at the University of Chicago Divinity School; Louis Menand. 2003, September 8. Comment: Moses in Alabama. *New Yorker*, pp. 31–32; Martin E. Marty. 2003, September 20. Moore commandments. Sightings. Chicago: Martin Marty Center at the University of Chicago Divinity School; Moore commandments. *Christian Century*, p. 55; God reigns—Even in Alabama. 2003, October. *Christianity Today*, p. 35.

45. Brian Ross and Rehab El-Suri. 2008, March 13. Obama's pastor: God damn America, U.S. to blame for 9/11. *ABC News*. Retrieved June 5, 2008, from http://abcnews.go.com/Blotter/Story?id=4443788.

46. Ibid.

47. Robert M. Franklin. 2007, May 31. Obama's faith: A civil and social gospel. *Sightings*. Chicago: Martin Marty Center at the University of Chicago Divinity School.

48. Andrew R. Murphy. 2001, October 17. Pat Robertson and the rhetoric of decline. *Sightings*. Chicago: Martin Marty Center at the University of Chicago Divinity School.

49. Martin E. Marty. 2008, April 2. Keeping the faith at Trinity United Church of Christ. *Sightings*. Chicago: Martin Marty Center at the University of Chicago Divinity School; Dwight N. Hopkins. 2008, Spring. The Wright neighborhood. *Religion in the News*, pp. 7–8, 25.

50. Eric Gorski. 2008, March 18. Message of Obama pastor forged in civil rights movement. *Atlanta Journal and Constitution*. Retrieved June 5, 2008, from http://www.ajc.com/news/content/news/stories/2008/03/18/wright_0319.html; Franklin, Obama's faith; Marty, Keeping the faith; R. Stephen Warner. 2008, Spring. Civil religious revival. *Religion in the News*, pp. 2–4, 21.

51. Wright's wrongs. 2008, May 3. *The Economist*, p. 44.

52. Crisis of faith. 2008, June 7. *The Economist*, p. 46; Martin E. Marty. 2008, April 14. Rod Parsley on Islam. *Sightings*. Chicago: Martin Marty Center at the University of Chicago Divinity School.

53. Suzanne Sataline. 2008, November 6. Democrats gain with religious voters. *Wall Street Journal*. Retrieved November 7, 2008, from http://online.wsj.com.

54. Karl Rove. 2008, November 6. How the president-elect did it. *Wall Street Journal*. Retrieved November 7, 2008, from http://online.wsj.com. See also, Monica Langley. 2008, November 5. As economic crisis peaked, tide turned against McCain. *Wall Street Journal*. Retrieved November 7, 2008, from http://online.wsj.com.

CHAPTER 7

1. John Somerville and Ronald E. Santoni, eds. 1963. *Social and political philosophy*. Garden City, NJ: Anchor Books, p. 250.

2. Noonan and Gaffney Edward McGlynn, *Religious* Freedom: History, cases, and other materials on the interaction of religion and government, 2nd ed. New York: Foundation Press, p. 292.

3. Elizabeth Hayes Alvarez. 2004, May 27. Neighbors, fences, and religion in America. *Sightings*. Chicago: Martin Marty Center at the University of Chicago Divinity School.

4. Dee Brown. 1972. *Bury my heart at Wounded Knee*. New York: Bantam Books, p. 12; John Tebbel and Keith Jennison. 2006. *The American Indian wars*. Edison, NJ: Castle Books, p. 291.

5. Tebbel and Jennison, *The American Indian wars*, pp. 291–293.

6. Brown, *Bury my heart at Wounded Knee*, p. 403; Stanley Vestal. 1932/1989. *Sitting Bull: Champion of the Sioux*. Norman: University of Oklahoma Press, p. 276.

7. Tebbel and Jennison, *The American Indian wars*, pp. 291–293.

8. Brown, *Bury my heart at Wounded Knee*, p. 410; Tebbel and Jennison, *The American Indian wars*, pp. 293–294.

9. Brown, *Bury my heart at Wounded Knee*, p. 410.

10. Ibid., pp. 410–411.

11. Ibid., pp. 414–415.

12. Ibid., p. 416.

13. Tebbel and Jennison, *The American Indian wars*, p. 298.

14. Vestal, *Sitting Bull*, p. 280.

15. Weston LaBarre. 1962. *They shall take up serpents: Psychology of the southern snake-handling cult*. St. Paul: University of Minnesota Press, pp. 11, 15; Ralph W. Hood, Jr., and W. Paul Williamson. 2008. *Them that believe: The power and meaning of the Christian serpent-handling tradition*. Berkeley: University of California Press, p. 38.

16. Hood and Williamson, *Them that believe*, pp. 37–51.

17. LaBarre, *They shall take up serpents*, p. 12; Hood and Williamson, *Them that believe*, pp. 47, 49.

18. Hood and Williamson, *Them that believe*, pp. 39, 50; Holiness faith healers. 1944, July 3. *Life*, pp. 59–64.

19. LaBarre, *They shall take up serpents*, p. 23; Hood and Williamson, *Them that believe*, p. 212.

20. Hood and Williamson, *Them that believe*, p. 212

21. LaBarre, *They shall take up serpents*, pp. 35–37.

22. Ibid., pp. 41–42.

23. Noonan and Gaffney, *Religious freedom*, pp. 553–554.

24. Ibid.; Hood and Williamson, *Them that believe*, pp. 213–214; Ban on snake handling is upheld in Tennessee. 1975, September 9. *New York Times*, p. 37.

25. Hood and Williamson, *Them that believe*, pp. 214–215.

26. Dennis Covington. 1995. *Salvation on Sand Mountain.* New York: Penguin Books, pp. 4, 42–43.

27. Garrett Epps. 2001. *To an unknown god: Religious freedom on trial.* New York: St. Martin's Press, pp. 107, 133–134.

28. Ibid., pp. 100–101.

29. Ibid., pp. 107–109.

30. Ibid., pp. 109–110.

31. Ibid.

32. Ibid., p. 125.

33. Ibid., pp. 140–141.

34. Ibid., pp. 143–144.

35. Ibid., p. 220; Noonan and Gaffney, *Religious freedom*, pp. 480–487; Linda Greenhouse. 1990, April 18. Use of drugs in religious rituals can be prosecuted, justices rule. *New York Times*, p. A22.

36. David M. O'Brien. 2004. *Animal sacrifice and religious freedom: Church of the Lukumi Babalu Aye v. City of Hialeah.* Lawrence: University of Kansas Press, p. 33.

37. Ibid., pp. 33–37.

38. Ibid., p. 37.

39. Ibid., pp. 35–36.

40. Ibid., pp. 39–41.

41. Ibid., p. 23.

42. Ibid., pp. 44, 163–164.

43. Ibid., pp. 46–47, 164.

44. Ibid., pp. 47, 164–168.

45. Ibid., pp. 90–93.

46. Ibid., p. 100.

47. Ibid., p. 138; Noonan and Gaffney, *Religious freedom*, pp. 535–547; Linda Greenhouse. 1993, June 12. Court, citing religious freedom, voids a ban on animal sacrifice. *New York Times*, pp. 1, 9.

48. Kim Sue Lia Perke. 1999, May 11. Practicing their old-time religion. *Austin American-Statesman*, p. A1.

49. Mark Silk. 1999, Summer. Something Wiccan this way comes. *Religion in the News* 2(2): 9–10.

50. Perke, Practicing their old-time religion.

51. Silk, Something Wiccan this way comes, p. 9; S. C. Gwynne. 1999, July 5. "I saluted a witch." *Time*, p. 59; Charles S. Clifton. 2000, November 20. Fort Hood's Wiccans and the problem of pacifism. Nashville, TN: Paper presented to the annual meeting of the American Academy of Religion. Retrieved April 27, 2007, from http://www.chasclifton.com/papers/hood.html.

52. Silk, Something Wiccan this way comes; Clifton, Fort Hood's Wiccans.

53. Ibid.

54. Associated Press. 1999, May 18. Barr blasts Army for allowing Wiccan celebration at Texas base. Retrieved April 27, 2007, from http://www.rickross.com/reference/wicca/wicca1.html.

55. Silk, Something Wiccan this way comes, p. 10; Clifton, Fort Hood's Wiccans.

56. Joe Holley. 1999, June 14. A genuine witch hunt. *U.S. News & World Report*, p. 27.

57. Clifton, Fort Hood's Wiccans.

58. Associated Press. 1999, June 11. Religious groups urge Christians to boycott Army over Wiccans. Retrieved April 27, 2007, from the First Amendment Center, http://www.firstamendmentcenter.org/news.aspx?id=9729; Silk, Something Wiccan this way comes, p. 10.

59. Silk, Something Wiccan this way comes; Jeremy Leaming. 1999, June 29. Senate Republicans join call to end military accommodation of Wicca. *First Amendment topics.* Retrieved April 27, 2007, from http://www.firstamendmentcenter.org/news.aspx?id=9708.

60. Silk, Something Wiccan this way comes, p. 10.

61. Ibid.

62. Charles C. Haynes. 2007, April 1. Witch trials and tribulations in the land of the free. *First Amendment topics.* Retrieved 2008, March 14, from http://www.firstamendmentcenter.org/commentary.aspx?id=18355.

CHAPTER 8

1. Lawrence Foster. 1981 *Religion and sexuality: The Shakers, the Mormons, and the Oneida Community.* Urbana: University of Illinois Press, p. 73.

2. Ibid., p. 82; Hillenbrand, Randall. (undated) The Oneida Community. *New York History Net.* Retrieved March 14, 2008, from http://www.nyhistory.com/central/oneida.html.

3. Spencer Klaw. 1993. *Without sin: The life and death of the Oneida Community.* New York: Penguin Books, pp. 3, 57–58; Hillenbrand, The Oneida Community.

4. Klaw, *Without sin*, p. 66.

5. Ibid., p. 243.

6. Ibid., p. 244.

7. Ibid., p. 245.

8. Church of Jesus Christ of Latter-day Saints. (undated). Polygamy (plural marriage). Retrieved June 25, 2008, from http://www.lds.org/ldsorg; see also Noonan and Gaffney Edward McGlynn, *Religious* Freedom: History, cases, and other materials on the interaction of religion and government, 2nd ed. New York: Foundation Press, pp. 290–291; Horace Greeley. 1859, August 29. Two hours with Brigham Young. *New York Tribune.* In Buddenbaum and Mason, *Readings on religion as news*, pp. 127–133.

9. Noonan and Gaffney, *Religious freedom*, pp. 288–289.

10. Ibid., pp. 289–290.

11. Ibid., p. 293.

12. Ibid., p. 294.

13. Ibid., pp. 297–298.

14. Ibid., p. 304.

15. Church of Jesus Christ of Latter-day Saints. 1890, September. Manifesto. Retrieved June 25, 2008, from http://www.lds.org/ldsorg; Church of Jesus Christ of Latter-day Saints. 1890, October 6. Official Declaration I and Excerpts from three addresses by President Wilford Woodruff regarding the Manifesto. Retrieved June 25, 2008, from http://www.lds.org/ldsorg.

16. Jon Krakauer. 2004. *Under the banner of heaven.* New York: Anchor Books.

17. Andrew Murr and Kevin Peraino. 2002, June 17. "A man took Elizabeth." *Newsweek*, p. 37.

18. Family offers new reward for info about Smart. 2003, February 4. *Court TV.* Retrieved June 23, 2008, from http://www.courttv.com/news/smart; Jodie Morse. 2003, March 24. The missing nine months. *Time*, pp. 44–48.

19. Smart found alive nine months after abduction. 2003, March 12. *Court TV.* Retrieved June 23, 2008, from http://www.courttv.com/news/smart; Morse, The missing nine months.

20. Andrew Murr. 2006, March 22. Polygamist on the lam. *Newsweek*, p. 37.

21. Eugene V. Gallagher. 2008, Fall. FLDS 1, Texas 0. *Religion in the News* 11(2), p. 8; Martha Bradley. 2008, October 18. Repeat of history: The raid on the Fundamentalist Latter Day Saint Community of El Dorado. Paper presented to the annual convention of the Society for the Scientific Study of Religion, Louisville, Kentucky.

22. Gallagher, FLDS 1, Texas 0, pp. 6, 25.

23. Stephanie Simon. 2008, May 23. Court overrules polygamist raid. *Wall Street Journal*, p. A3.

24. James T. Richardson and Tamatha L. Schreinert. 2008, October 18. The courts finally speak in Texas: An analysis of the Appeal Court opinions concerning the FDLS children. Paper presented to the annual convention of the Society for the Scientific Study of Religion, Louisville, Kentucky.

25. David Von Drehle. 2008, May 5. The sins of the fathers. *Time*, pp. 32, 35; Gallagher, FLDS 1, Texas 0, pp. 7–8, 25.

26. Shawn Francis Peters. 2008. *When prayer fails: Faith healing, children, and the law.* New York: Oxford University Press, p. 73.

27. Ibid., p. 72.

28. Ibid., pp. 73, 75–77.

29. Ibid., p. 73.

30. Ibid., p. 75.

31. Ibid., p. 79.

32. Ibid.

33. Ibid., p. 80.

34. Ibid.

35. Ibid., pp. 89–90.

36. Ibid., pp. 94–97.

37. Ibid., p. 95.

38. Ibid.

39. Ibid., pp. 91, 107–108.

40. Ibid., p. 116.

41. Ibid., pp. 11–14; see also p. 160.

42. Ibid., pp. 167–173; Noonan and Gaffney, *Religious freedom*, pp. 554–557.

43. Ellen Goodman. 2000, September 10. Just how far can the state go in protecting an "unborn child"? *Boston Globe*, p. F7; Peters, *When prayer fails*, pp. 160–163.

44. Sun Myung Moon: Religious martyr or tax cheat? 1984, May 28. *U.S. News & World Report*, p. 14.

45. Douglas E. Cowan and David G. Bromley. 2008. *Cults and new religions: A brief history.* Malden, MA: Blackwell Publishing, pp. 93–94, 97, 111–116.

46. John McClaughry. 1983, December 23. The uneasy case against Reverend Moon. *National Review*, pp. 1611–1612; Noonan and Gaffney, *Religious freedom*, pp. 576–577.

47. McClaughry, The uneasy case against Reverend Moon, p. 1612; Noonan and Gaffney, *Religious freedom*, p. 579.

48. Garrett Epps. 2001. *To an unknown god: Religious freedom on trial.* New York: St. Martin's Press, p. 68.

49. Ibid., p. 67.

50. Steve Twomey. 1982, April 17. Oregon town seeing red over Bhagwan and his cult. *Washington Post*, p. C12; Laura Parker. 1983, July 30. Culture clash in Oregon. *Washington Post*, p. A3.

51. Epps, *To an unknown god*, pp. 76–77.

52. Ibid., p. 77.

53. Ibid., p. 78.

54. Ibid., pp. 77–79; Barry Von Driel and Jacob Van Belzen. 1990, March. The downfall of Rajneeshpuram in the print media: A cross-national study. *Journal for the Scientific Study of Religion* 29(1): 76–90.

55. Epps, *To an unknown god*, p. 77.

56. Michael Marriott Washington. 1984, September 15. Homeless taken to commune of Indian mystic. *Washington Post*, p. A1; Michael Marriott Washington. 1984, September 21. D.C.'s homeless line up for Oregon commune bus. *Washington Post*, p. B1; William Raspberry. 1984, September 24. The bus to Rajneeshpuram. *Washington Post*, p. A19.

57. Epps, *To an unknown god*, p. 84.

58. Ibid., pp. 85–86.

59. Kenneth G. C. Newport. 2006. *The Branch Davidians of Waco: The history and beliefs of an apocalyptic sect.* New York: Oxford University Press, p. 202.

60. Ibid., pp. 202, 299; Robert S. Fogarty. 1993, April 12. "Cults," guns, and the Kingdom. *The Nation*, p. 485.

61. Lawrence Lilliston. 1994. Who committed child abuse at Waco? In James R. Lewis, ed. *From the ashes: Making sense of Waco.* Lanham, MD: Rowman & Littlefield, 1994, pp. 169–173; George Robertson. 1994. Suffer the little children. In Lewis, *From the ashes*, pp. 179–180.

62. Newport, *The Branch Davidians of Waco*, p. 202; Fogarty, "Cults," guns, and the kingdom.

63. Jill Smolowe. 1993, May 3. February 28: Sent into a deathtrap? *Time*, p. 33.

64. Michael Riley, Richard Woodbury, Julie Johnson, and Elaine Shannon. 1993, May 3. Tragedy in Waco. *Time*, p. 40; Aric Press. 1993, May 3. Day of judgment. *Newsweek*, p. 24.

65. Fred Bruning. 1993, May 10. The FBI and other Washington wackos. *Macleans*, p. 9.

66. Elaine Shannon. 1993, October 11. Tripped up by lies. *Time*, pp. 39–40.

67. Andrew Milne. 1994. The cult awareness network: Its role in the Waco tragedy. In Lewis, *From the ashes*, pp. 137–142; James M. Wall. 1993, May 5. Eager for the end. *Christian Century*, pp. 475–476. Edward McGlynn Gaffney, Jr. 1993, May 21. Reaction to Waco: Enforcing the law, consider the Bill of Rights. *Commonweal*, pp. 5–6.

68. Michael Barkun. 1993, June 2–9. Reflections after Waco: Millennialists and the state. *Christian Century*, pp. 596–600.

BIBLIOGRAPHY

Abelman, Robert. 1991, Spring/Summer. Influence of news coverage of the "Scandal" on PTL viewers. *Journalism Quarterly* 68(1/2): 101–110.

Abortion foes will borrow page from Nazi trials. 1996, December 31. *Oregonian.* Retrieved January 18, 2008, from http://nl.newsbank.com.

According to John. 1966, August 12. *Time,* p. 38.

Aimee and the media. No date. Retrieved April 1, 2007, from http://.xroads.virginia.edu/~UG00/robertson/asm/media.html.

Ali up. 1966, February 25. *Time,* p. 26.

Alter, Jonathan, and Michael Isikoff. 1996, October 28. The real scandal is what's legal. *Newsweek,* pp. 30–31.

Alvarez, Elizabeth Hayes. 2004, May 27. Neighbors, fences, and religion in America. *Sightings.* Chicago: Martin Marty Center at the University of Chicago Divinity School.

Aman, John. 2004, July. It's about God. *Christianity Today,* p. 58.

Associated Press. 1999, May 18. Barr blasts Army for allowing Wiccan celebration at Texas base. Retrieved April 27, 2007, from http://www.rickross.com/reference/wicca/wicca1.html.

Associated Press. 1999, June 11. Religious groups urge Christians to boycott Army over Wiccans. Retrieved April 27, 2007, from the First Amendment Center, http://www.firstamendmentcenter.org/news.aspx?id=9729.

Atlas, Pierre M. 2007, January 4. Religious tolerance means allowing oath on Quran. *Indianapolis Star,* p. A8.

Bakker, Jim. 1996. *I was wrong.* Nashville, TN: Thomas Nelson.

Ban on snake handling is upheld in Tennessee. 1975, September 9. *New York Times,* p. 37.

Barkun, Michael. 1993, June 2–9. Reflections after Waco: Millennialists and the state. *Christian Century,* pp. 596–600.

Bell, Walter. 2007. Malcolm X: Plots, theories and facts. *TruTV Crime Library.* Retrieved May 15, 2008, from http://www.crimelibrary.com/terrorists_spies/assassins/malcolm_x/4.index.html.

Bell, Walter. 2007. Malcolm X: The legend emerges. *TruTV Crime Library.* Retrieved May 15, 2008, from http://www.crimelibrary.com/terrorists_spies/assassins/malcolm_x/index.html.

Berger, Peter. 1967. *The Sacred Canopy.* New York: Doubleday.

Berrigan, Dan. 1966, April 9. *Commonweal,* pp. 34–35.

Berrigan, Dan. 1968, April 26. My brother, the witness. *Commonweal,* p. 646.

Berrigan, Dan. 1968, September 27. From the Catonsville Nine: Greetings. *Commonweal,* pp. 195–196.

Berrigan, Dan. 1969, October 10. The bishop and the ghosts of Filetto. *Commonweal*, pp. 39–42.

Berrigan, Philip. 1967, November 17. Musings from Baltimore City Jail. *Commonweal*, pp. 180–182.

Berrigan, Philip. 1968, December 6. Berrigan from jail: "Truth creates its own room." *Commonweal*, pp. 333–334.

The Berrigan Brothers: They rob draft boards. 1968, June 7. *Time*, p. 62.

The Berrigan case. 1968, June 14. *Commonweal*, p. 373.

Bilger, Burkhard. 2004, December 6. God doesn't need Ole Anthony. *New Yorker*, pp. 70–81.

Bird, J. Malcolm. 1924, July. Our next psychic: A preliminary account of the case that now comes before us, as it appears to the naked eye. *Scientific American*, pp. 28–29.

Bird, J. Malcolm. 1924, August. The "Margery" mediumship. *Scientific American*, pp. 88–89, 126.

Bissell, Shelton. 1928, May 23. Vaudeville at Angelus Temple. *The Outlook*, pp. 126–127, 158.

Bjerga, Alan. 2001. The trials of faith: Discussion of religion and the Beecher adultery scandal, 1870–1880. *American Journalism* 18(1): 73–94.

Black America. 1970, April 6. *Time*, p. 13.

Bliven, Bruce. 1926, November 3. Sister Aimee. *The New Republic*, pp. 289–291.

Bloom, Stephen G. 2000. *Postville: A clash of cultures in heartland America*. New York: Harcourt.

Blues for the Beatles. 1966, August 23. *Newsweek*, p. 94.

Blumhofer, Edith L. 1987, May 6. Divided Pentecostals: Bakker v. Swaggart. *Christian Century*, pp. 430–431.

Bound, tortured, killed—and captured? 2005, March 7. *Newsweek*, p. 35.

Boys Town bonanza. 1972, April 10. *Time*, pp. 17–18.

Bradley, Martha. 2008, October 18. Repeat of history: The raid on the Fundamentalist Latter Day Saint Community of El Dorado. Paper presented to the annual convention of the Society for the Scientific Study of Religion, Louisville, Kentucky.

Brown, Dee. 1972. *Bury my heart at Wounded Knee*. New York: Bantam Books.

Brown, Douglas R., Wesley R. Iversen, H. Michael Rood, Douglas D. Smith, and Paul N. Williams. 1972. Boys Town: Lucrative income of a well-known child-care home. In Heinz Dietrich Fischer, ed. *Local reporting, 1947–1987: From a county vote fraude [sic] to a corrupt city council*. New York: K. G. Saur, 1989, pp. 170–180.

Bruning, Fred. 1993, May 10. The FBI and other Washington wackos. *Macleans*, p. 9.

BTK archive. 2007. *Wichita Eagle*. Retrieved May 10, 2007, from http://www.kansas.com/215.

Buddenbaum, Judith M. 1987. "Judge … what their acts will justify": The religion journalism of James Gordon Bennett. *Journalism History* 14(2–3): 54–67.

Buddenbaum, Judith M., and Debra L. Mason, eds. 2000. *Readings on religion as news*. Ames: Iowa State University Press.

Carpenter, Ronald H. 1998. *Father Charles E. Coughlin: Surrogate spokesman for the disaffected*. Westport, CT: Greenwood Press.

Carter, Paul A. 1971. *The spiritual crisis of the Gilded Age*. DeKalb: Northern Illinois University Press.

Christian, Carol, and Lisa Teachey. 2002, March 6. Yates believed children doomed. *Houston Chronicle*. Retrieved February 20, 2008, from http://www.chron.com/disp/story.mpl/special/drownings/1268306.html.

Chronology: From a synagogue to a murder trial. 2001, October 16. *New York Times.* p. D1.

Church of Jesus Christ of Latter-day Saints. 1890, September. Manifesto. Retrieved June 25, 2008, from http://www.lds.org/ldsorg.

Church of Jesus Christ of Latter-day Saints. 1890, October 6. Official Declaration I and Excerpts from three addresses by President Wilford Woodruff regarding the Manifesto. Retrieved June 25, 2008, from http://www.lds.org/ldsorg.

Church of Jesus Christ of Latter-day Saints. N.d. Polygamy (plural marriage). Retrieved June 25, 2008, from http://www.lds.org/ldsorg.

Church releases statement on Mark Hofmann interviews. 1987, July 31. *Church News,* pp. 78–79.

Clancy, William T. 1951, March 16. Freedom of the Screen Commonweal. Retrieved June 27, 2007, from http://www.commonwealmagazine.org.

Cleave, Maureen. 1966, March 4. How does a Beatle live? John Lennon lives like this. *London Evening Standard.* Retrieved April 16, 2007, from http://www.standard.co.uk.

Cleave, Maureen. 2005, October 5. The John Lennon I knew. *London Telegraph.* Retrieved April 16, 2007, from http://Telegraph.co.uk.

Cleaver and Berrigan. 1968, June 14. *Commonweal,* pp. 372–373.

Clifton, Charles S. 2000, November 20. Fort Hood's Wiccans and the problem of pacifism. Paper presented to the annual convention of the American Academy of Religion, Nashville, Tennessee. Retrieved April 27, 2007, from http://www.chasclifton.com/papers/hood.html.

Clinic killings. 1995, January 27. *Commonweal,* pp. 3–4.

Clinic shootings interpreted. 1995, January 18. *Christian Century,* p. 4.

The clue in the letter. 1996, August 12. *Newsweek,* p. 49.

Comments on Andres Serrano. 1989, May 8. *Congressional Record.* P. 2, no. 15 in online version retrieved April 18, 2007, from http://www.csub/~jvancamp/361_r7.html.

Comstock, Sarah. 1927, December. Aimee Semple McPherson: Prima donna of revivalism. *Harper's Monthly Magazine,* pp. 11–19.

Conservative groups raise uproar over art funding. 1990, April 23. *Christianity Today,* p. 53.

Cooperman, Alan. 2003, June 2. Is terrorism tied to Christian sect? *Washington Post,* p. A3.

Cooperman, Alan. 2004, December 31. USDA investigating kosher meat plant: Advocacy group's grisly video sparked outcry. *Washington Post,* p. A3.

Cooperman, Alan. 2007, July 7. Eco-kosher movement aims to heed tradition, conscience. *Washington Post,* p. A1.

Coughlin's "communists": Fellow churchmen embarrassed but radio priest talks on. 1938, December 26. *Newsweek,* pp. 26–27.

Council for America's First Freedom. 2008, September 14–21. Newsclips. Retrieved September 20, 2008, from http:www//firstfreedom.org.

Covington, Dennis. 1995. *Salvation on Sand Mountain.* New York: Penguin Books.

Cowan, Douglas E., and David G. Bromley, 2008. *Cults and new religions: A brief history.* Malden, MA: Blackwell Publishing.

Crisis of faith. 2008, June 7. *The Economist,* p. 46.

Cronin, Mary M. 2006, Autumn. The liberty to argue freely: Nineteenth-century obscenity prosecutions and the emergence of modern libertarian free speech discourse. *Journalism Monographs* 8(3): 190–195.

Darman, Jonathan, and Andrew Murr. 2006, November 13. A pastor's fall from grace. *Newsweek,* pp. 34–37.

Dart, John. 2003, September 6. Courts order judge's monument moved. *Christian Century*, pp. 12–13.

Death and transfiguration. 1965, March 5. *Time*, p. 13.

Deedy, John. 1968, January 12. News and views. *Commonweal*, p. 426.

Deedy, John. 1968, May 10. News and views. *Commonweal*, p. 220.

Deedy, John. 1968, June 7. News and views. *Commonweal*, p. 346.

Deedy, John. 1968, June 21. News and views. *Commonweal*, p. 394.

Denno, Deborah W. 2003. Who is Andrea Yates? A short story about insanity. *Duke Journal of Gender Law and Policy* 10(1): 1–84.

Dew, Spencer. 2006, July 20. New World blood libel. *Sightings*. Chicago: Martin Marty Center at the University of Chicago Divinity School.

Dickinson, James R., and Kathy Sawyer. 1984, June 28. Mr. Farrakhan—and reaction. *Washington Post*, p. A23.

Dobson, James. 2006, November 2. News release from Focus on the Family, Colorado Springs.

Dominguez, Alex. 2008, November 1. Funeral protesters hit with verdict nearing $11M. *Indianapolis Star*, p. A5.

A double life. 2005, December 2. BTK history. *Wichita Eagle*. Retrieved May 2, 2007, from http://www.kansas.com/216.

Downing, Larry. 1996, October 28. The Asian connection. *Newsweek*, pp. 25–32.

Doyle, Arthur Conan. 1926. *The history of spiritualism, Vol. 1*. New York: G. H. Doran.

Drinan, Robert. 1990, December 29. Religious freedom and the incoming Congress. *America*, pp. 512–514.

Eastland, Terry, ed. 1995. *Religious liberty in the Supreme Court: The cases that define the debate over church and state*. Grand Rapids, MI: Wm. B. Eerdmans Publishing Company, pp. 25–58.

Eilperin, Julie. 2004, May 3. Kosher meat plant sets off Iowa feud: Some fear release of salt water into river. *Washington Post*, p. A2.

Entrepreneurs R us. 2006, December. *Christianity Today*, pp. 22–23.

Episcopal coffers plundered. 1995, May 17. *Christian Century*, pp. 533–534.

Epps, Garrett. 2001. *To an unknown god: Religious freedom on trial*. New York: St. Martin's Press.

Faithful cling to waning hope: Men and women followers of Mrs. McPherson grouped on sands at Venice pray that leader will return to them. 1926, May 20. *Los Angeles Times*. Retrieved April 10, 2007, from http://xroads.virginia.edu/~UG00/robertson/asm/latimes.html.

Family offers new reward for info about Smart. 2003, February 4. Court TV. Retrieved June 23, 2008, from http://www.courttv.com/news/smart.

Finley, Peter, Laura Finley, and Jeffrey Fountain. 2008. *Sports Scandals*. Westport, CT: Greenwood Press.

First "Hofmann" history-mystery. 1987, February 15. *Salt Lake Tribune*. Retrieved March 5, 2008, from http://www.utlm.org/onlinebooks/tracingreview.htm?FACT.

Fisher, Carrie. 1991, June 27. True confessions: The *Rolling Stone* interview with Madonna, part two. *Rolling Stone*, pp. 45–49, 78.

Fogarty, Robert S. 1993, April 12. "Cults," guns and the Kingdom. *The Nation*, pp. 485–487.

Fonda, Daren. 2003, June 9. How luck ran out for a most wanted fugitive. *Time*, p. 8.

Foster, Lawrence. 1981. *Religion and sexuality: The Shakers, the Mormons, and the Oneida Community*. Urbana: University of Illinois Press.

Fox, Richard Wightman. 1999. *Trials of intimacy: Love and loss in the Beecher-Tilton scandal.* Chicago: University of Chicago Press.

Foy, Paul M. 2007, January 9. Judge tosses lawsuit over Hughes will. Associated Press. Retrieved May 2, 2007, from http://www/signonsandiego.com/news/nation/20070109-1151-wst-dummar-hughes.html.

Fraker, Susan. 1976, May 17. Howard Hughes: Heirs apparent? *Newsweek*, pp. 39–40.

Fraker, Susan. 1976, May 24. Howard Hughes: A wealth of wills. *Newsweek*, p. 30.

Franklin, Robert M. 2007, May 31. Obama's faith: A civil and social gospel. *Sightings*. Chicago: The Martin Marty Center at the University of Chicago Divinity School.

Free cinema. 1952, June 2. *Time*, p. 22.

Frisken, Amanda. 2004. *Victoria Woodhull's sexual revolution: Political theater and the popular press.* Philadelphia: University of Pennsylvania Press.

Gado, Mark. 2006. *Killer Priest.* Westport, CT: Praeger.

Gaffney, Edward McGlynn, Jr. 1993, May 21. Reaction to Waco: Enforcing the law; Consider the Bill of Rights. *Commonweal*, pp. 5–6.

Gallagher, Eugene V. 2008, Fall. FLDS 1, Texas 0. *Religion in the News* 11(2): 6–8, 25.

Gelman, David. 1976, October 4. The great *Playboy* furor. *Newsweek*, pp. 70–71.

Geselman, Anne Belli, and Lynette Clemetson. 2002, March 25. A crazy system. *Newsweek*, p. 30.

Gillis, Chester. 2002, July 29–August 5. Cultures, codes and publics. *America*, pp. 8–11.

Givens, Ron. 1988, June 6. Back in the limelight again. *Newsweek*, p. 7.

Glassroth v. Moore. 2002. 229F Supp 2d (M.D. Ala. 2002). Online version retrieved April 15, 2008, from http://www.findlaw.com.

Globe Spotlight Team. 2002, January 31. Scores of priests involved in sex abuse cases. *Boston Globe*, p. A1.

God reigns—even in Alabama. 2003, October. *Christianity Today*, p. 35.

Goldstein, Patrick. 1989, March 12. Are Pepsi, Madonna on the rocks? *Los Angeles Times*, p. C76.

Goodman, Ellen. 2000, September 10. Just how far can the state go in protecting an "unborn child"? *Boston Globe*, p. F7.

Gorski, Eric. 2006, November 5. Disgraced Haggard: I am a "deceiver and a liar." *Denver Post.* Retrieved January 22, 2008, from http://www.denverpost.com/search/ci_4607865.

Gorski, Eric. 2007, February 6. Haggard says he is "completely heterosexual." *Denver Post.* Retrieved January 22, 2008, from http://www.denverpost.com/search/ci_5164921.

Gorski, Eric. 2008, March 18. Message of Obama pastor forged in civil rights movement. *Atlanta Journal and Constitution.* Retrieved June 5, 2008, from http://www.ajc.com/news/content/news/stories/2008/03/18/wright_0319.html.

Gorski, Eric, and Mike McPhee. 2006, November 3. Haggard admits meth buy. *Denver Post.* Retrieved January 22, 2008, from http://www.denverpost.com/search/ci_4597552.

Green, Joshua. 2005, October. Roy and his rock. *The Atlantic*, pp. 70–71, 74–76, 78–82.

Greenhouse, Linda. 1990, April 18. Use of drugs in religious rituals can be prosecuted, justices rule. *New York Times*, p. A22.

Greenhouse, Linda. 1993, June 12. Court, citing religious freedom, voids a ban on animal sacrifice. *New York Times*, pp. 1, 9.

Gwynne, S. C. 1999, July 5. "I saluted a witch." *Time*, p. 59.

Hackett, George. 1988, February 29. A sex scandal breaks over Jimmy Swaggart. *Newsweek*, p. 30.

Haggard, Gayle. 2006, November 5. Gayle Haggard's letter to New Life Church. *The Gazette* (Colorado Springs). Retrieved January 22, 2008, from http://www2.gazette. com/display.php?id+1326185&secid=1.

Haggard, Ted. 2004, April. Decalogue debacle. *Christianity Today,* p. 98.

Hanley, Robert. 1996, July 11. Judge gives church treasurer more than maximum sentence. *New York Times*, p. B6.

Hanley, Robert. 2002, November 23. Rabbi gets jail, not death, for hired murder of wife. *New York Times*, pp. A1, B5.

Haynes, Charles C. 1999, June 27. Witches test our religious tolerance. *First Amendment.* Retrieved March 14, 2008, from http://www.freedomforum.org/templates/document. asp?documentID=9013.

Haynes, Charles. 2007, April 1. Witch trials and tribulations in the land of the free. *Freedom Forum topics.* Retrieved March 14, 2008, from http://www.firstamendmentcenter.org/ commentary.aspx?id=18355.

Hein, Marjorie. 2005. The "Miracle" of *Burstyn v. Wilson.* In Joseph Russomanno, ed., *Defending the First: Commentary on First Amendment issues and cases.* Mahwah, NJ: Lawrence Erlbaum, pp. 61–84.

High, Stanley. 1940, September 14. Armageddon, Inc. *Saturday Evening Post,* pp. 18–19, 50, 52–54, 58.

Hillenbrand, Randall. N.d. The Oneida Community. *New York History Net.* Retrieved March 14, 2008, from http://www.nyhistory.com/central/oneida.html.

Hinckley, Gordon B. 1985, September. First Presidency message: Keep the faith. *Ensign,* pp. 3–6. Retrieved March 5, 2008, from http://www.ids.org.

Hochman, Steve. 1989, February 18. Madonna poised for big media blitz. *Los Angeles Times,* Sec. 5, pp. 1, 7.

Holiness faith healers. 1944, July 3. *Life,* pp. 59–64.

Hollenhorst, John. 2005, February 23. Dummar may have told truth after all. *Deseret News,* Retrieved May 2, 2008, from http://deseretnews.com/dn/view/0,1249,600114069,00. html.

Holley, Joe. 1999, June 14. A genuine witch hunt. *U.S. News & World Report,* p. 27.

Holmes, David L. 2006. *The faith of the founding fathers.* New York: Oxford University Press.

Honan, William H. 1989, August 16. Artist who outraged Congress lives amid Christian symbols. *New York Times.* Retrieved August 18, 2008, from http://www.nytimes. com.

Hood, Ralph W., Jr., and W. Paul Williamson. 2008. *Them that believe: The power and meaning of the Christian serpent-handling tradition.* Berkeley: University of California Press.

Hopkins, Dwight N. 2008, Spring. The Wright neighborhood. *Religion in the News,* pp. 7–8. 25.

Houdini, Harry. 1922, November. "Margery" the medium exposed. Retrieved May 2, 2007, from http://www.pbs.org/wgbh/amex/houdini/sfeature/margery1/html.

Houghland, James G., Jr., Dwight Billings, and James R. Wood. 1990, September. The instability of support for television evangelists: Public reactions during a period of embarrassment. *Review of Religious Research* 32(1): 56–64.

An interview with Wendy Beckett. 1990. PBS. Retrieved April 18, 2007, from http://www. pbs.org/wgbh/sisterwendy.

Investigative staff of the *Boston Globe.* 2002. *Betrayal: The crisis in the Catholic Church.* Boston: Little, Brown.

Isikoff, Michael. 1985, August 26. New Moon. *The New Republic*, pp. 14–16.

Isikoff, Michael. 2003, June 9. Flushed from the woods. *Newsweek*, p. 35.

Is terrorism tied to Christian sect? 2003, June 2. *Washington Post.*

Jenkins, Philip. 2004. *The new anti-Catholicism.* New York: Oxford University Press.

Jim Jones: Man who would be "God." 1978, December 15. *Christianity Today*, pp. 370–371.

Johnson, Pat. 2008, May 13. Biggest kosher meatpacker started by Jews in 1987. *Des Moines Register.* Retrieved November 6, 2008, from http://search.desmoinesregister.com.

Johnson, Paul E., and Sean Wilentz. 1994. *The kingdom of Matthias.* New York: Oxford University Press.

Jones and the disciples. 1978, December 13. *Christian Century*, p. 1176.

Joseph Burstyn v. Wilson. 1952. 343 U.S. 495. Online version retrieved April 16, 2007, from http://caselaw.1p.findlaw.com.

Kantrowicz, Barbara. 1993, May 3. Day of judgment: How the cult standoff with the FBI escalated into a fiery finale. *Newsweek*, pp. 22–27.

Kennedy, John W. 1993, September 13. End of the line for Tilton? *Christianity Today*, pp. 78–82.

Kennedy, John W. 1994, September 12. Killings distort pro-life message. *Christianity Today*, pp. 56–57.

Kerstetter, Todd. 2003. "Mobocratic feeling": Religious outsiders, the popular press, and the American West. *American Journalism* 20(1): 57–72.

Kiener, Ronald C. 2008, Fall. The Postville raid. *Religion in the News* 11(2): 2–5, 24.

Kilduff, Marshall, and Phil Tracey. 1977, August 1. Inside Peoples Temple. *New West*, pp. 30–38. Retrieved February 20, 2008, from http://jonestown.

Killer of rabbi's wife says he was told to fake a robbery. 2001, February 20. *New York Times*, p. D2.

Klaw, Spencer. 1993. *Without sin: The life and death of the Oneida Community.* New York: Penguin Books.

Kopkind, Andrew. 1987, April 6. Jim Bakker's lost America. *Esquire*, pp. 175–183.

Krakauer, Jon. 2004. *Under the banner of heaven.* New York: Anchor Books.

LaBarre, Weston. 1962. *They shall take up serpents.* Minneapolis: University of Minnesota Press.

Langford, Terri. 2002, March 8. Doctor: Yates knew killing was wrong. *Dallas Morning News*, p. 35A.

Langley, Monica. 2008, November 5. As economic crisis peaked, tide turned against McCain. Psychology of the southern snake-handling cult. *Wall Street Journal.* Retrieved November 7, 2008, from http://online.wsj.com.

Lattin, Don. 2003, November 18. How spiritual journey ended in destruction. *San Francisco Examiner.* Retrieved February 20, 2008, from http://www.sfgate.com/cgi-bin/article.cgi?f=/c/a/2003/11/18/JONESTOWN.TMP.

Lawton, Kim A. 1990, June 18. Taking aim at art. *Christianity Today*, pp. 52–55.

Lawton, Kim A. 1992, January 13. Broadcasters face ethics questions—again. *Christianity Today*, pp. 42–43.

Leaming, Jeremy. 1999, June 29. Senate Republicans join call to end military accommodation of Wicca. *First Amendment topics.* Retrieved April 27, 2007, from http://www.firstamendment center.org/news.aspx?id=9708.

Lee, Andrew. 2006, January 5. Christian groups in Colorado Springs. *Sightings.* Martin Marty Center at the University of Chicago.

Lemonick, Michael D. 1995, January 9. An armed fanatic raises the stakes. *Time*, pp. 34–35.

Lentz, Richard. 1993. The incorporation of Malcolm X. *American Journalism* 10(3–4): 38–69.

Levy, Leonard W. 1993. *Blasphemy: Verbal offense against the sacred, from Moses to Salman Rushdie.* Chapel Hill: University of North Carolina Press.

Lewis, James R., ed. 1994. *From the ashes: Making sense of Waco.* Lanham, MD: Rowman & Littlefield.

Lewis, Michael. 1996, July 8. Crucifixion. *The New Republic*, pp. 20–24.

Ley, Tony. 2008, August 26. Packers taking advantage of workers nettles Obama. *Des Moines Register.* Retrieved November 6, 2008, from http://search.desmoinesregister.com.

Ley, Tony. 2008, September 10. Kosher group: Change plant's leadership. *Des Moines Register.* Retrieved November 6, 2008, from http://search.desmoinesregister.com.

Lilliston, Lawrence. 1994. Who committed child abuse at Waco? In James R. Lewis, ed. *From the ashes: Making sense of Waco.* Lanham, MD: Rowman & Littlefield, pp. 169–173.

Lincoln, C. Eric. 1961. *The Black Muslims in America.* Boston: Beacon.

Lincoln, C. Eric. 1965, April 7. The meaning of Malcolm X. *Christian Century*, pp. 431–433.

Lindner, Eileen W., ed. 2008. *2008 Yearbook of American and Canadian Churches.* Nashville, TN: Abingdon Press.

Lippard, Lucy R. 1990, April. The spirit and the letter. *Art in America*, pp. 230, 238–245.

Long, Carolyn N. 2000. *Religious freedom and Indian rights: The case of Oregon v. Smith.* Lawrence: University of Kansas Press.

Loomis, James. 1965, February 27. Death of Malcolm X. *New York Times*, p. 24.

Malcolm's brand X. 1964, March 23. *Newsweek*, p. 32.

Marty, Martin E. 2002, July 31. Facing the fallout. *Sightings.* Martin Marty Center at the University of Chicago.

Marty, Martin E. 2003, September 20. Moore commandments. *Sightings.* Martin Marty Center at the University of Chicago.

Marty, Martin E. 2006, August 7. Extra Ecclesiam. *Sightings.* Martin Marty Center at the University of Chicago.

Marty, Martin E. 2008, January 14. Statistics. *Sightings.* Martin Marty Center at the University of Chicago.

Marty, Martin E. 2008, April 2. Keeping the faith at Trinity United Church of Christ. *Sightings.* Martin Marty Center at the University of Chicago.

Marty, Martin E. 2008, April 14. Rod Parsley on Islam. *Sightings.* Martin Marty Center at the University of Chicago.

Mathews, Tom. 1990, July 2. Fine art or foul? *Newsweek*, pp. 46–51.

McCabe, Nancy. 2005, October 17. A bogeyman with supernatural powers. *Newsweek*, p. 26.

McCarten, John. 1939, June. Father Coughlin: Holy medicine man. *American Mercury*, pp. 129–141.

McClaughry, John. 1983, December 12. The uneasy case against Reverend Moon. *National Review*, pp. 1611–1612.

McCrimmon, Katie Kerwin. 2006, November 4. Polygraph results indicate deception. *Rocky Mountain News.* Retrieved January 22, 2008, from http://www.rockymountainnews.com/news/2006/nov/04.

McGuigan, Cathleen. 1989, August 7. Art grants under fire. *Newsweek*, p. 23.

McGuigan, Cathleen. 1989, July 3. When taxes pay for art. *Newsweek*, p. 68.

Melton, J. Gordon, ed. 2002. *Encyclopedia of American Religions*, 7th ed. Detroit: Gale Cengage.

Menand, Louis. 2003, September 8. Comment: Moses in Alabama. *New Yorker*, pp. 31–32.

Messiah from the Midwest. 1978, December 4. *Time*, p. 23.

Miller, William Lee. 1976, October 9. Defending Carter's heresies. *New Republic*, pp. 17–19.

Miller-McLemore, Bonnie J. 2007, May 3. Christian discipline of children. *Sightings*. Chicago: Martin Marty Center at the University of Chicago Divinity School.

Milne, Andrew. 1994. The cult awareness network: Its role in the Waco tragedy. In James R. Lewis, ed. *From the ashes: Making sense of Waco*. Lanham, MD: Rowman & Littlefield, pp. 137–142.

"The Miracle" decision. 1952, June 13. *Commonweal*, pp. 235–236.

The money machine. 1972, April 10. *Newsweek*, p. 55.

Moore, Jonathan. 1996, November 18. Buddhism gets down to business—and politics. *Business Week*, p. 31.

Moore commandments. 2003, September 20. *Christian Century*, p. 55.

Morse, Jodie. 2003, March 24. The missing nine months. *Time*, pp. 44–48.

Murphy, Andrew R. 2001, October 17. Pat Robertson and the rhetoric of decline. *Sightings*. Chicago: Martin Marty Center at the University of Chicago Divinity School.

Murr, Andrew. 2006, March 22. Polygamist on the lam. *Newsweek*, p. 37.

Murr, Andrew. 2006, September 11. The polygamist's life. *Newsweek*, p. 25.

Murr, Andrew, and Kevin Peraino. 2002, June 17. "A man took Elizabeth." *Newsweek*, p. 37.

NCC's FaithfulAmerica delegation meets with Rep. Virgil Goode. 2007, January 30. *NCC News*. Received January 31, 2007, from mccnews@nccusa.org.

Neff, David. 1990, June 18. When religion makes us nervous. *Christianity Today*, p. 17.

New Life Church. 2006, November 2. News release from New Life Church, Colorado Springs.

Newport, Kenneth G. C. 2006. *The Branch Davidians of Waco: The history and beliefs of an apocalyptic sect.* New York: Oxford University Press.

Nightmare in Jonestown. 1978, December 4. *Time*, pp. 16–21.

Noonan, John T., Jr., and Edward McGlynn Gaffney, Jr. 2001. *Religious freedom: History, cases, and other materials on the interaction of religion and government*, 2nd ed. New York: Foundation Press.

Notes and comment. 1966, August 27. *New Yorker*, pp. 21–22.

Nuckols, Ben. 2007, December 12. Gay-hating church scrutinized. *Indianapolis Star*, p. 12.

Oaks, Dallin H. 1987, October. Recent events involving Church history and forged documents. *Ensign*, pp. 63–69.

O'Brien, David M. 2004. *Animal sacrifice and religious freedom: Church of the Lukumi Babalu Aye v. City of Hialeah.* Lawrence: University of Kansas Press.

Olsen, Jack. 1966, April 11. Cassius Clay: The man, the Muslim, the mystery: Part I, A case of conscience. *Sports Illustrated*, pp. 88–90, 92, 95–96, 101–102, 104.

O'Malley, Suzanne. 2004. *Are you there alone? The unspeakable crime of Andrea Yates.* New York: Simon & Schuster.

O'Malley, Suzanne. 2004, March. Horror in Houston. *Readers Digest*, pp. 132–139.

Orthodox Union. 2006, June 30. Prof. Grandin is satisfied with AgriProcessors slaughter practices. Retrieved November 6, 2008, from http://www.ou.org/news.

Ostling, Richard N. 1985, May 20. Challenging Mormonism's roots. *Time*, p. 44.

Ostling, Richard N. 1988, March 7. Now it's Jimmy's turn. *Time*, pp. 46–48.

Overseers Board. 2006, November 4. News release from New Life Church, Colorado Springs.

Packer, George. 2008, March 31. Comment: Native son. *New Yorker*, p. 39.

Parker, Laura. 1983, July 30. Culture clash in Oregon. *Washington Post*, p. A3.

Pazstor, David. 1995, December 7. Goofin' on God. *Dallas Observer.* Retrieved March 3, 2008, from http://www.dallasobserver.com/1995-12-07/news/goofin-on-god.

Pepsi cancels Madonna ad. 1989, April 5. *New York Times*, p. D2.

Perke, Kim Sue Lia. 1999, May 11. Practicing their old-time religion. *Austin American-Statesman*, p. A1.

Perry, Seth. 2008, April 17. Look at this tangle of thorns. *Sightings.* Chicago: Martin Marty Center at the University of Chicago Divinity School.

Peters, Shawn Francis. 2000. *Judging Jehovah's Witnesses.* Lawrence: University of Kansas Press.

Peters, Shawn Francis. 2008. *When prayer fails: Faith healing, children, and the law.* New York: Oxford University Press.

Peterson, Iver. 1995, February 27. Resignation adds to mystery in bludgeoning of rabbi's wife. *New York Times*, pp. B1, B3.

Peterson, Iver. 2001, November 16. Trial begins for a rabbi in New Jersey accused in his wife's killing in 1994. *New York Times*, pp. D1, D7.

Pew Forum on Religion and Public Life. 2008, February 25. The U.S. landscape survey. Retrieved September 29, 2008, from http:www//Pewforum.org/surveys.

Pfeiffer, Sacha. 2002, January 31. Famed "street priest" preyed upon boys. *Boston Globe*, p. A21.

Plimpton, George. 1964, June. Miami notebook: Cassius Clay and Malcolm X. *Harper's Magazine*, pp. 54–61.

Preliminary report of the Commission appointed by the University of Pennsylvania to investigate modern spiritualism in accordance with the request of the late Henry Seybert. 1887. New York: J. B. Lippincott.

Press, Aric. 1993, May 3. Day of judgment. *Newsweek*, p. 24.

Purnick, Joe. 1995, May 8. An unlikely matchmaker for Shabazz and Farrakhan. *New York Times*, pp. B1, B6.

Raspberry, William. 1984, September 24. The bus to Rajneeshpuram. *Washington Post*, p. A19.

Richardson, James T., and Tamatha L. Schreinert. 2008, October 18. The courts finally speak in Texas: An analysis of the Appeal Court opinions concerning the FDLS children. Paper presented to the annual convention of the Society for the Scientific Study of Religion, Louisville, Kentucky.

Riley, Michael, Richard Woodbury, Julie Johnson, and Elaine Shannon. 1993, May 3. Tragedy in Waco. *Time*, pp. 27–45.

Robertson, George. 1994. Suffer the little children. In James R. Lewis, ed. *From the ashes: Making sense of Waco.* Lanham, MD: Rowman & Littlefield, pp. 175–180.

Roche, Timothy. 2002, January 28. The Yates odyssey. *Time*, pp. 42–50.

Roche, Timothy. 2002, March 18. Andrea Yates: More to the story. *Time*, Retrieved February 20, 2008, from http://www.time/nation/article/0,8599,218445,00.html.

The Rochester rappers. 1853, April. United States Democratic Review. Retrieved February 11, 2008, from http://www.victorian-magic-blogspot.com/a006/rochester.rappers.

Rogers, Patrick. 1994, August 8. Is murder "justifiable" homicide? *Newsweek*, p. 22.

Ross, Brian, and Rehab El-Suri. 2008, March 13. Obama's pastor: God damn America, U.S. to blame for 9/11. *ABC News.* Retrieved June 5, 2008, from http://abcnews.go.com/Blotter/Story?id=4443788.

Rossetti, Stephen J. 2002, April 22. The Catholic Church and child sexual abuse. *America,* pp. 9–15.

Rove, Karl. 2008, November 6. How the president-elect did it. *Wall Street Journal.* Retrieved November 7, 2008, from http://online.wsj.com.

Rowe, Sean. 2006, June 11. Second coming: A jet-settin', Scotch-sippin' Robert Tilton washes up in South Florida and he still wants your money. *Dallas Observer.* Retrieved March 3, 2008, from http://www.dallasobserver.com/2006-11-06/news/second-coming.

Royal Ontario Museum. 2003, July 23. Royal Ontario Museum: Oded Golan's arrest/James Ossuary. Retrieved March 12, 2008, from http://www.rom.on.ca/news/releases/public.php?mediakey=vhggdo3048.

Rudolph, Eric. 2004. Statement. Retrieved February 12, 2007, from http://www.armyofgod.com/EricRudolphHomepage.html.

Ryan, John A. 1938, December 30. Anti-Semitism in the air. *Commonweal,* pp. 260–262.

Ryder, David Warren. 1926, July 28. Aimee Semple McPherson. *The Nation,* pp. 81–82.

Sanchez, Rene. 1999, January 15. Abortion foes' Internet site on trial. *Washington Post,* p. A3.

Sanneh, Kelefa. 2008, April 7. Project Trinity. *New Yorker,* pp. 30–36.

Sargent, Edward D. 1984, June 30. Metropolitan A.M.E. pastor blasts Farrakhan statements. *Washington Post,* p. B1.

Sataline, Suzanne. 2008, November 6. Democrats gain with religious voters. *Wall Street Journal.* Retrieved November 7, 2008, from http://online.wsj.com/article.

Scheer, Robert. 1976, November. *Playboy* interview Jimmy Carter. *Playboy,* pp. 63–86.

Schwartz, John. 1988, April 11. Jimmy Swaggart: Breaking away. *Newsweek,* p. 6.

Scotchmer, Paul, with Edward Plowman. 1978, December 15. Jim Jones: Man who would be "God." *Christianity Today,* pp. 38–40.

The search for the phantom will. 1976, April 20. *Time,* p. 21.

Seligman, Jean. 1987, June 8. The inimitable Tammy Faye. *Newsweek,* p. 69.

Serial killer's big mistake. 2005, December 2. *Wichita Eagle.* Retrieved May 2, 2007, from http://www.kansas.com/215/story/19184.html.

Sevig, Julie. 2005, May. Images of hope: Congregation echoes pastor. *The Lutheran.* Retrieved May 10, 2007, from http://www.thelutheran.org/article/article.cfm?article-id/=5092&key=25928462.

Sevig, Julie. 2005, August. After the Rader guilty plea: "Take note of what we do with evil," pastor urges. *The Lutheran.* Retrieved May 10, 2007, from http://www.thelutheran.org/article/article.cfm?article-id/=5259&key=2765709.

Sevig, Julie. 2006, February. Beyond BTK—Wichita pastor: Blessings amid the "muck and mire." *The Lutheran.* Retrieved May 10, 2007, from http://www.thelutheran.org/article/article.cfm?article-id/=5723&key=32752727.

Shannon, Elaine. 1993, October 11. Tripped up by lies. *Time,* pp. 39–40.

Shapiro, Samantha M. 2008, October 12. Kosher wars. *New York Times,* Retrieved October 31, 2008, from http://www.nytimes.com/2008/10/12/magazine/12kosher-t.html.

Shepard, Charles. 1987, March 20. Jim Bakker resigns from PTL. *Charlotte Observer,* p. 1A.

Shepard, Charles. 1987, March 7. Bakker treated for drug dependency. *Charlotte Observer,* p. 1A.

Shipps, Jan. 1985, November 13. The salamander and the saints. *Christian Century*, pp. 1020–1021.

Sidey, Ken. 1992, February 10. Addicted to broadcasting. *Christianity Today*, p. 12.

Silk, Mark. 1999, Summer. Something Wiccan this way comes. *Religion in the News* 2(2): 9–10.

Simon, Stephanie. 2008, May 23. Court overrules polygamist raid. *Wall Street Journal*, p. A3.

Simpson, Kevin, and Eric Gorski. 2006, November 12. Pastor's case stirs debate. *Denver Post*. Retrieved January 22, 2008, from http://www.denverpost.com/search-ci4644918.

Sins of the fathers. 2002, March 4. *Newsweek*, pp. 48–53.

Smart found alive nine months after abduction. 2003, March 12. Court TV. Retrieved June 23, 2008, from http://www.courttv.com/news/smart.

Smolowe, Jill. 1993, May 3. February 28: Sent into a deathtrap? *Time*, p. 33.

Smolowe, Jill. 1995, January 16. Fear in the land. *Time*, pp. 34–36.

Somerville, John, and Ronald E. Santoni, eds. 1963. *Social and political philosophy*. Garden City, NJ: Anchor Books.

Southwick, Albert B. 1963, June 5. Malcolm X: Charismatic demagogue. *Christian Century*, pp. 740–741.

Springer, John. 2003, January 18. Rabbi gets life in prison, still professes innocence in wife's slaying. Court TV. Retrieved August 16, 2007, from http://www.courttv.com/trials/revlander/sentencing_ctv.html.

Stashower, Daniel. 1999, August. The medium and the magician. *American History*, pp. 38–46.

Stern, Madeline B., ed. 1974. *The Victoria Woodhull reader*. Weston, MA: M&S Press.

Stern, Marc. 2008, Spring. IRS: Bipartisan tool. *Religion in the News*, pp. 9–11, 26.

Sun Myung Moon: Religious martyr or tax cheat? 1984, May 28. *U.S. News & World Report*, p. 14.

Szegedy-Maszak, Marianne. 2002, March 18. Mothers and murder. *U.S. News & World Report*, p. 23.

Talk of the town. 1966, August 27. *New Yorker*, pp. 21–22.

Tebbel, John, and Keith Jennison. 2006. *The American Indian wars*. Edison, NJ: Castle Books.

The Hughes will: Is it for real? 1976, May 10. *Time*, p. 30.

The psychic investigation: Claims of "Margery" to produce supernatural phenomena are rejected by the Committee. 1925, April. *Scientific American*, p. 229.

Timeline: U.S. Church sex scandal. 2008. *BBC News*. Retrieved January 21, 2008, from http://www.newsvote.bbc.co.uk/1/hi/world/americas/3872499.stm.

T.N.D. 1966, August 20. Of many things. *America*, p. 164.

Two families. 1996, February 23. *Commonweal*, p. 5.

Twomey, Steve. 1982, April 17. Oregon town seeing red over Bhagwan and his cult. *Washington Post*, p. C12.

Unitarian Universalist Association. N.d. Abner Kneeland. Retrieved April 16, 2007, from http://www25.uua.org/uuhs/duub/articles/abnerkneeland.html.

Updike, John. 2007, April 30. Famous Aimee. *New Yorker*, pp. 76–79.

Vance, Carole S. 1989, September. The war on culture. *Art in America*, pp. 39–42.

Vatican shifts on expulsion of sex abusers. 2002, May 13. *America*, p. 5.

Vestal, Stanley. 1932/1989. *Sitting Bull: Champion of the Sioux*. Norman: University of Oklahoma Press.

The violent end of the man called Malcolm X. 1965, March 5. *Life*, pp. 26–31.

Von Drehle, David. 2008, May 5. The sins of the fathers. *Time*, pp. 32–35.

Von Driel, Barry, and Jacob Van Belzen. 1990, March. The downfall of Rajneeshpuram in the print media: A cross-national study. *Journal for the Scientific Study of Religion* 29(1): 76–90.

Walczak, Lee. 1996, August 12. Campaign-finance reform needs a miracle. *Business Week*, p. 31.

Wall, James M. 1987, April 8. The fall of the House of Bakker. *Christian Century*, pp. 323–324.

Wall, James M. 1993, May 5. Eager for the end. *Christian Century*, pp. 475–476.

Walters, Fred. 1952, August. The Supreme Court ruling on *The Miracle* and *Pinky* gives censorship a punch in the nose. *Theater Arts*, pp. 74–77.

Wang, Judy. 2007, Fall. Chipping away. *Student Press Law Center Report*, pp. 20–23.

Ward, Christopher. 1934, December 8. Mr. Pierson and the new Messiah. *New Yorker*, pp. 43–48.

Warner, R. Stephen. 2008, Spring. Civil religious revival. *Religion in the News*, pp. 2–4, 21.

Warren, Donald. 1996. *Radio priest Father Charles Coughlin: The father of hate radio.* New York: The Free Press.

Washington, Michael Marriott. 1984, September 15. Homeless taken to commune of Indian mystic. *Washington Post*, p. A1.

Washington, Michael Marriott. 1984, September 21. D.C.'s homeless line up for Oregon commune bus. *Washington Post*, p. B1.

Watson, Russell. 1987, June 8. Heaven can wait. *Newsweek*, pp. 58–72.

Webb, Lawrence. 2003, August 29. Seven suggestions and three commandments. *Sightings.* Chicago: Martin Marty Center at the University of Chicago Divinity School.

Week by week: *The Miracle* decision. 1952, June 13. *Commonweal*, pp. 235–236.

Wilkinson, Peter. 2003, July 10. The making of a maniac. *Rolling Stone*, pp. 31–32, 34.

Williams, Dennis A., Phyllis Malamud, and Anthony Mabro. 1976, May 17. Howard Hughes: Heirs apparent. *Newsweek*, pp. 39–40.

Woodward, Kenneth L. 1976, June 7. Carter's cross to bear. *Newsweek*, p. 56.

Woodward, Kenneth L. 1977, August 15. Temple trouble. *Newsweek*, p. 79.

Wright's wrongs. 2008, May 3. *The Economist*, p. 44.

Zagoria, Sam. 1984, February 22. What Jesse Jackson said. *Washington Post*, p. A20.

Index

About the Author

JUDITH M. BUDDENBAUM is professor emerita in the Department of Journalism and Technical Communication at Colorado State University where she taught seminars on religion and media and courses in First Amendment law, media research and reporting. She is founder and past president of the Association for Education in Journalism and Mass Communication's Religion and the Media Interest Group and co-founder and co-editor of the *Journal of Media and Religion*. A former religion reporter, she has conducted media research for the Lutheran World Federation, Geneva, Switzerland. She has also served on boards for *The Lutheran* magazine and the First Amendment Congress and on the American Academy of Religion's committee for the Public Understanding of Religion. She holds an A.B. in chemistry, M.A. in journalism, and Ph.D. in mass communication from Indiana University, Bloomington.